ART AT AUCTION 1977-78

ENGLISH SCHOOL, SIXTEENTH CENTURY
Queen Elizabeth I in her coronation robes
On panel, 50in by 39½in (127cm by 100cm)
London £35,000 ($64,750). 14.XII.77

This painting is now in the National Portrait Gallery, London

ART AT AUCTION

The Year at Sotheby Parke Bernet 1977-78

Two hundred & forty-fourth season

SOTHEBY PARKE BERNET

© Sotheby Parke Bernet Publications Ltd, 1978

First published by
Sotheby Parke Bernet Publications, Philip Wilson Publishers Ltd,
Russell Chambers, Covent Garden, London WC2E 8AA

First published in the USA by
Sotheby Parke Bernet Publications, c/o Biblio Distribution Center,
81 Adams Drive, Totowa, New Jersey 07512

Edited by Diana de Froment and Lynn Lewis
Assistant: Betsy Pinover (USA)
Production: Peter Ling, Heather Scutt, Harry Tyler
Jacket photograph: Norman G. Jones, AMPA, ARPS

ISBN: 0 85667 049 9

Printed in England by Jolly & Barber Ltd, Rugby,
and bound by Webb Son & Co Ltd, Glamorgan, Wales

The publishers would like to acknowledge the following for their
kind permission to reproduce illustrations:
The Mansell/Alinari Collection, p21; The Albertina, Vienna, p38;
Cie Internationale des Wagons-Lits, Paris, p466

Endpaper illustrations A repeating pattern of a detail from a pair of
printed chintz curtains in the Honeysuckle pattern by Morris & Co,
circa 1880. From the collection of Mrs Oliver Owen and sold in
London for £280 on 7 April 1978

Contents

A Louis XV/Louis XVI transitional guéridon tripod table with Sèvres porcelain plaques, stamped
M. Carlin, the plaques painted and signed by Dodin and marked *V* for 1774, height 2ft 7½in (80cm)
Monte Carlo FF580,000 (£66,286 : $122, 629). 22.V.78
From the collection of Madame Bethsabée de Rothschild and Madame Jacqueline Piatigorsky

Note

Prices given throughout this book are the hammer prices exclusive of any buyer's premium or sales tax which may have been applicable in any of the salerooms. These prices are shown in the currency in which they were realised. The sterling and dollar equivalent figures, shown in brackets, are for guidance only and are based on average rates for the season. These rates, for each pound sterling, are as follows:

U.S. dollars, 1.85; Canadian dollars, 2.07; Hong Kong dollars, 8.65; French francs, 8.75; Swiss francs, 3.71; Dutch guilders, 4.25; Italian lire, 1,590; South African rand, 1.60; German marks, 3.95

The main gallery in Bond Street with Peter Wilson, the Chairman, selling the *armilla* on the
memorable morning of 22 June 1978; Dr Wille is in the foreground and his son is immediately
on Peter Wilson's left

Items from the Robert von Hirsch Collection are illustrated throughout the book in their appropriate sections

'But where would you get another?'
The sale of the Robert von Hirsch Collection

Frank Herrmann

'One hundred thousand to start it is bid. I have £100,000. £150,000 . . . £200,000 . . . £250,000.' The accent of the gently coaxing voice is always on the *fifty* thousand. In the shortest possible time the lullingly rhythmic incantation has reached £600,000. '£600,000 against you in the centre, Sir. £650,000 . . . £700,000 . . . £750,000.' The bidder hesitates. The sum is truly enormous. He nods. '£800,000.' '£850,000,' shoots back without hesitation. The bidding goes over £1,000,000. Surely no-one can top that? But they do. '£1,100,000.' The hammer comes down, slowly, hesitantly, very deliberately, in case someone changes his mind. No-one does. '£1,100,000. Agnew.'

There is a moment of genuinely stunned silence; then a low babble of conversation erupts all over the gallery. Two dealers beside me look at each other in astonishment. One of them explodes, 'Preposterous'. 'Perhaps,' his friend replies, 'but where would you get another like it?' He was referring to a *champlevé* enamel arm ornament, probably from the coronation vestment of the Emperor Frederick I Barbarossa. Where indeed? That was the message from the magical series of seven sales of the Robert von Hirsch Collection held in the Bond Street galleries in June 1978. Such an assemblage was a marvel that had survived out of its time. So perhaps it was not surprising that when it came to objects of such surpassing quality, money did not basically matter.

The arm ornament, or *armilla*, was the twenty-second lot of ninety-seven sold on the morning of Thursday, 22 June in the session devoted to medieval and Renaissance works of art. By and large they consisted of the contents of the glass-fronted cabinet and the table in front that stood in von Hirsch's library and workroom in his house in the Engelgasse in Basle. This was a small, intimate room in which this shrewdest of collectors also kept an extensive collection of first editions and other rare books and which he delighted in showing to visitors. He had acquired the majority of the works of art between 1925 and 1935 at some of the most important continental sales and dispersals of that period: from the Guelph treasure in Brunswick; from the Hermitage Collection; from the collections of Prince Karl Anton von Hohenzollern-Sigmaringen in particular, and from other collectors such as Figdor of Vienna, Trivulzio of Milan, Passavant-Gontard of Frankfurt-am-Main and Rütschi of Zurich. In their turn these collectors had bought them from celebrated collections of an earlier generation such as Lanna, Spitzer and Baron von Rothschild at Grüneburg. Von Hirsch made many of these acquisitions in close consultation with his friend and mentor, the art historian, George Swarzenski, then director of the Städelsche Kunstinstitut in Frankfurt. They included the early bronze aquamaniles and candlesticks, the enamels, the Venetian glass, various reliquary caskets and an incomparable series of ivory carvings.

In just over one and a half hours these ninety-seven items sold for £6,368,150 – more than the total for the nine days and eighteen sessions it took to sell the contents of Mentmore in what had been Sotheby's most exciting sale up to this year. It was an altogether remarkable occasion and left all of us who attended it (and were not too *blasé* to admit it) breathless and shaken with excitement. The extraordinary total made front-page news on most English newspapers the following morning. So did the fact that many of the most important items had been bought by dealers on behalf of a consortium of German museums. The cream of the collection had been exhibited long before the sale in Frankfurt at the Städelsche Kunstinstitut, then in the Kunsthaus in Zurich and eventually for a week at the Royal Academy in London. While the material was in Germany a number of museum directors had viewed it and had been deeply impressed by its quality. After many consultations, the German Ministry of Interior decided to make DM10,000,000 available for purchases at the sale and the museums raised a similar sum from their own resources. A number of dealers were briefed on the bidding but the German contingent of museum officials was also accompanied to each of the sales by Dr Hermann Abs, the Honorary Chairman of the Deutsche Bank and for many years Adenauer's confidant and adviser on financial and economic affairs. It was a shrewd move and observers soon began to notice that Dr Abs took an active role in controlling the bidding. At first he was reticent about the reason for his presence but by the end of the first sales it had become clear and he seemed to enjoy giving interviews to innumerable press, radio and television reporters. The ultimate consensus was one of admiration for the use of public funds in this way and for the skill with which the buying strategy had been planned and executed.

Robert von Hirsch, an affluent leather goods manufacturer, had left his native Germany to live in Switzerland at the time when the Nazis came into power. He had then been collecting for about thirty-six years – since the age of fourteen. As a condition of the removal of another major painting he had to donate Cranach's *Judgement of Paris* to the authorities. The picture was in fact restored to him after the war (still bearing the label 'The Property of the Reichsmarschall Goering') and he bequeathed it to the Kunstmuseum in Basle. Von Hirsch gave much thought to the eventual fate of his collection. There were memorable precedents in Switzerland of private collections becoming public museums on the owners' death, such as the Oskar Reinhart Collection at Wintherthur, and the Bührle Collection and the Rietberg Museum in Zurich. But towards the end of his life he found himself at loggerheads with certain of the museum authorities in Basle and he determined that the bulk of his art treasures should be sold at auction and thus be allowed to recirculate, although he did bequeath certain major items to museums and private collections. It was indeed at von Hirsch's house, some years before his death, that Peter Wilson met Dr George Wille, then a neighbour of the collector. Dr Wille later became Sotheby's representative in Switzerland, and now he and his son, David, laboured mightily through every stage of the negotiations, preparation and execution of the sale to make it a success.

Of course the German buyers faced fierce competition from collectors and museums in every other part of the world. This became evident from the very beginning of the opening evening sale devoted to Old Master drawings. H. P. Krauss dominated the early part by walking away with five of the seven medieval miniatures at prices that were way above expectations and set completely new standards in the field.

The glass-fronted cabinet and table in the Small Library of Robert von Hirsch's house in Basle, showing many of the major medieval and Renaissance works of art and, above, a Gothic altar frontal

With lot 11, a charming drawing of *Two angels, one with a trumpet* by Fra Bartolomeo it became apparent how complex was the auctioneer's job when the bidding came not only from the crowded central gallery in front of him but also from four other galleries in Bond Street and the Westbury Hotel linked by closed circuit television, as well as from the United States by satellite and at times from Tokyo and elsewhere. The outside bids were taken by no fewer than eleven members of Sotheby's staff each on a separate telephone. Excitement grew with the sale of lot 13, the curiously memorable drawing of a young man setting his compendium by the sun by Urs Graf. The bidding nearly stopped at £92,000. A new bidder came in at £95,000 in the main auction room. Counter-bids poured in rapidly over the telephones. The hammer fell at £122,000 to Segal, a Swiss dealer who had bought the portrait for the Basle museum. The next lot was the one remaining watercolour landscape by Dürer still in private ownership. The opening bid was £50,000. Competition thereafter was so intense that Peter Wilson took the bidding to an unbelievable £640,000 at the fastest speed that anyone could remember, in just over thirty seconds. The buyer was Mrs Marianne Feilchenfeldt, a leading Swiss dealer, on behalf of a yet unknown German museum. Not for a moment did the tempo slacken thereafter. An American museum bought a sheet of studies by Raphael for £95,000. A Swiss private collector acquired a sketch by Palma Vecchio of a *Virgin and Child* for £12,000. Mrs Feilchen-

A view of the Renaissance Room showing *The Branchini Madonna* flanked by two large Italian wood polychrome figures and, to the right, some of the Old Master drawings

feldt scored again with the Dürer drawing of *Christ on the Mount of Olives* at £300,000 and also took the next lot of Wolf Huber's *Portrait of a man wearing a soft broad-brimmed hat* for £105,000, this time on behalf of the Städelsche Kunstinstitut in Frankfurt. Two New York dealers bought Pintoricchio's classic *Head of a youth looking upwards* and Hans Burgkmair's illustration of a strange mythological duel for £65,000 and £80,000 respectively. In the light of what had gone before it was no surprise that a small landscape drawing by Rembrandt, which closely resembled one of his famous etchings, should fetch £154,000, again to H. P. Krauss or that his sketch of *Shah Jahan*, which Duveen had bought for £680 at the Lord Brownlow sale at Sotheby's in 1926, should now fetch £160,000. It was bought by the Cleveland Museum. The total for that first evening sale was £2,777,100.

The highlights of the sale of the Old Master paintings on the next morning, were the marvellous *Branchini Madonna* by Giovanni di Paolo, bought by Speelman for the Norton Simon Foundation at £500,000; *The Annunciation* by Bernhard Strigel which sold for £120,000 and Hans Baldung's *The Virgin as Queen of Heaven* which fetched £245,000; the two latter bought for European private collections.

A fact that would have delighted von Hirsch himself was that throughout the series of sales, clever bidding often won the day. On many occasions the winning bid came from a new bidder who had held back until the very last moment when the competition had virtually exhausted itself. One amusing sidelight at the evening sale of the Impressionist paintings, when the pace in general was very much slower than it

Robert von Hirsch (1883–1977)

Right
A view of the Main Reception Room
showing *Les adieux de Roméo et Juliette* by
Delacroix, and in the distance one of the
Meissen vases decorated with English birds

Below
Another view of the Main Reception Room,
showing the major Impressionist and
modern paintings as displayed by Robert
von Hirsch

Robert von Hirsch's Study, showing his arrangement of six of the watercolours by Cézanne

had been for some of the other sales, occurred when a continental dealer waved insistently with his blue entrance card to a friend who had just entered the gallery. Unsuspectingly he made the final bid for a sculpture by Daumier at £3,600. But the story ended happily when the piece was put up for sale again and fetched £3,900.

At the last sale of all, of Impressionist and modern drawings, the sheer quality of many of the items, such as those by van Gogh and Cézanne, led to the establishment of innumerable new records and brought the total for the sale to the gigantic figure of just under £18,500,000. Von Hirsch had acquired the majority of these drawings and the Impressionist and modern paintings after his marriage to Martha Dreyfus-Koch in 1945. Perhaps the drawings reflected most perspicuously the enjoyment that he derived from the collection with which he surrounded himself. A common factor among the more than eight hundred objects included from it in the sale was that they were on a scale that any lover of the arts could instantly understand. Von Hirsch was one of the rare survivors of a generation who possessed the scholarship, the regard for provenance, the discerning eye and the long purse that made it possible to assimilate what was really outstanding at a time when prices were still pitched at a completely different level. Until this year his name was known to few except a small circle of friends and art historians. Now the acclaim which the sale received will give it a hallowed niche in the history of great art connoisseurs. It also seemed delightfully appropriate that Peter Wilson's greatest triumph should have occurred exactly twenty years after his appointment as Chairman of Sotheby's.

Paintings, Drawings and Sculpture

LUCA DI TOMMÈ
The Adoration of the Magi
On panel, 16⅛in by 16½in (41cm by 42cm)
London £75,000($138,750). 21.VI.78
From the collection of the late Robert von Hirsch

SCHOOL OF THE VENETO, LATE THIRTEENTH CENTURY
Two wings of a portable reliquary triptych
A pair, on panel, each $7\frac{3}{8}$in by $2\frac{3}{4}$in (18.5cm by 7cm)
London £31,000($57,350). 21.VI.78
From the collection of the late Robert von Hirsch

ANDREA DI NICCOLÒ
The Madonna and Child with Saints
On panel, 15½in by 11½in (39.4cm by 29.2cm)
London £26,000($48,100). 21.VI.78
From the collection of Douglas Cory-Wright

GIOVANNI DI PAOLO
The Branchini Madonna
On panel, inscribed, signed and
dated *MCCCCXXVII,* 71¾in by
36¾in (182cm by 93.5cm)
London £500,000($925,000).
21.VI.78
From the collection of the late
Robert von Hirsch

The Branchini Madonna by Giovanni di Paolo

John Pope-Hennessy

At first sight *The Branchini Madonna* by Giovanni di Paolo from the Robert von Hirsch Collection looks like other Sienese fifteenth-century paintings. The central panel of an altarpiece painted for the chapel of the Branchini family in the church of San Domenico, it shows a Virgin of Humility supporting the Child at her side. Over her head is a small dove and above, at the apex of the panel, is God the Father in benediction. Only when we look at the painting more carefully do we become conscious of its singularity. The Virgin is indeed a Madonna of Humility but she is also represented as Queen of Heaven wearing a gesso crown and a cloak lined with ermine; she does not rest on the ground but is supported by four seraphim whose wings protrude beneath her dress. Indeed properly speaking there is no ground on which she could reasonably be sitting, for the base of the painting is strewn with flowers with severed stems. The seraphim continue above, three at each side, their wings outstretched against the gold background. The original blue surface of the Virgin's cloak has been renewed – it seems to have been reduced to its present form between 1904, when the panel was in the Chigi-Saracini Collection and the time of its purchase for the von Hirsch Collection which was not later than February 1923 – but the edge of the ermine lining is original and falls with extraordinary elegance and freedom. The ermine tails break what might otherwise have been a hard uninterrupted line and are visible once more at the base on the right and at a point on the left where the cloak is turned back on itself.

That the image has a rather special devotional intention is confirmed by the inscription in the Virgin's halo, *HIC QUI TE PINXIT PROTEGE VIRGO VIRUM* (Protect, O Virgin, the man who has painted thee), the more so that the name of 'the man who has painted thee' appears beneath on the frame: *JOHANNES SENENSIS PAULI FILIUS PINXIT MCCCCXXVII*. The most notable precedent for such an inscription occurs not in a halo but on the step of the central panel of Duccio's *Maesta* where the painter's name is also associated with an invocation to the Virgin: *MATER SCA DEI/SIS CAUSA SENIS REQUIEI/SIS DUCCIO VITA/TE QVIA PINXIT ITA*. The flowers at the bottom of the present panel are attributes of the Virgin and include white roses, marigolds and cornflowers.

The 1420s in Tuscany were a period of stylistic revolution. In Florence the innovators were two sculptors, Donatello and Ghiberti, and four painters, Gentile da Fabriano, the young Fra Angelico, Masolino and Masaccio; in Siena they were a sculptor, Jacopo della Quercia; and three painters, Domenico di Bartolo, Sassetta and Giovanni di Paolo. The interconnection between the two centres must have been much closer than modern art historians allow. Jacopo della Quercia may have worked in Florence; Domenico di Bartolo is traditionally supposed to have painted the high altarpiece for the church of the Carmine; Ghiberti seems to have been responsible for the design of the base of the baptismal font in San Giovanni in Siena and visited the city repeatedly in connection with this work, and in 1425 Gentile da Fabriano, his Florentine commissions completed, moved to Siena on his way to Orvieto and Rome. There is no evidence that Giovanni di Paolo visited Florence before 1427, though he must have done so in the 1430s when he studied the Florentine works of Gentile and Fra Angelico, but he was closely associated with Gentile da Fabriano in Siena in 1425. The work commissioned from Gentile for Siena, the so-called *Madonna dei Notai*, has disappeared, but we can form an impression of its general character from the two great altarpieces he produced in Florence immediately before, *The Adoration of the Magi* for the Strozzi Chapel of Santa Trinita and the Quaratesi Polyptych for San Niccolò, as well as from the small *Virgin and Child with Saints* of the same date, now in the Frick Collection. The idiosyncrasies of these three paintings, their linear rhythms, their firm modelling, their latent naturalism and their opulent decorative style are all reflected in Giovanni di Paolo's earliest works.

The first work by Giovanni di Paolo that we know, the Pecci altarpiece, dates from a year before the von Hirsch *Madonna* and was also painted for the church of San Domenico. The central panel, a *Madonna and Child enthroned with angels*, is now in the church at Castelnuovu Berardenga (see opposite) and two of its side panels are in the Pinacoteca at Siena. Its central group derives from that in an altarpiece painted by the leader of conservatism in Siena, Taddeo di Bartolo, in 1400 for the chapel of Santa Caterina della Notte, but the differences between them, the cursive line of the Virgin's cloak, the soft inclination of her head and the decorative music-making angels disposed in the depth at the two sides, are the first fruits of Giovanni di Paolo's contact with Gentile. At the front is an entirely novel feature, a pavement of large foliated tiles with orthogonals directed not centrally but towards the left of the panel. Three of the tiles show thistles, a symbol of the Passion of Christ, and four represent a small plant, perhaps a daisy. The tiles are fanciful, insofar as no tiles of this type produced in Italy at so early a date are known, but they reflect the influence of Gentile and look forward to the floreated base of the panel on which Giovanni di Paolo started work as soon as the Pecci altarpiece was complete.

The influence of Ghiberti in Siena has not been adequately analysed. His first recorded contacts with the city date from 1416 and 1417 when he paid three visits in connection with the designing of the baptismal font. Despite repeated urging, his two bronze reliefs were still unfinished in 1425 and were completed only in 1427. The linear rhythms in the work of the young Giovanni di Paolo, especially in the von Hirsch *Madonna*, bear a direct relation to one of these reliefs, *The Baptism of Christ*.

One of the most beautiful features of the von Hirsch *Madonna* is the Child, who is shown standing with his left leg extended on the Virgin's thigh. His right foot rests on her hand and his right arm reaches up diagonally in an unsuccessful effort to touch or stroke her face. There is no precedent for this beautiful figure in Sienese painting but it has parallels in Florence in the work of Masolino. In 1423 Masolino, in a well-known *Madonna*, now at Bremen, depicted the Child with his left foot on the Virgin's knee, the other in the Virgin's hand and his left arm thrown round her neck. A few years later, in a *Madonna* (now lost but known from photographs) which was once at Novoli

GIOVANNI DI PAOLO
The Pecci Madonna
On panel, signed and dated *MCCCCXXVI*,
64¾in by 34⅝in (170cm by 88cm)
In the church at Castelnuovo Berardenga,
near Siena

and formed part of an altarpiece in Santa Maria Maggiore, a climbing Child is again shown, this time clothed; his feet and head are disposed much as they are in Giovanni di Paolo's painting with the right elbow bent against the Virgin's neck. Possibly Giovanni di Paolo knew these paintings at first hand, but nowhere is the relationship so clear as to compel us to believe that this was so and it is far more likely that they have a common source in a terracotta by Ghiberti.

About 1430 both in Florence and Siena, for reasons that cannot be reconstructed, the springs of inspiration started to dry up. When Gentile da Fabriano's Quaratesi predella was copied by Bicci di Lorenzo, what was imitated was its content not its style. With Masaccio's death in 1428 work in the Brancacci Chapel came to a sudden halt, and thereafter his style, or such aspects of it as were apprehensible, was translated into terms of decoration by Fra Filippo Lippi, while in Siena after 1432 Sassetta retreated from the *Madonna of the Snow* to the pinched, schematic forms of the *Madonna* from the Borgo San Sepolcro altarpiece, now in the Louvre. With Giovanni di Paolo, a less great painter but doctrinally a more serious, more committed artist, the same process occurs, first in the fragments surviving from the Fondi altarpiece in Siena, now at Houston and in the Metropolitan Museum, and then in the third of his polyptychs for San Domenico, the Guelfi altarpiece of 1445 which is now in the Uffizi. Impressive his later works unquestionably are, but when confronted by their jagged silhouettes how fervently one wishes that he had painted other works as yielding, as graceful, as tender as the von Hirsch *Madonna*.

PAOLO VENEZIANO
The Madonna and Child enthroned
On panel, 13⅛in by 8in (33.2cm by 20.3cm)
London £36,000($66,600). 21.VI.78
From the collection of the late Dr Raimond van Marle

SCHOOL OF NUREMBERG, LATE FOURTEENTH CENTURY
The Bishop of Assisi handing a palm to St Clare
On panel, 13¼in by 8⅝in (33.6cm by 22cm)
London £55,000($101,750). 21.VI.78
From the collection of the late Robert von Hirsch

BERNHARD STRIGEL
*The Annunciation to Saints Anne
and Joachim*
On panel, 23in by 11¾in
(58.4cm by 30cm)
London £120,000($222,000). 21.VI.78
From the collection of the late Robert
von Hirsch

HANS BALDUNG called GRIEN
The Virgin as Queen of Heaven
On panel, 14in by 10in (35.5cm by 25.5cm)
London £245,000($453,250). 21.VI.78
From the collection of the late Robert von Hirsch

DOMENIKOS THEOTOCOPULI called EL GRECO
The Flight into Egypt
On panel, 6¼in by 8½in (15.8cm by 21.5cm)
London £90,000($166,500). 21.VI.78
From the collection of the late Robert von Hirsch

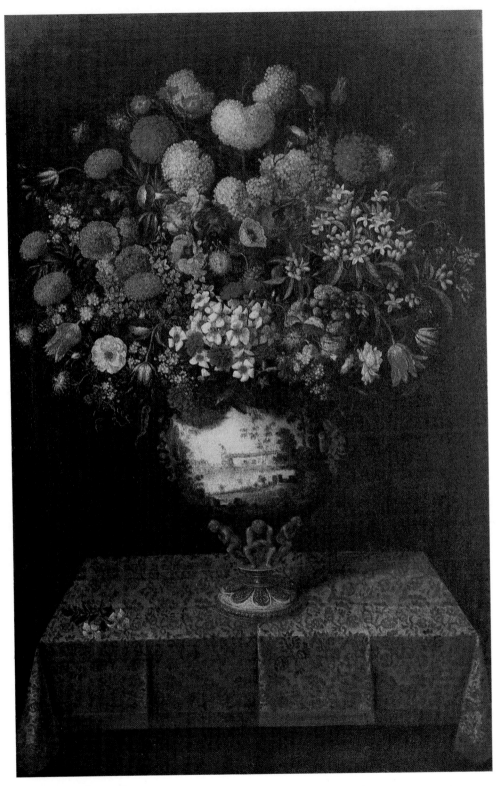

TOMAS YEPES (HIEPES)
Flowers in a painted vase
One of a pair, signed and dated *1664*, 59in by 38½in (150cm by 98cm)
London £40,000($74,000). 14.XII.77

JAN MASSYS
Susannah and the Elders
On panel, signed and dated *1556*, 50¾in by 43¼in (129cm by 110cm)
London £32,000($59,200). 14.XII.77

JAN GOSSAERT called MABUSE
The Virgin and Child with Saints
On panel, 33¼in by 27¼in (84.5cm by 69.2cm)
London £60,000($111,000). 14.XII.77
From the collection of the Barons de Moffarts

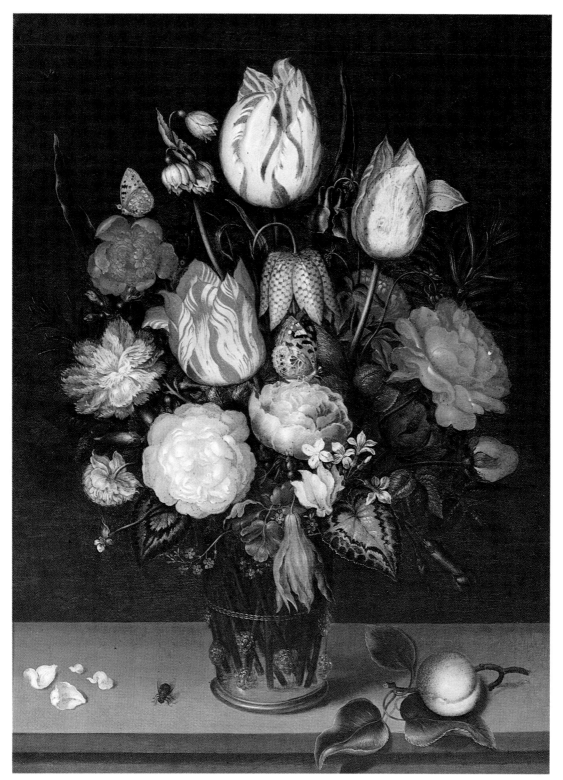

AMBROSIUS BOSSCHAERT THE YOUNGER
Flowers in a glass beaker
On copper, $17\frac{3}{4}$in by $13\frac{1}{4}$in (45.5cm by 33.5cm)
London £48,000($88,800). 12.VII.78

JAN BRUEGHEL THE ELDER
Flowers in a glass beaker
On panel, 16¼in by 13¼in (41.3cm by 33.6cm)
New York $560,000(£302,703). 13.I.78

MARTEN RYCKAERT
The Flight into Egypt
On panel, signed and dated *1631*, 14¼in by 22¾in (36cm by 57.5cm)
New York $130,000(£70,270). 7.VI.78
From the collection of S. de Swann

JAN BRUEGHEL THE YOUNGER
A river landscape
On copper, 15$\frac{1}{4}$in by 24$\frac{1}{2}$in (38.7cm by 62cm)
London £60,000($111,000). 12.VII.78

JOOS DE MOMPER
A mountain landscape
On panel, 24¾in by 44¼in (63cm by 112cm)
London £62,000($114,700). 12.VII.78
From the collection of Madame C. Tiranti

CLAUDE-JOSEPH VERNET
A southern harbour scene
Signed and dated *Roma 1745*, 34½in by 47¼in (88cm by 120cm)
London £24,000($44,400). 12.VII.78
From the collection of John Astor

ALBRECHT DÜRER
Doss' Trento with the Romanesque church of Sant' Apollinare di Piedicastello
Watercolour and bodycolour, inscribed *trintperg*, probably 1494, $6\frac{5}{8}$in by $8\frac{3}{8}$in (16.8cm by 21.2cm)
London £640,000($1,184,000). 20.VI.78
From the collection of the late Robert von Hirsch

Dürer's Doss' Trento landscape

John Rowlands

Albrecht Dürer's interest in the natural world always remained strong and vital and his recording of it affords us one of the most exciting features of the whole Renaissance period. When under nature's spell, he drew with a freshness and spontaneity and a sureness of hand unsurpassed by any of his contemporaries. The vitality of his brushwork was legendary in his lifetime and an examination of his surviving work, both paintings and drawings, bears ample testimony to it. From the beginning of his career, such skilful handling is evident, as in his watercolour of a single pine tree, one of the famous group of watercolours by Dürer in the British Museum. Without the faintest preliminary outline in chalk, Dürer unhesitatingly builds up with washes, strengthened here and there with bodycolour, a tree which is the very essence of a pine. From his self-portraits and correspondence Dürer gives us a clear picture of a highly sensitive, very self-conscious artist, fully aware of his prodigious talents. While he recognised them as heaven-sent he was equally sure that only diligence would see that he received his due from the world. His confident assurance strikes us forcibly even when he was still only a journeyman.

His desire for discovery of himself and the world was given full scope when he made his first journey over the Brenner Pass to Italy in 1494. Many from north of the Alps had experienced their initial taste of Italy and the novelty of the south with a sense of heightened excitement but Dürer was one of the first to translate these stirrings on to paper. The results are revolutionary and sensational. The watercolours that we can reasonably assign to this trip are the beginning of a new development not only in Dürer's style but also in European art. The sketches he made *en route* are among the first autonomous landscapes in European art and they show the artist beginning to free himself from the rather dull palette and cool rigidity of his earlier views, for instance, those of Nuremberg which are characterised by too heavy a dependence on bodycolour. In these first Italian views he moves away gradually from a miniaturist-like technique and uses less and less bodycolour. Transparent washes shine at us from the paper even today, and in the Alpine valleys he first produced views which show signs of an almost romantic *rapport* with nature. Dürer encountered here spirits which did not rise again until the time of Goethe.

Among these watercolours is a view of the fortified rock, Doss' Trento, high above the Italian city of Trent, with the small Romanesque church of Sant' Apollinare di Piedicastello at its foot. Robert von Hirsch's choice collection of Old Master drawings

ALBRECHT DÜRER
View of Innsbruck
Watercolour and bodycolour, probably 1494, 5in by 7$\frac{3}{8}$in (12.7cm by 18.7cm)
In the collection of the Albertina, Vienna

was distinguished for the number of important drawings by the leading German masters but this watercolour by Dürer, one of only thirty or so that still exist, had held pride of place since its acquisition in 1950. Not only was it the last remaining known watercolour landscape by Dürer still in private hands but it was also the only such drawing by Dürer sold at auction this century. Indeed his last watercolour landscape to pass through the salerooms was *The Watermill*, from the collection of Edward Cheney, auctioned at Sotheby's in 1885 and now in the Berlin Print Room.

It seems quite likely that Dürer executed the von Hirsch watercolour after the famous miniature-like *View of Innsbruck* (see above) now at Vienna. In the von Hirsch drawing there is a similar precise attention to the portrayal of architectural details but in drawing natural features, such as the rock and wooded areas, Dürer works with the brush more freely. The handling is also closely akin to that of his larger panoramic *View of Trent seen from the north*, formerly at Bremen, which was probably executed at the time of the von Hirsch drawing; however, in none of these drawings had Dürer as yet achieved the spontaneity of his *Castle of Trent* at the British Museum, where the use of wash entirely prevails. The mastery here is more apparent because Dürer had the courage to work on a larger scale and it could be, too, that the drawing was done a year later, possibly on the return journey in the spring of 1495. But nothing can detract from the exquisite quality and fine precision of the von Hirsch drawing, in which Dürer has created, evidently for its own sake, a study of the world vividly fresh in observation and skilled in execution.

WOLF HUBER
Portrait of a man wearing a soft broad-brimmed hat
Black, red and white chalks, dated *1522* and inscribed with a Dürer monogram which has been added at a later date, $10\frac{7}{8}$in by $8\frac{7}{16}$in (27.6cm by 21.5cm)
London £105,000($194,250). 20.VI.78
From the collection of the late Robert von Hirsch

REMBRANDT HARMENSZ, VAN RIJN

Landscape with the house with the little tower
Pen and brown ink and wash, $3\frac{13}{16}$ in by $8\frac{7}{16}$ in (9.7 cm by 21.5 cm)
London £154,000 ($284,900). 20.VI.78
From the collection of the late Robert von Hirsch

This drawing is dated by Benesch *circa* 1651–52 as it closely approaches in style the etching dated 1651, *The goldweigher's field* (Hollstein B234). The view, first recognised by Hind (1932–33), shows the house which once belonged to the Receiver General, Jan Uytenbogaert. It is situated beside the road running along the river Schinckel from Amsterdam to Amstelveen which was one of Rembrandt's favourite excursions outside the city

REMBRANDT HARMENSZ. VAN RIJN
The beheading of St John the Baptist
Pen and brown ink and brown, grey and black wash, heightened with white,
$6\frac{5}{16}$in by 10in (16.1cm by 25.3cm)
London £130,000($240,500). 20.VI.78
From the collection of the late Robert von Hirsch

Benesch considers this drawing to be one of the most important of Rembrandt's compositions of many figures and agrees with the suggestions of earlier scholars that it was probably executed *circa* 1640

Left
FRA BARTOLOMEO
Two angels, one with a trumpet
Pen and brown ink, $6\frac{3}{4}$in by $5\frac{1}{16}$in (16.8cm by 12.9cm)
£36,000($66,600)

This is an early work of *circa* 1505–6

Right
BERNARDINO DI BETTO called PINTORICCHIO
Head of a youth looking upwards
Metalpoint heightened with white on pinkish-grey prepared paper, 10in by $7\frac{5}{8}$in (25.5cm by 19.4cm)
£65,000($120,250)

PAOLO VERONESE
Sheet of studies for 'The Martyrdom of St George'
Pen and brown ink and wash, $11\frac{3}{8}$in by $8\frac{5}{8}$in (28.9cm by 21.9cm)
£75,000($138,750)

These studies are first ideas for Veronese's altarpiece in San Giorgio, Verona, executed *circa* 1566

GIOVANNI BATTISTA TIEPOLO
The Holy Family
Pen and brown ink and wash, $11\frac{7}{8}$in by $8\frac{1}{8}$in (30.2cm by 20.7cm)
£20,000($37,000)

The drawings on this page are from the collection of the late Robert von Hirsch and were sold in London on 20 June 1978

ALBRECHT DÜRER
Christ on the Mount of Olives
Pen and brown ink, signed with
monogram and dated *1520*,
8⅜in by 11in (20.8cm by 27.9cm)
£300,000 ($555,000)

This drawing was executed during
Dürer's visit to the Netherlands
and is one of the three mentioned
in his diary on 26 May 1521

HANS BURGKMAIR
The encounter between Valentin and Oursson in the Forest of Orleans
Pen and black ink, circa 1521–23, 8¼in by 11$\frac{3}{16}$in (21cm by 28.5cm)
£80,000 ($148,000)

The subject of this drawing comes from a Carolingian legend. It depicts the
struggle between Valentin, the nephew of King Pepin, and Oursson, a wild
man living in the forest of Orleans who plagued travellers. Later it was
discovered that the two combatants were twin brothers and the sons of
Empress Bellisant and Alexander of Greece

The drawings on this page are from the collection of the late Robert von Hirsch and were sold in London on
20 June 1978

REMBRANDT HARMENSZ. VAN RIJN
Shah Jahan
Pen and dark brown ink and wash, $8\frac{7}{8}$in by $6\frac{3}{4}$in (22.5cm by 17.1cm)
London £160,000($296,000). 20.VI.78
From the collection of the late Robert von Hirsch

This is one of twenty-one copies by Rembrandt of Indian miniatures of the Mogul school which are
all dated by Benesch in the period of 1654–56

URS GRAF
A man holding a compendium
Pen and black ink, signed, $7\frac{9}{16}$in by $5\frac{1}{8}$in (19.2cm by 13cm)
London £122,000($225,700). 20.VI.78
From the collection of the late Robert von Hirsch

This is an early work, dated by K. T. Parker *circa* 1508. It is one of Graf's finest portrait drawings and is signed with the detached initials and the borax box, emblem of the goldsmith's craft, which frequently forms part of his signature prior to 1511

RAFFAELLO SANTI called RAPHAEL
A seated female nude, three studies of the infant Christ lying down, and a study of a child's head
Metalpoint on pink prepared paper, $4\frac{11}{16}$in by 6in (11.9cm by 15.3cm)
£95,000($175,750)

Oskar Fischel dated these studies *circa* 1508 during Raphael's early Roman period

JAN BRUEGHEL THE ELDER
View of Heidelberg
Pen and brown ink and blue and brown wash, $7\frac{7}{8}$in by $11\frac{15}{16}$in (19.9cm by 30.4cm)
£58,000($107,300)

The drawings on this page are from the collection of the late Robert von Hirsch and were sold in London on 20 June 1978

GIOVANNI FRANCESCO BARBIERI
called IL GUERCINO
*Study of a youth holding a piece
of drapery*
Red chalk, $10\frac{11}{16}$in by $8\frac{11}{16}$in
(27.1cm by 22cm)
London £4,600 ($8,510).
5.XII.77

FRANCESCO DEI ROSSI called IL
SALVIATI
A design for an elaborate helmet
Pen and brown ink and wash,
$8\frac{1}{8}$in by $7\frac{1}{4}$in (20.7cm by 18.5cm)
London £3,600 ($6,660). 5.XII.77

ANNIBALE CARRACCI
Faun holding a mascaroon
Black chalk on grey-blue paper,
$15\frac{1}{16}$in by $10\frac{3}{16}$in (38.3cm by 25.9cm)
London £13,000 ($24,050) 25.IV.78
From the collection of David Daniels

This drawing is related to those finished figure
studies by Annibale Carracci for the ceiling
frescoes of 1597–1600 in the Gallery of the
Palazzo Farnese, Rome

STEFANO DELLA BELLA
The fall of Phaeton
Pen and brown ink and wash over black chalk,
16in by $10\frac{7}{8}$in (40.7cm by 27.7cm)
London £7,400 ($13,690). 5.XII.77
From the collection of Mrs Don Forrest

Left FRANÇOIS BOUCHER
Apollo
Black and white chalk,
signed, 21⅜in by 14⅜in
(54.3cm by 36.5cm)
£35,000 ($64,750)

This is a study for the figure
of Apollo in *The Raising of
the Sun*, 1753, in the Wallace
Collection, London

Right CORRADO GIAQUINTO
*The translation of the relics of
SS Acutius and Eutyches*
Pen and black ink and grey
wash, heightened with white
over black chalk on washed
grey-pink paper, 17⅜in by
11 5/16 in (44.2cm by 28.7cm)
£11,500 ($21,275)

This is a preparatory study
for the canvas in the Duomo
in Naples, painted 1744–45

JOACHIM WTEWAEL
The Bishop and the Persecutions
Pen and black ink and grey wash,
heightened with white, signed
and numbered *Jo Wte Wael 2*,
7½in by 9⅞in (19.1cm by 25cm)
£6,000 ($11,100)
Now in the Utrecht Museum, Holland

This drawing forms part of an allegorical
series of *circa* 1609–10 illustrating fifty
years of Netherlandish history from the
point of view of a Dutch Calvinist patriot

The drawings on this page are from the collection of David Daniels and were sold in London on 25 April 1978

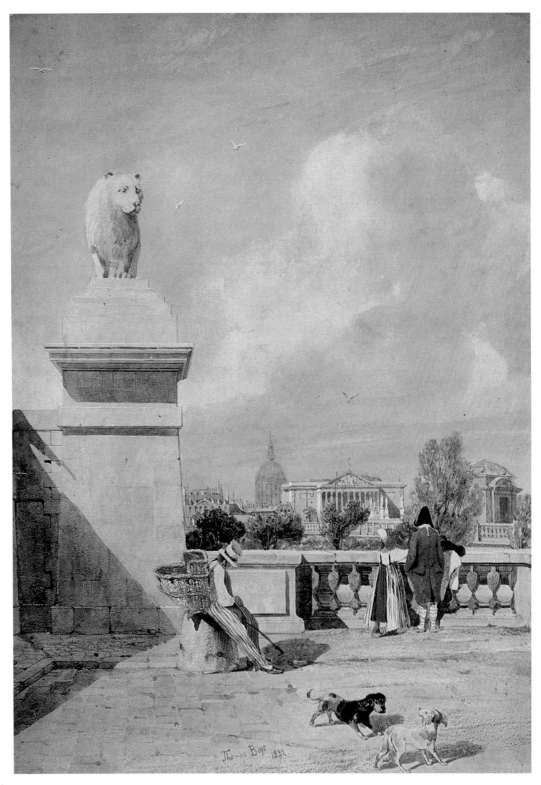

THOMAS SHOTTER BOYS
Near the Tuileries Gardens, Paris, the dome of Les Invalides in the distance
Signed and dated *1832*, 13¾in by 9½in (35cm by 24.2cm)
London £10,500($19,425). 24.XI.77

Formerly in the collection of J. Leslie Wright

THOMAS GAINSBOROUGH, RA
A wooded landscape with village scene
Pencil, pen and black ink, watercolour and oil on reddish-brown toned paper mounted on canvas,
16in by 21in (40.6cm by 53.3cm)
London £17,000 ($31,450). 24.XI.77

THOMAS GIRTIN
Conway Castle, Caernarvonshire
Pencil and watercolour, 12¼in by 18¾in (31cm by 47.5cm)
London £17,000($31,450) .16.III.78
From the collection of Sir Francis Beaumont, Bart

Girtin visited North Wales in the company of Sir George Beaumont in the summer of 1800. From June until October they stayed near Conway, where a number of artists including John Sell Cotman were entertained by Beaumont

ISAAC OLIVER
Madonna and Child
Pen and brown ink, blue wash, on blue-grey
paper, 7in by 5¼in (18cm by 13.5cm)
London £3,000 ($5,550). 24.XI.77
From the collection of Thomas Cottrell-Dormer

This drawing was executed between 1597 and
1605 after Oliver's first visit to Italy. The use
of pen and brown ink is typical of the
drawings by Oliver executed after his first
continental journey but the use of wash is rare
at this date, becoming more common later. The
style reflects the influence of artists working
in the Courts of Fontainebleau and Prague, a
style also found in the group of portrait
miniatures executed around 1600

ROBERT DIGHTON
Snipe shooting
One of a pair with *Pheasant shooting*, pen and black ink and watercolour, signed and dated *1790*,
10in by 14¼in (25.5cm by 36.2cm)
London £3,000 ($5,550). 23.II.78
From the collection of the late Jeffrey Rose

BEN MARSHALL
Skiff, a racehorse held by a groom, with John Howe the owner of the stables
Signed and dated *1829*, 38in by 49in (96.5cm by 124.5cm)
London £54,000 ($99,900). 23.XI.77
From the collection of Miss G. E. Hodges

Skiff, a bay colt by Pactisan out of a Gohanna mare, was bred in 1821 by the Duke of Grafton. He was unplaced in the Derby of 1824 which was won by Cedric. Skiff was then sold to Lord Kennedy and won many races in Scotland. In 1827 and 1828 he won at Newmarket, the Hoo and Stamford, and was then taken out of training after becoming the property of Mr Sowerby and advertised as a stallion at John Howe's stables, Newmarket

JAMES POLLARD
Hyde Park Corner, coaches, horses and figures in front of the Wellington Arch
Signed and dated 1838, 12¼in by 20in (31cm by 51cm)
London £40,000($74,000). 19.VII.78

This painting was formerly in the collection of Mr and Mrs Jack R. Dick and was sold at Sotheby's
in 1974 for £33,000

JOHN FREDERICK HERRING, SNR
The Yeoman cavalry of the Richmondshire militia on manoeuvres near Richmond
Signed and dated 1820, 41in by 54¼in (104.2cm by 139cm)
London £40,000($74,000). 19.VII.78
From the collection of Mrs Michael Speir

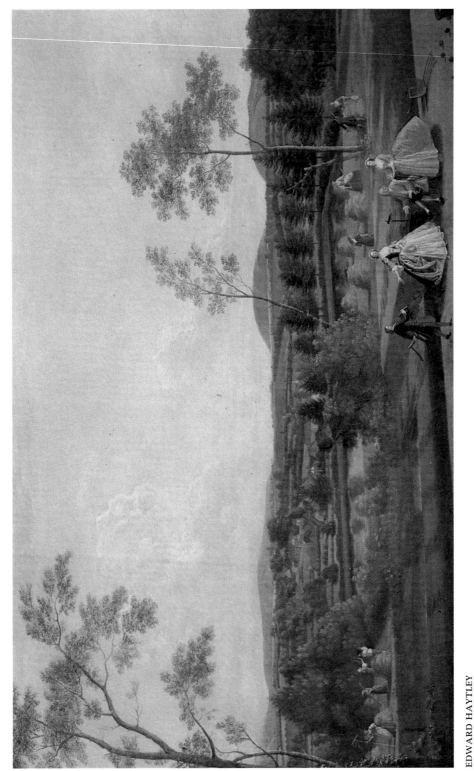

EDWARD HAYTLEY
An extensive view from Sandleford Priory towards Newtown and the Hampshire Downs, Edward
Montagu and his wife Elizabeth in the foreground
35¼in by 59in (89.5cm by 150cm)
London £84,000($155,400). 15.III.78
From the collection of Mrs John Bennett and Julian and Nigel Inglis-Jones

This painting was sold as by George Lambert (1710–65) and subsequently established by the
purchaser, The Leger Gallery, to be indisputably by the almost unknown Edward Haytley.
Mrs Montagu's unpublished correspondence in the Henry E. Huntingdon Library, San Marino,
California, mentions Haytley's visit to Sandleford Priory and his work on this painting

GEORGE LAMBERT
An extensive wooded valley with gentlemen picnicking and sketching and lovers on a haycart
Signed and dated *1733*, 35in by 52¼in (89cm by 133.5cm)
London £34,000($62,900). 19.VII.78
From the collection of Mrs E. O. Evans

This painting is a companion to the landscape in the Tate Gallery, London

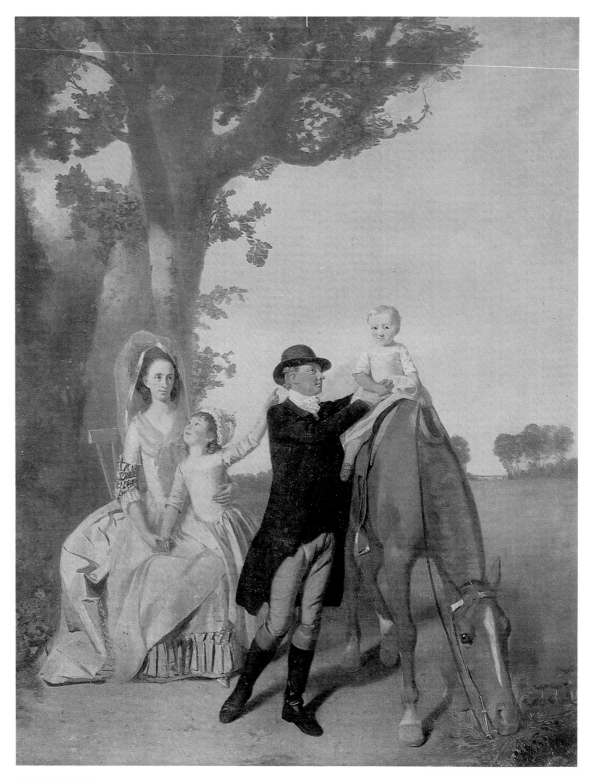

HENRY WALTON
The Rev. Charles Tyrell of Thurlow, Suffolk with his family
44½in by 34½in (113cm by 87.7cm)
London £23,000($42,550). 15.III.78
From the collection of the late John Walter Harvey

HENRY WALTON
Portrait of the Rev. Charles Tyrell of Thurlow, Suffolk seated under a tree
$29\frac{1}{2}$in by $24\frac{1}{4}$in (75cm by 61.5cm)
London £21,000($38,850). 15.III.78
From the collection of the late John Walter Harvey

BENJAMIN WEST, PRA
The Ascension
49½in by 34in (125.8cm by 86.4cm)
London £20,000 ($37,000). 19.VII.78
From the collection of The Lord Egremont and Leconfield

BENJAMIN WEST, PRA
The triumph of Death
Signed and dated *1796*, 23½in by 50½in (59.5cm by 128.3cm)
London £38,000($70,300). 19.VII.78
From the collection of The Lord Egremont and Leconfield

WILLIAM ASHFORD
Figures with cattle and sheep by a stream in a wooded landscape
Signed, 36¾in by 48¼in (93.4cm by 122.5cm)
London £17,000($31,450). 19.VII.78
From the collection of J. A. S. Russell

AUGUSTUS LEOPOLD EGG, RA
The life and death of Buckingham
One of a pair, 29½in by 36in (75cm by 91.4cm)
London £6,000($11,100). 6.XII.77

These two paintings were exhibited at the Royal Academy in 1855, the International Exhibition of 1862 and the London International Exhibition of 1874

EMILY MARY OSBORN
Home thoughts, 'One heart heavy, one heart light'
Signed, 27½in by 35½in (70cm by 90cm)
London £4,800 ($8,880). 6.XII.77

This painting was exhibited at the Royal Academy in 1856

WILLIAM PARROTT
Bal de la ville de Paris pour les blessés
Signed and dated *1851*, 45in by 59in (114cm by 150cm)
London £9,500($17,575). 18.IV.78

JOHN RODDAM SPENCER STANHOPE
Procris and Cephalus
37½in by 66in (95.3cm by 167.6cm)
London £8,300($15,355). 18.IV.78

This painting was exhibited both at the Royal Academy and Liverpool in 1872

EDWARD JOHN GREGORY, RA
A duet
Signed with monogram, 10¾in by 8¾in (27.3cm by 22cm)
London £4,500($8,325). 18.IV.78

JAMES JACQUES JOSEPH TISSOT
Study for 'The ball on shipboard'
37$\frac{1}{4}$in by 26in (94.6cm by 66cm)
London £10,000 ($18,500). 25.X.77

The finished painting, exhibited at the Royal Academy in 1874, is now in the
Tate Gallery, London

Fig 1
FRANCIS CAMPBELL BOILEAU CADELL, RSA, RSW
Recto: *Portrait in pink*
On board, signed and dated '11, 27in by 23in (68.5cm by 58.5cm)
Scone Palace £3,200($5,920). 11.IV.78

The Scottish Colourists

A. Lawrence

In order to show how the Scottish Colourists fit into the main tradition of Scottish art and how they make their own special contribution, it is necessary to say a brief word about the course of Scottish painting from its sources in the early nineteenth century. The most obvious and relevant thread that runs through all Scottish painting is the love of colour and its use in forming sensitive designs and patterns by building up interesting shapes and planes in their gradations. After the Nasmyths and John Thomson (1778–1840), John Wintour (1825–82) probably did the most to widen the palette and broaden the sensibility to outdoor colours. Sam Bough (1822–78), Alexander Fraser (1828–99) and Horatio McCulloch (1805–65) also shared in developing the emphasis. About 1880 began the most momentous movement of all, the Glasgow Group. This included some twenty painters, about half of whom can claim real eminence, who were in active contact at first as to their aims and theories. They were concerned to break away from the then prevailing practice of art-school teaching which produced narrative studio pictures. They were determined to go out into the fresh country air, to derive inspiration from the actual colours they saw and to heighten the emotional impact of their compositions by developing beautifully-combined and imaginative, graded patterned backgrounds. This gave great scope to their acute sense of colour without losing the sense of outdoor freshness. In these ambitious aims they certainly succeeded.

It is the Glasgow Group that provided the ideal seedbed for all four Scottish Colourists in the early years. Their example enabled the Colourists to make full use of the rich growths in French painting from Cézanne onwards, in colour, light and the designing of coloured spaces into forceful arrangements of planes and balanced compositions. These developments were successfully absorbed by the Colourists who worked them into the Scottish oil painting tradition. The subjects they chose, portraits, still lives and the landscape around them, were always subordinate to this search for expression through colour balance and harmony. Just how their success came about can be sketched by looking at their work.

First come Samuel John Peploe (1871–1935) and George Leslie Hunter (1879–1935) as they are generally considered the most eminent of the group and because they present such an intriguing contrast. Artists all work through their emotions and intellects. Their vision of each picture corresponds to what they see heightened by their imaginations and they capture a response from their viewers through the same channels. Taking this premise, Peploe makes his appeal rather more to our intellects,

Fig 2   SAMUEL JOHN PEPLOE, RSA
A reclining girl reading
Coloured chalks, signed, 14½in by 18¾in (37cm by 48cm)
Gleneagles £480($888). 30.VIII.77

Hunter rather more to our emotions. Hunter has more immediate impact on our feelings, while Peploe arouses our mental enthusiasm more slowly, though of course both painters used both approaches, Peploe being an exquisite colourist.

Although they were good friends, as indeed were all four painters, they were very different men and lived in different circumstances. Peploe set himself problems of design, composition, balance and drawing and solved them slowly and intensely to his own exacting standards. A good Peploe will keep you thinking about it and finding new delicacies of colour, balance and proportion for many years. Hunter will continue to give you emotional joy and excitement for as many. Peploe, being blessed by a controlled temperament and an ideal home and wife, seldom painted a weak picture. Hunter never married and was apt to be swept away by such excitement that he worked in long spells driving his nervous system to exhaustion to the ultimate detriment of his health. As a result, while Peploe kept near a steady high average, Hunter painted many more weak pictures. Yet it could be argued that if you judged them on their finest examples, it would be difficult to match Hunter's best work. Both were outstanding in their use of colour, Hunter in its impact, Peploe in the delicacy of tones and their gradations and harmonies, and with these qualities they developed the colours of the Glasgow Group. As to range, Hunter had probably the greater, as his landscapes are seen in bad weather as well as good; for Peploe the sun usually shines and the sky receives less emphasis. But Peploe could also have been an outstanding portrait painter if he had wished. What record he has left of his family and his favourite models proves this through the tonal delicacy, the truth of drawing and especially in the dewy bloom of the flesh colours. Also there is no doubt about his power to penetrate his sitters' characters (Fig 2).

Fig 3   JOHN DUNCAN FERGUSSON
Highland road
Black chalk and watercolour, signed, 11in by 15¼in (28cm by 38.7cm)
Gleneagles £140. 30.VIII.74

With the work of Francis Campbell Boileau Cadell (1883–1937) we are in a rather different world. He was the quickest painter of them all and the master sketcher. The fast accuracy of his eye and its keen response to the beauties he saw around him incite an immediate reaction from the viewer. Over all his works, colours reign supreme (Fig 5) and we share his joy in the harmonies and light they reflect. He found all the inspiration he wished in his own country, being the least of the four to be influenced by French art and will always, like Peploe, be particularly associated with Iona. From his work was handed on to his fellow painters the unique spirit of the Scottish islands, which we now so much appreciate. In his best pictures, especially in some of his very sensitive (but too scarce) watercolours and in oils such as the *Portrait in pink* (Fig 1) Cadell approaches the heights of his art.

John Duncan Fergusson (1874–1961) demands individual study, for while the other three definitely remained in the Scottish tradition and kept their base in Scotland, Fergusson spent the most important part of his life in Paris and on the Riviera and there was influenced by contemporary French painters. He was friendly with them all and so was naturally apt to absorb some of their continually changing and often experimental characteristics. For this reason he has often wrongly been excluded from accounts of the Scottish Colourists. Was he in fact too influenced by French art? Would his strong individualism have blossomed more brightly if he had kept more to the Scottish tradition and base, as did the others? Any answer is pure speculation. Certainly in his pre-French painting we see his Scottish character and also in the work produced during return visits, for instance during a tour of the Highlands in 1925. The mountain views that resulted, especially of the Cairngorms, show a return in full strength to his Scottish style (Fig 3). One further word, he and

Fig 4
SAMUEL JOHN PEPLOE, RSA
Ile de Brehat, Brittany
On board, signed, 1911, 12½in by 15½in (32cm by 39.3cm)
Gleneagles £1,900($3,515). 30.VIII.77

Hunter added a special value to the group – that of power. Fergusson's portraits and drawings have an immediate impact which lasts in our memories.

Fergusson raises the whole subject of the French influence on the Scottish Colourists, for he was a main link. He certainly helped Peploe and, less so, Hunter to appreciate and use some of the best traits in the French schools. He introduced them to many of the most eminent French artists and became the catalyst through which the exciting French freshness and zeal found its way into their work. Peploe began with beautifully-painted tonal still-life studies which owe nothing to the French painters, except possibly Manet. They excel in the smooth pure enamel texture of their paint and the balance of their objects. But by 1910 he had exhausted this vein so his first long visit to France (encouraged by Fergusson) was providential. Inspired by the brighter and bolder colours of French artists, his palette suddenly exploded into a rich fullness, first seen in sketches around Etaples and Paris-Plage (Fig 4) and also in the fruits of tours in the south of France with Fergusson. The ferment of experiment in the French schools captured Peploe also, though he was most influenced by heavy dark outlines balancing strong coloured shapes and the associated efforts to harmonise these colour planes. Such ventures raised for Peploe constant problems of design with which he wrestled for some years but the departures gradually became less strident and were assimilated into his natural, more delicate variations in tone, colour and grading of planes, to their enrichment (Fig 6).

For Hunter, French influence took a different course. He was an explosive, emotional painter at the easel, though always controlled by a strong sense of design. But his love of strong clear lights and colours was obviously stimulated by the south of France and its interpretations by Cézanne and especially van Gogh. Although he

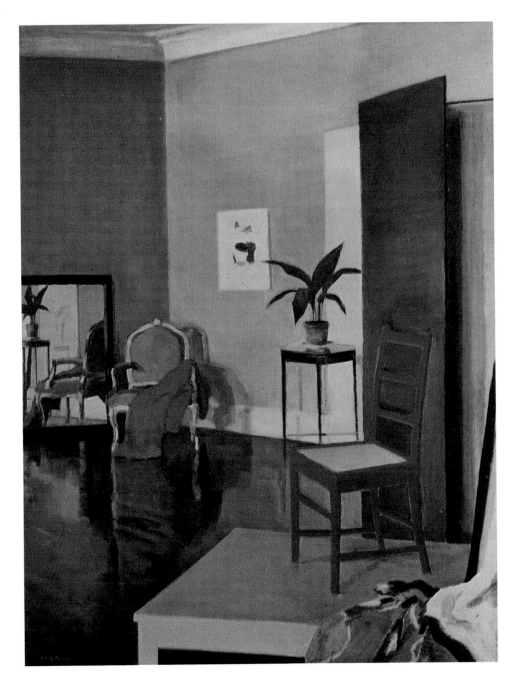

Fig 5
FRANCIS CAMPBELL BOILEAU CADELL, RSA, RSW
An interior
Signed, 39½in by 29½in (100cm by 75cm)
Gleneagles £2,000. 24.VIII.76

Fig 6
SAMUEL JOHN PEPLOE, RSA
Summer
Signed, 21½in by 29in (54.5cm by 74cm)
Scone Palace £1,500. 19.IV.77

never lost this affinity he always remained himself as can be seen in the still life illustrated opposite (Fig 7).

The colour tradition has continued to be stressed until our own day by such painters as Sir William Gillies, Sir William MacTaggart, Anne Redpath, John Maxwell, Robin Philipson and David Donaldson. The Colourists created a body of distinguishable work within the Scottish tradition which will always deserve a chapter in art history and a place in any exhibition of art illustrating it. For their traditional virtues they have secured an honoured place in Scottish painting. [1]

[1] Extensive literature on the subject includes: Sir James Caw, *Scottish Painting Past and Present*, 1908; David and Francina Irwin, *Scottish Painters, 1700–1900*, 1975; Stanley Cursiter, *Samuel John Peploe*, 1900; T. J. Honeyman,. *Introducing Leslie Hunter*, 1947, *Three Scottish Colourists*, 1950; Margaret Morris, *The Art of J. D. Fergusson*, 1974

Fig 7
GEORGE LESLIE HUNTER
Still life
On board, signed, 27in by 21½in (68.5cm by 54.5cm)
Gleneagles £1,100. 13.IV.76

BAREND CORNELIS KOEKKOEK
Winter landscape with peasants gathering wood
Signed and dated *1856*, 32in by 43in (81.3cm by 109.2cm)
New York $57,500(£31,081). 7.X.77

ANDREAS SCHELFHOUT
Skaters on a frozen river
On panel, signed and dated *1851*, 28½in by 35¾in (72.5cm by 91cm)
Amsterdam Fl 250,000 (£58,824:$108,824). 31.X.77

GIROLAMO INDUNO
The wounded Garibaldi on a stretcher
Signed and dated *1863*, 59in by 89¼in (150cm by 227cm)
London £28,000($51,800). 19.IV.78

This picture shows Garibaldi surrounded by his principal companions after their surrender to King
Victor Emanuel at the skirmish of Aspromonte on 29 August 1862

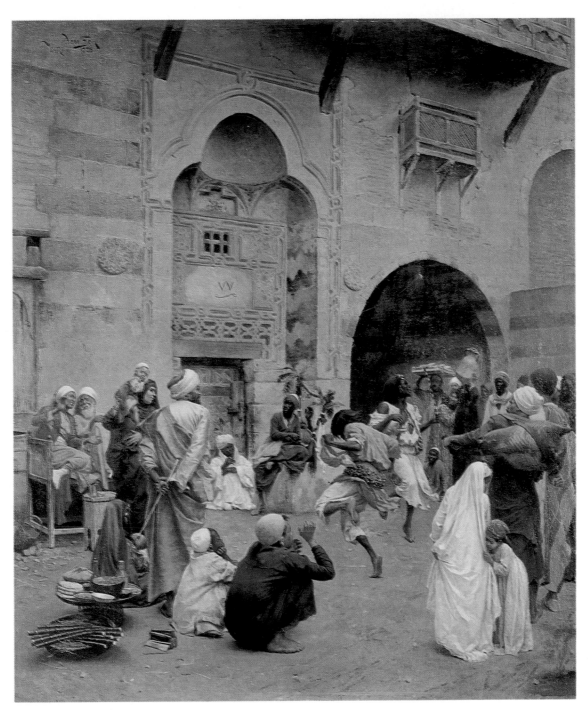

LUDWIG DEUTSCH
Nubian dancers watched by a crowd in the square
On panel, signed and dated *Cairo 1886*, 39in by 33½in (99cm by 85cm)
London £29,000($53,650). 19.IV.78
From the collection of the Royal Scottish Automobile Club

ALFRED DE DREUX
The departure for the hunt
Signed, 108in by 166in (274cm by 422cm)
London £20,000 ($37,000). 19.IV.78

GIOVANNI FATTORI
Adolescent courtship
Signed, *circa* 1880–90, 41in by 20¼in
(104cm by 51.4cm)
London £20,500($37,925). 19.IV.78
From the collection of
Mrs A. D. F. Newton

HANS THOMA
Die Quelle
Signed with monogram and dated *1895*, 43¾in by 34in (111cm by 86cm)
London £15,000($27,750). 30.XI.77

FELIX SCHLESINGER
Kindergarten
On panel, signed, 27½in by 39in (70cm by 99cm)
New York $65,000(£35,135). 12.V.78

GERARD PORTIELJE
The card game
Signed and inscribed
Antwerpen, dated *1896* on
the reverse, 17¾in by 23¼in
(45cm by 59cm)
New York
$46,000(£24,865). 20.I.78

ALFRED VON WIERUSZ-KOWALSKI
A Lithuanian sleigh ride
Signed, 28¾in by 46¾in (73cm by 119cm)
New York $67,500(£36,486). 12.V.78

FRIEDRICH VOLTZ
Cattle watering
On panel, signed and dated *München '871*, 18in by 46½in (46cm by 118cm)
New York $62,500(£33,784). 12.V.78

LUDWIG HARTMANN
Arrival at the inn
On panel, signed and dated *1871*, 15½in by 30¾in (39.4cm by 78cm)
New York $55,000(£29,730). 12.V.78

PAUL CAMILLE GUIGOU
The banks of the river Durance
Signed and dated '64, 24½in by 58¼in (62cm by 148cm)
New York $60,000 (£32,432). 12.V.78

LESSER URY
Berlin – der Tiergarten
Signed, *circa* 1921–22, 10¾in by 15in (27.3cm by 38cm)
London £10,000 ($18,500). 30.XI.77

JEAN-FRANÇOIS RAFFAELLI
Les vieux officiers
On panel, signed, 22½in by 15¾in (57cm by 40cm)
London £14,000($25,900). 30.XI.77

GUSTAVE MOREAU
L'Apparition
Signed, *circa* 1876, 13in by 9in (33cm by 23cm)
London £20,000 ($37,000). 19.IV.78

LUCIEN LEVY-DHURMER
Quietude
Pastel, signed and dated '96, 13¼in by 10¾in (34cm by 27cm)
London £14,000 ($25,900). 30.XI.77

GUSTAVE COURBET
Demoiselle des bords de la Seine
Signed, 1856, 35¼in by 43½in (89.5cm by 110.5cm)
London £250,000($462,500). 28.VI.78

This is a complete study for the blonde girl in Courbet's painting of the same title in the Petit Palais, Paris

HENRI MATISSE
Nature morte à la dormeuse
Signed and dated '40, 31⅛in by 39⅞in (81cm by 101.3cm)
London £310,000($573,500). 26.VI.78
From the collection of the late Robert von Hirsch

JEAN AUGUSTE DOMINIQUE INGRES
Monsieur et Madame Ingres
Signed, inscribed *à Ses bons amis Taurel* and dated *1830*,
7½in by 5½in (19cm by 14cm)
New York $55,000(£29,730). 28.X.77
From the collection of the late Edith Kane Baker

THEODORE GERICAULT
Deux hommes nus s'efforçant d'arrêter un taureau
Pen and sepia ink and wash, drawn in Rome *circa* 1817, 8½in by 12⅜in (21.5cm by 31.5cm)
London £23,000($42,550). 27.VI.78
From the collection of the late Robert von Hirsch

EDOUARD MANET
Portrait de Claude Monet
Brush and indian ink heightened with white,
signed, 1880, 5⅜in by 4¾in (13.6cm by 12cm)
London £21,000($38,850). 27.VI.78
From the collection of the late Robert von
Hirsch

Manet drew this portrait to illustrate the
catalogue of the *Exposition des oeuvres de
Claude Monet* held in Paris in June 1880

HONORE DAUMIER
Don Quichotte au clair de la lune
Charcoal and stump, 7¼in by 10in (18.5cm by 25.5cm)
London £22,000($40,700). 27.VI.78
From the collection of the late Robert von Hirsch

GUSTAVE COURBET
Fleurs sur un banc
Signed and dated '62, 28in by 43in (71.2cm by 109.2cm)
New York $200,000(£108,108). 19.X.77
From the collection of Mr and Mrs Sidney F. Brody

HENRI FANTIN-LATOUR
Vase de fleurs
Signed and dated '72, 17¾in by 19½in (45cm by 49.5cm)
New York $90,000(£48,649). 19.X.77
From the collection of the Pennsylvania Academy of the Fine Arts

CAMILLE PISSARRO
Portrait de Paul Cézanne
Probably 1874, 28¾in by 23½in (73cm by 59.7cm)
London £300,000($555,000). 26.VI.78
From the collection of the late Robert von Hirsch

This portrait was probably painted when Pissarro and Cézanne were working together at Pontoise in the early months of 1874. Hanging on the wall behind is part of Pissarro's landscape *La maison du Père Galien à Pontoise* and above it is a caricature of Courbet. The portrait was one of Pissarro's favourite pictures and was still hanging in his studio at Eragny towards the end of his life

PAUL CEZANNE
Portrait de Fortuné Marion
Circa 1871, 16in by 12¾in (40.6cm by 32.5cm)
London £150,000 ($277,500). 26.VI.78
From the collection of the late Robert von Hirsch

Fortuné Marion was a close friend of Cézanne from his school days in Provence and was a great supporter of his in the early years

BERTHE MORISOT
Jeune femme en robe noire
Watercolour and pencil, signed, 1876, 5in by 3⅛in
(12.7cm by 8cm)
£21,000($38,850)

Opposite above
GEORGES SEURAT
Pêcheuse à la ligne au bord de la Seine
Oil on panel, stamped with signature, *circa* 1884–85,
6⅛in by 9¾in (15.5cm by 24.8cm)
£75,000($138,750)
This is a study for the woman fishing in the left of the
painting *Un dimanche à la Grande Jatte* in the Art Institute,
Chicago

Opposite below
CLAUDE MONET
Etude d'enfants
Pastel, signed, executed in Normandy in 1864,
8¾in by 9¼in (22.2cm by 23.5cm)
£23,000($42,550)

EDGAR DEGAS
Au théâtre, le duo
Pastel over monotype in black ink, signed, 1877,
4⅝in by 6⅜in (11.7cm by 16.2cm)
£62,000($114,700)

The studies on these two pages are from the collection of the late Robert von Hirsch and were sold in London on 26 and 27 June 1978

EDGAR DEGAS
Lyda, femme à la lorgnette
Peinture à l'essence on paper laid down on canvas, signed and inscribed *Lyda*,
circa 1869–72, 14¼in by 9in (36.2cm by 23cm)
London £100,000($185,000). 26.VI.78
From the collection of the late Robert von Hirsch

Degas did three other studies of this figure, the one most closely related to
the above is in the Burrell Collection, Glasgow

PIERRE-AUGUSTE RENOIR
La danse, étude pour 'Le Moulin de la Galette'
Signed, 1876, 17⅛in by 10½in (43.3cm by 26.7cm)
London £80,000($148,000). 26.VI.78
From the collection of the late Robert von Hirsch

This is a study for the couple dancing in the foreground on the left-hand side
of *Le Moulin de la Galette* in the Jeu de Paume, Paris

VINCENT VAN GOGH
Mas à Saintes-Maries
Reed pen and sepia ink and pencil, June 1888, 12in by 18½in (30.5cm by 47cm)
London £205,000($379,250). 27.VI.78
From the collection of the late Robert von Hirsch

PAUL CEZANNE
Nature morte au melon vert
Watercolour and pencil, circa 1900–1905, 12⅜in by 18¾in (31.5cm by 47.5cm)
London £300,000($555,000) 27.VI.78
From the collection of the late Robert von Hirsch

VINCENT VAN GOGH
Arles, vue des champs de blé
Reed pen and sepia ink, signed, 1888, 12¼in by 9½in (31.2cm by 24.2cm)
London £200,000($370,000). 27.VI.78
From the collection of the late Robert von Hirsch

There are two other drawings of the same subject, and a related painting now in the Musée Rodin, Paris

PAUL GAUGUIN
Baigneuses sous l'arbre
Watercolour, inscribed with a poem from *Sagesse* by Verlaine, *circa* 1891–92,
9¾in by 12⅜in (24.8cm by 31.5cm)
London £52,000($96,200). 27.VI.78
From the collection of the late Robert von Hirsch

This watercolour was executed shortly after Gauguin's arrival in Tahiti. Earlier in 1891 a group of friends had tried unsuccessfully to raise money for both Gauguin and Verlaine who were in dire financial distress. Gauguin finally raised the money for the trip by auctioning thirty of his paintings at the Hôtel Drouot. The poem by Verlaine inscribed above the drawing reflects not only the tranquillity and beauty that Gauguin found in Tahiti but also his own preoccupation with the passing of time which was to be one of the main themes of his later pictures. The subject is very similar to that of his painting *Fatata Te Miti* in the National Gallery of Art, Washington

PAUL CEZANNE
Baigneuses, la montagne Sainte-Victoire au fond
Watercolour and pencil, *circa* 1902–1906, 5in by 8½in (12.7cm by 21.6cm)
£140,000($259,000)

GEORGES SEURAT
Ensemble, étude pour 'La Parade'
Pen and sepia ink, 1887, 5in by 7⅜in (12.7cm by 18.7cm)
£79,000($146,150)

This is a complete study for the painting in the Metropolitan Museum of Art, New York

PAUL CEZANNE
Arbres au bord d'une route
Watercolour and pencil, *circa* 1900–1905, 18⅜in by 12in (46.7cm by 30.5cm)
£110,000($203,500)

The drawings on these two pages are from the collection of the late Robert von
Hirsch and were sold in London on the 27 June 1978

HENRI DE TOULOUSE-LAUTREC
La rousse au caraco blanc
Signed, 1889, 23⅜in by 19in (59.5cm by 48.2cm)
London £230,000($425,500). 26.VI.78
From the collection of the late Robert von Hirsch

The model was Carmen Gaudin, a young working girl who posed for Lautrec, Rachou and Gauzi.
Lautrec painted her a number of times during the late 1880s

EDOUARD VUILLARD
Fillettes se promenant
Signed, *circa* 1891, 32in by 25⅝in (81.2cm by 65cm)
New York $190,000 (£102,703). 17.V.78
From the collection of Mrs Adelaide Ross Stachelberg

GEORGES SEURAT
Une promeneuse
Conté crayon, *circa* 1882, 12$\frac{1}{8}$in by 9$\frac{1}{2}$in (30.8cm by 24.2cm)
London £60,000($111,000). 27.VI.78
From the collection of the late Robert von Hirsch

HENRI DE TOULOUSE-LAUTREC
Le Divan Japonais
Black crayon, signed, 1892, $31\frac{3}{8}$in by $25\frac{1}{4}$in (79.8cm by 64.1cm)
London £70,000($129,500). 27.VI.78
From the collection of the late Robert von Hirsch

This is a preparatory drawing for the poster of the same title

CLAUDE MONET
Matinée sur la Seine, temps net
Signed and dated '97, 33½in by 38in (85cm by 96.5cm)
New York $330,000(£178,378). 17.V.78

AUGUSTE RODIN
Deux mains
White marble, signed, *circa* 1909–10, height 35in (88.8cm)
New York $125,000 (£67,568). 17.V.78

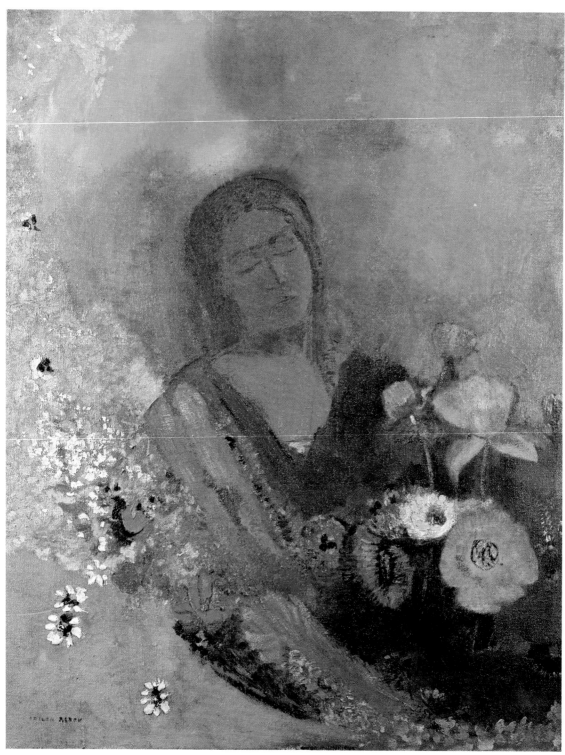

ODILON REDON
Les yeux clos
Signed, *circa* 1900, 25½in by 19¾in (64.8cm by 50cm)
London £90,000($166,500). 7.XII.77

HENRI MATISSE
Le luth
Signed and dated *2/43*, 23¾in by 32in (60.4cm by 81.3cm)
New York $440,000(£237,837). 19.X.77
From the collection of Mr and Mrs Sidney F. Brody

PAUL KLEE
Gestirn über bösen Häusern
Tempera on linen laid down on board, signed, titled and dated *1916* on the mount,
7⅞in by 8⅝in (20cm by 22cm)
London £70,000($129,500). 26.VI.78
From the collection of the late Robert von Hirsch

PABLO PICASSO
Homme assis au verre
Signed, painted in Avignon in 1914, 94in by 66in (238.7cm by 167.6cm)
New York $600,000 (£324,324). 19.X.77

PABLO PICASSO
Costume design for the Chinese Conjuror in 'Parade'
Pen and brown ink, signed, 10¾in by 7¾in (27.3cm by 19.7cm)
New York $10,250(£5,540). 15.XII.77

This drawing is a study for Léonide Massine's costume for the part of the
Chinese Conjuror in the ballet *Parade*, first performed by the Diaghilev
Ballet at the Théâtre du Châtelet, Paris on 18 May 1917. The libretto was
written by Jean Cocteau, the music was by Erik Satie and Massine did the
choreography. The decor and costumes were designed by Picasso and
mark his debut as a theatrical designer

LEON BAKST
Costume design for the Queen's Fiancé in 'Le Dieu Bleu'
Pencil and watercolour, signed, inscribed *Dieu Bleu le Fiancé* and dated
1911, 11⅛in by 7¾in (28.2cm by 19.7cm)
London £4,400 ($8,140). 17.V.78

This design is for the ballet *Le Dieu Bleu* which was produced by the
Diaghilev Ballet at the Théâtre du Châtelet, Paris on 13 May 1912. The
libretto was written by Jean Cocteau, the music was by Reynaldo Hahn,
the choreography was by Fokine and Bakst designed the decor and
costumes

WASSILY KANDINSKY
Improvisation mit Pferden
Signed, titled and dated *1911* on the stretcher, 28in by $38\frac{7}{8}$in (71.2cm by 98.8cm)
New York $365,000(£197,297). 17.V.78
From the collection of Mrs Adelaide Ross Stachelberg

EGON SCHIELE
Zwei Mädchen
Pencil and watercolour, signed and dated *1911*, 20¼in by 14⅞in (51.3cm by 37.7cm)
New York $60,000(£32,432). 18.V.78

JEAN ARP
Composition abstraite
Painted wood relief, signed and dated *1915* on the reverse, 29¼in by 35½in (74cm by 90cm)
London £57,000($105,450). 7.XII.77
From the collection of Madame Ruth Tillard-Arp (the artist's niece)

RENE MAGRITTE
La trahison des images (Ceci n'est pas une pipe)
Signed, *circa* 1928–29, 23⅝in by 32in (60cm by 81.3cm)
New York $115,000(£62,162). 17.V.78
From the collection of William N. Copley

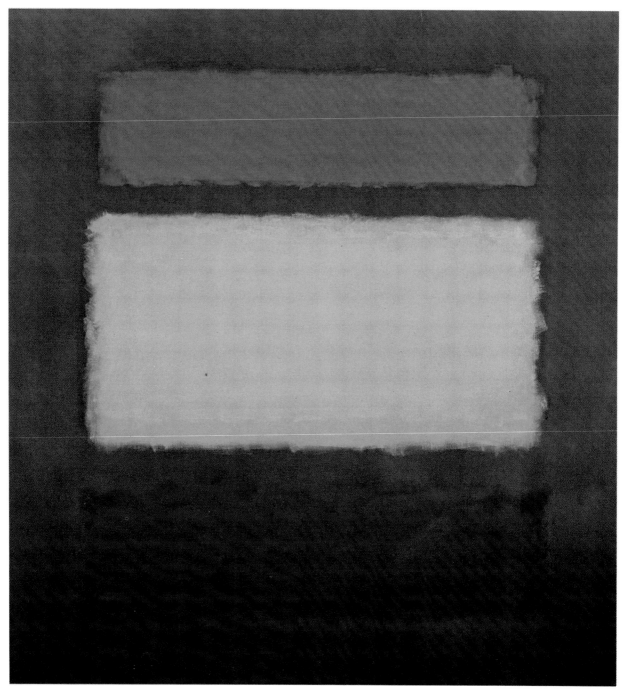

MARK ROTHKO
Brown, orange, blue on maroon
Signed and dated *1963* on the reverse, 81in by 76in (206cm by 193cm)
New York $130,000(£70,270). 20.X.77
From the collection of the late Barbara Wescott

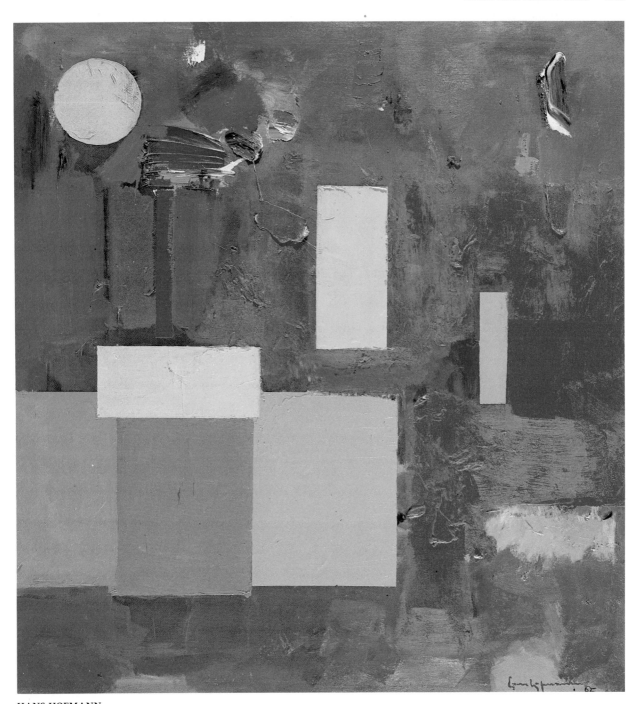

HANS HOFMANN
Rising moon
Signed and dated '65, titled on the reverse, 84in by 78in (213cm by 198cm)
New York $220,000(£118,919). 20.X.77
From the collection of Samuel M. Kootz

CLAES OLDENBURG
Giant blue shirt with brown tie
Cotton and canvas filled with kapok, plexiglas buttons and chromed metal rack with wheels, 1963,
height 65⅝in (166.5cm)
New York $95,000(£51,351). 18.V.78
From the collection of Peter M. Brant

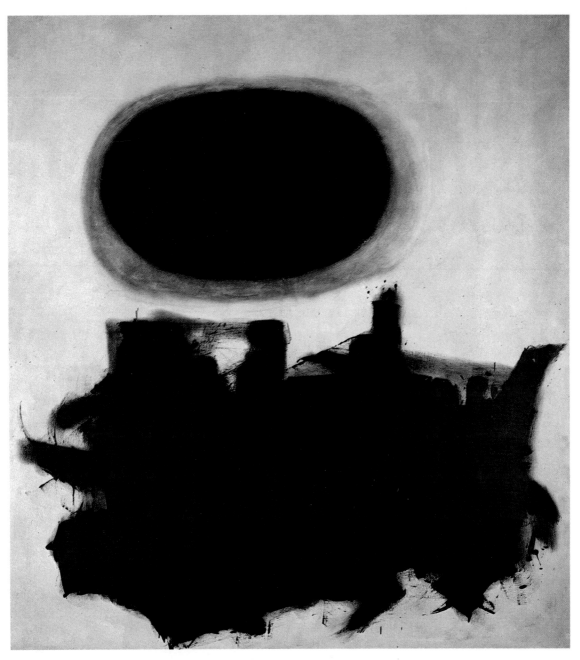

ADOLPH GOTLIEB
Black and black
Acrylic on canvas, signed and dated *1959* on the reverse, 79½in by 72in (202cm by 183cm)
London £17,000($31,450). 5.IV.78

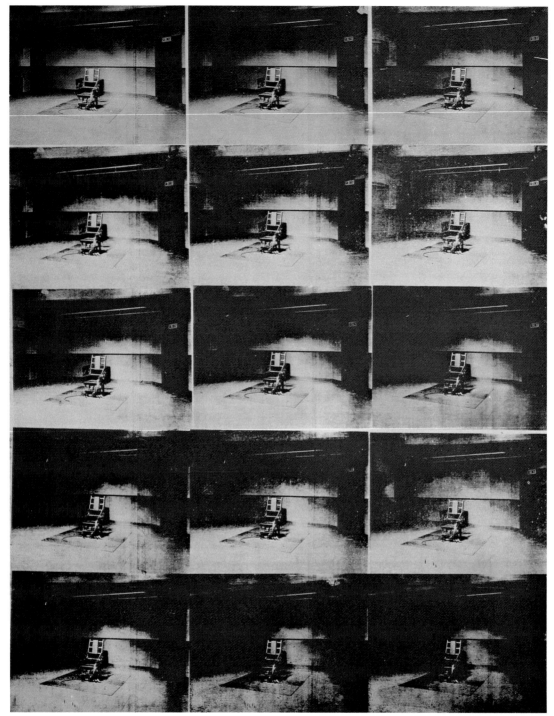

ANDY WARHOL
Lavender disaster
Silkscreen on canvas, 1964, 108in by 82in (274cm by 208cm)
New York $100,000(£54,054). 18.V.78
From the collection of Peter M. Brant

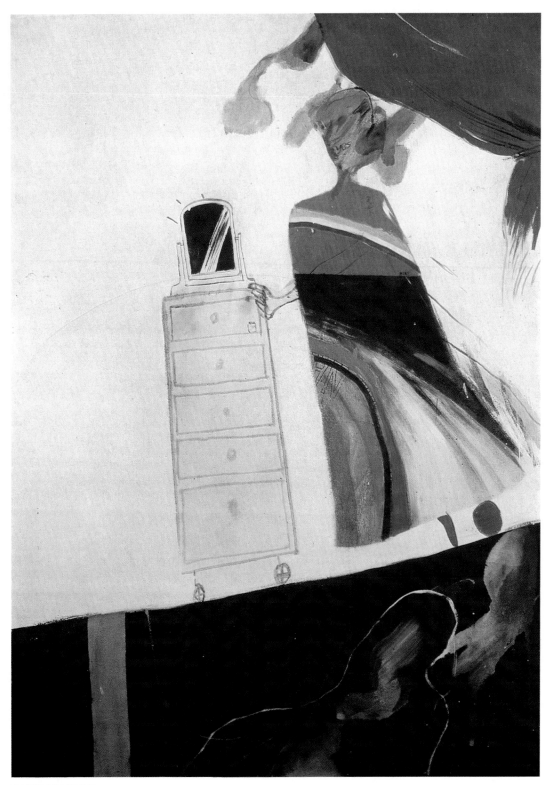

DAVID HOCKNEY
Boy with a portable mirror
Signed, titled and dated *'61* on the reverse, 55in by 39in (140cm by 99cm)
London £16,900($31,265). 5.IV.78

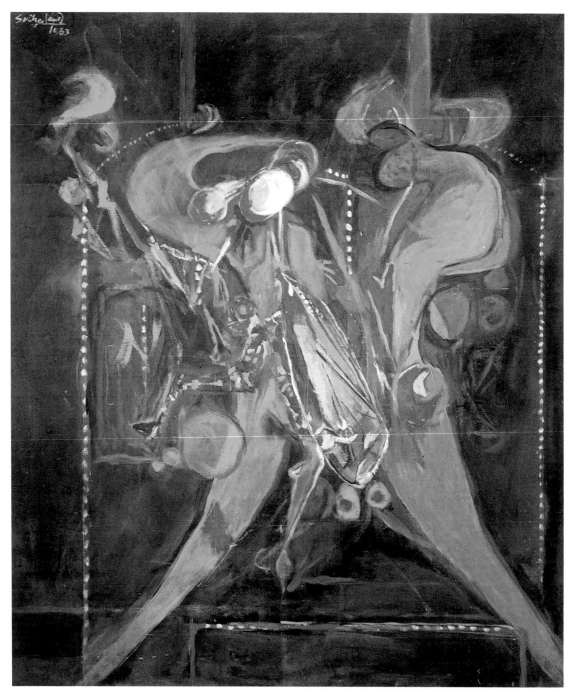

GRAHAM SUTHERLAND, OM
Insect
Signed and dated *1963*, 56½in by 47½in (142.5cm by 120.7cm)
London £14,000 ($25,900). 8.III.78

JOHN PETER RUSSELL
L'Aiguille, soleil d'hiver
Signed and dated *1903*,
25in by 25in (63.5cm by 63.5cm)
London £6,900 ($12,765). 16.XI.77
From the collection of the late
Dr A. B. Pastel

CHARLES CONDER
Children on the beach, Dieppe
Signed, inscribed *To Dal Young Nov. 96* and dated *Dieppe '95*, 14½in by 23½in (37cm by 60cm)
London £9,000 ($16,650). 7.VI.78
From the collection of Miss Sylvia Harrison

WALTER RICHARD SICKERT, ARA
L'Ennui
Signed, inscribed *To Asselin* and dated *1916*, 17¾in by 14½in (45cm by 37cm)
London £13,000 ($24,050). 7.VI.78

This is a version of the painting in the Tate Gallery, London

PHILIP WILSON STEER, OM
The ermine sea
Signed and dated '90, 23¾in by 29½in (60.3cm by 75cm)
London £20,000 ($37,000). 7.VI.78
From the collection of N. M. Daniel, MC

This picture was painted when the artist was at Swanage. Some sketches of children playing in the surf executed at about the same time are now in the Victoria and Albert Museum, London

BEN NICHOLSON, OM
White relief, project, 1938
Oil on carved board, signed and dated *1938* on the reverse, 11in by 16in (28cm by 40.6cm)
London £13,000 ($24,050). 8.III.78

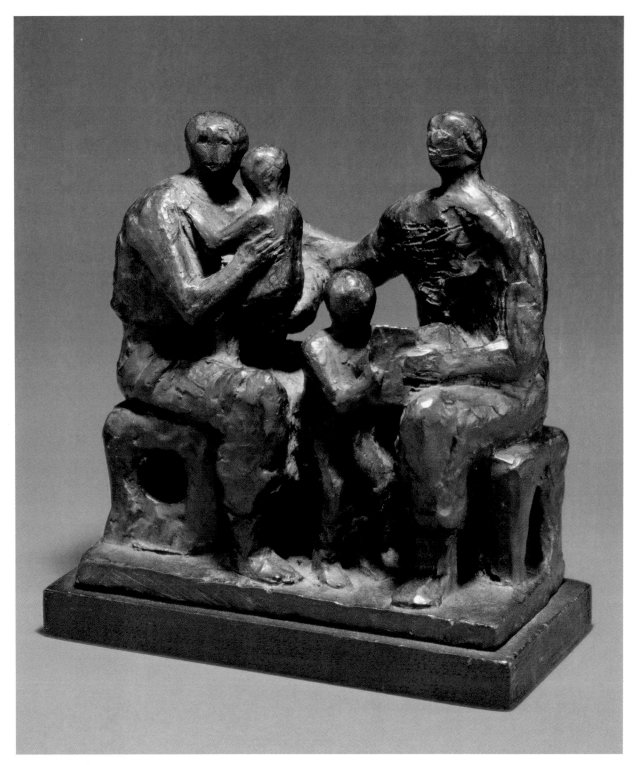

HENRY MOORE, OM, CH
Family group
Bronze on wood base, signed and dated '44, height of bronze 6⅜in (16.2cm)
New York $40,000 (£21,622). 19.V.78

This cast is number 1 from an edition of nine

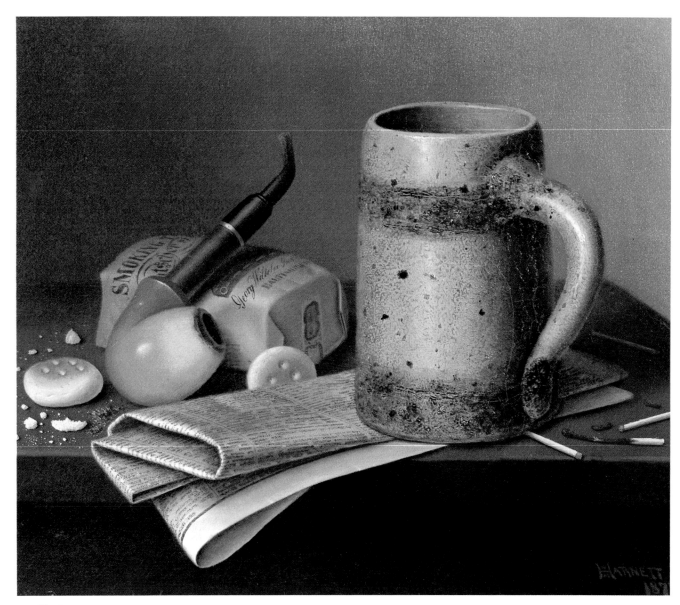

Fig 1
WILLIAM MICHAEL HARNETT
Still life
Signed and dated *1877*, 11½in by 13½in (29.2cm by 34.3cm)
New York $72,000(£38,919). 22.III.78

A landmark auction of American paintings

Thomas Norton

An atmosphere of optimistic, even cheerful, anticipation characterised the capacity audience gathered at the Madison Avenue salerooms for the dispersal of the collection of American paintings formed by Dr John J. McDonough of Youngstown, Ohio. Ever since the sale had been announced, dealers, collectors and interested observers of the art and auction scene had predicted that it would be a significant event. Both the strength of the market for American representational paintings and the extent to which collecting interest had spread beyond a few metropolitan centres would surely be put to the test when the sixty-three works were offered, and the feeling that a landmark auction was about to take place was measurably discernible in the room as the auction began.

Landmark auctions, those which continue to be used as reference points long after they occur, happen only rarely and are not always easily predictable, requiring, as they do, the right combination of circumstances and property. The quality of the collection as a whole, the individual works themselves, the reputation of the collector, the reasons for selling, the buoyancy of the market and the prevailing economic and political climates, must all come together in order to produce an event that will rise above the routine activities of the auction room. The sale of the McDonough Collection possessed most, if not all of the required ingredients: the paintings had been carefully chosen over a period of twelve years so that they formed an almost comprehensive cross-section of the principal artists, themes and periods of representational American Art; many of the individual works were of such outstanding quality that they would have caused excitement even in a mixed-owner sale; the collector was well known and had lent the pictures during 1975–76 for a travelling exhibition throughout the country[1] and there were sound personal reasons for selling. Further, the market for these nineteenth- and twentieth-century paintings had been steadily rising for a decade as more and more exhibitions, periodicals and books lavished attention on what had been the special province of a few private collectors and dealers and the economic and political background, while not euphoric, was stable enough to inspire confidence in the worth of investing devalued 1978 dollars in the solid and pleasantly nostalgic artistic creations of previous eras.

After an inauspicious start the sale's first surprises came when a superb little *trompe-l'oeil* still life by William Harnett (Fig 1), bought at Parke-Bernet in 1968 for

Fig 2
GEORGE INNESS
After the shower
Signed, *circa* 1863–65, 12¼in by 18½in (31.1cm by 47cm)
New York $52,000(£28,108). 22.III.78

$25,000, made $72,000; then George Inness' *After the shower* (Fig 2), purchased for $23,000 at Parke-Bernet in 1969, made $52,000 and Robert Reid's *Reverie* (Fig 7), acquired for what was thought to be a ridiculously high price of $5,000 in 1968, fetched $37,500. In fact, this charming early example by a relatively unknown artist, had gone from $50 to $500 to $5,000 in the 1960s and was later included in an influential exhibition of American Impressionist painting in 1973–74 before re-appearing in the saleroom this year. Only the early portraits by Robert Feke, C. W. Peale and Gilbert Stuart failed to elicit the predicted response showing again that the taste for these eighteenth-century paintings remains restricted to a small group.

The McDonough Collection was especially rich in typical and fine examples by the American Impressionists. The best-known member of the group was Childe Hassam, whose skilful landscapes of France and America, especially his city-scapes of New York inspired by Pissarro's views of Paris, have always been highly regarded by collectors of American painting. *Church of the Paulist Fathers* (Fig 4), provides a

Fig 3
JOHN SINGER SARGENT
Portrait of Charles Stuart Forbes
Signed and inscribed *to my friend Forbes, circa* 1889, 28¾in by 21¼in (73cm by 54cm)
New York $110,000(£59,459). 22.III.78

Fig 4
FREDERICK CHILDE HASSAM
Church of the Paulist Fathers, New York
Signed, 1907, 22in by 24in (55.9cm by 61cm)
New York $70,000(£37,838). 22.III.78

Fig 5
MAURICE BRAZIL PRENDERGAST
Summer day
Signed, 1918, 32in by 37in (81.3cm by 94cm)
New York $160,000(£86,486). 22.III.78

Fig 6
ALFRED H. MAURER
Jeanne
Signed, *circa* 1904, 74¾in by 39⅜in (189.9cm by 100cm)
New York $115,000(£62,162). 22.III.78

Fig 7
ROBERT REID
Reverie
On panel, signed and dated *'90*, 12in by 20in (30.5cm by 50.8cm)
New York $37,500(£20,270). 22.III.78

glimpse of New York City's West Side near what is now the Lincoln Center for the Performing Arts. When Hassam painted the scene from the window of his studio on 67th Street, he could look southwest over the anachronistically crenellated battlement of an armoury (now a television studio) towards the old Empire Hotel (demolished) and the Church of St Paul the Apostle, mother Church of the Paulists.[2] Today the view is blocked by highrise apartment buildings although the church still stands. Hassam enjoyed great success and fortune during his lifetime, but even his pictures were not immune to the slump in prices characteristic of the period from the 1930s to the '60s. *Church of the Paulist Fathers* had sold for $1,050 in a 1944 Parke-Bernet auction; this year it made over sixty times as much!

Although another Impressionist painting, Prendergast's *Summer day* (Fig 5), realised the highest price of the day, a masterpiece by a much less famous artist dominated the pre-sale exhibition and 'stole the show'. This was Alfred Maurer's *Jeanne* (Fig 6), painted in Paris before he became an Impressionist and curiously prophetic of the artist's tragic career.

Born in 1868, Maurer was the son of Louis Maurer, an enormously successful painter and printmaker for Currier & Ives in New York. His portrait of *Jeanne* is at once a brilliant depiction of a young woman, in the tradition of Velasquez and Manet, and a sardonic statement on the haughty female sitters of Sargent and Whistler whose fashionable portraits were much in vogue at the time. Jeanne was a model, 'alluring as a kitten, and as pettable'.[3] The painting sold for a record price, prompting a round of applause from the audience. Dr McDonough later commented:

> 'I'm pleased that *Jeanne* did so well. I have thought for a long time that Alfred Maurer's first period was far and away his best. Maybe future generations will accept his later, *avant-garde* work, but thus far they have not done so . . . Further, he had a miserable life – a father who upstaged him, a woman, possibly Jeanne, who could not be supported by him – and then he ultimately took his own life. It is a sad commentary, but [*Jeanne*] told the whole world what a truly great talent Maurer was.'

In reminiscing about the formation and subsequent sale of the paintings in the collection, Dr McDonough had also written:

> '. . . I really loved them all. I don't feel that I ever bought one with the idea of making a profit on it. I always hoped that I could buy intelligently . . . but I am afraid a lot of people who have contacted me since the sale are under the erroneous opinion that I bought for a profit. This couldn't be farther from the facts. [Every example in a collection] must be a work of art by an artist that you know very well and whose work you know thoroughly, as well as from the period in which he did his best work. Even more importantly, the picture must "come off" . . . must really speak for itself. There are so many intangibles in the selection of a work of art that I really don't believe there are any set formulas. Successful art-collecting is scholarship, *love*, and a moderate amount of money. Of the three, scholarship is the most important.'[4]

Indeed, Dr McDonough's collection did reflect these criteria: the range of subjects he had selected was impressive and he had also included examples from almost all periods of American art from early portraits, landscapes and genre paintings to the 'Ashcan' school and precursors of abstraction. Gaps such as the omission of works by Thomas Eakins or the Western painters like Thomas Moran and Frederic Remington were due to the unavailability of suitable examples within a relatively modest budget.

Many records were set and, along with such famous names as John Singer Sargent (Fig 3), Winslow Homer, Eastman Johnson, Thomas Sully, Rembrandt Peale and Andrew Wyeth, several under-appreciated and lesser-known artists enjoyed more widespread recognition. The sale brought a total of $1,892,750, surpassing expectations and turning pre-sale anticipation into post-sale jubilation. A landmark auction had indeed taken place.

[1] See John Bullard, *A Panorama of American Painting – The John J. McDonough Collection*, catalogue, 1975. John Bullard is Director of the New Orleans Museum of Art where the paintings were exhibited as well as in San Diego, San Antonio, Little Rock, Greensburg, Raleigh, Oklahoma City and Youngstown

[2] The Paulist Order was founded in 1858 by Father Issac Hecker (1819–1888) and was the first American order of Roman Catholic priests

[3] Elizabeth McCausland, *A. H. Maurer*, 1951, p83

[4] This quote and the one above are taken from a letter to the author, 18 April 1978

GEORGE CALEB BINGHAM
The jolly flatboatmen, no 2
Circa 1848, 25¼in by 37in (64.1cm by 94cm)
Los Angeles $980,000 (£529,730). 6.VI.78

This is the second of the three known depictions by Bingham of the subject and can probably be dated *circa* 1848. The artist, a largely self-taught limner who became America's greatest painter of life on the frontier, was born in Virginia in 1811 and died in Kansas City, Missouri in 1879. His achievement has been described by the art historian E. P. Richardson as 'one of the mysterious phenomena of the age . . . he was part of the life he painted . . . he saw the grand meaning of the commonplace'.

Roughly-built flatboats, piloted by farmboys from Indiana and other mid-Western states, were the principal means during the early nineteenth century of bringing American agricultural produce to market. A young Indiana farmboy, Abraham Lincoln, made two such trips 'downriver' to New Orleans and through engravings of Bingham's paintings, as well as through the stories of Mark Twain, the romantic life of the Mississippi bargemen became part of America's folklore

EDWARD HICKS
The Peaceable Kingdom
Signed and inscribed *The Peaceable Kingdom, Isa 11.6.7.8.,* 1847, 24in by 32in (61cm by 81.2cm)
New York $125,000 (£67,568). 27.X.77
From the collection of The Vineland Historical Society

Edward Hicks was a Quaker preacher whose art was a direct reflection of his religious meditations. His vision of a world without strife led to over sixty variations of the theme *The Peaceable Kingdom* which is found in Isaiah, chapter XI. In this version Hicks has included a vignette of William Penn's treaty with the Indians on the left of the canvas. He believed that Penn, in founding the Quaker community, had also achieved a peaceable kingdom on earth

R. W. AND S. A. SHUTE
Portrait of a young boy
Watercolour and pencil on paper, *circa* 1840, 27¼in by 18½in (69.2cm by 47cm)
New York $42,500 (£22,973). 27.IV.78
From the collection of Edgar William and Bernice Chrysler Garbisch

JOHN SINGLETON COPLEY, RA
Portrait of Mrs George Turner, née Elizabeth Cutty
Pastel, 22¼in by 16½in (56.5cm by 42cm)
London £31,000 ($57,350). 20.VII.78
From the collection of the late Mrs Wright Morrow

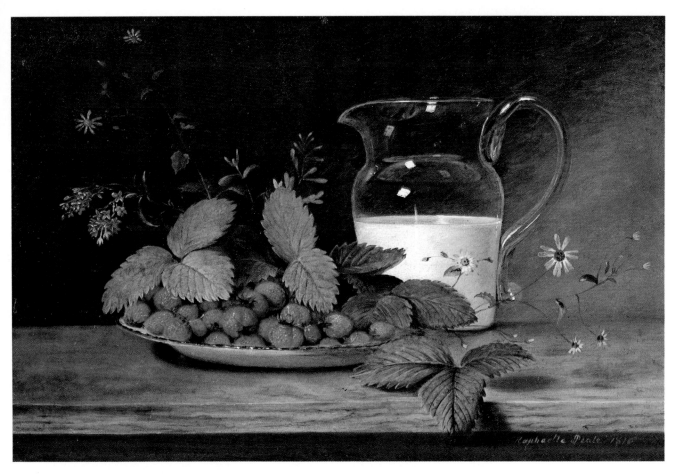

RAPHAELLE PEALE
Strawberries and cream
On panel, signed and dated *1816*, 13in by 19½in (33cm by 49.5cm)
New York $170,000(£91,892). 21.IV.78

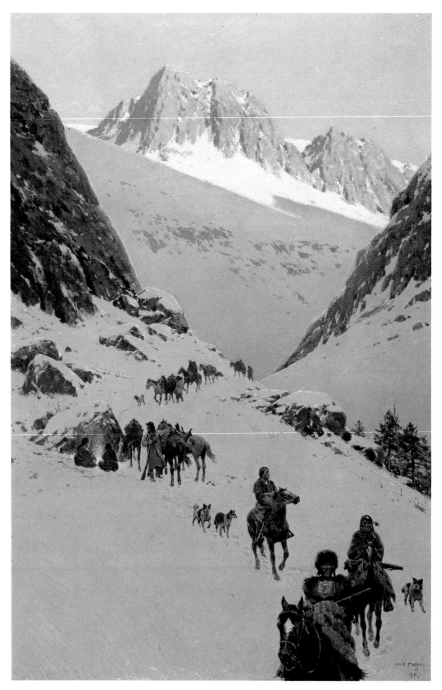

HENRY F. FARNY
Crossing the divide
Signed and dated *1907*, 28¼in by 18¼in (71.8cm by 46.4cm)
New York $195,000(£105,405). 21.IV.78

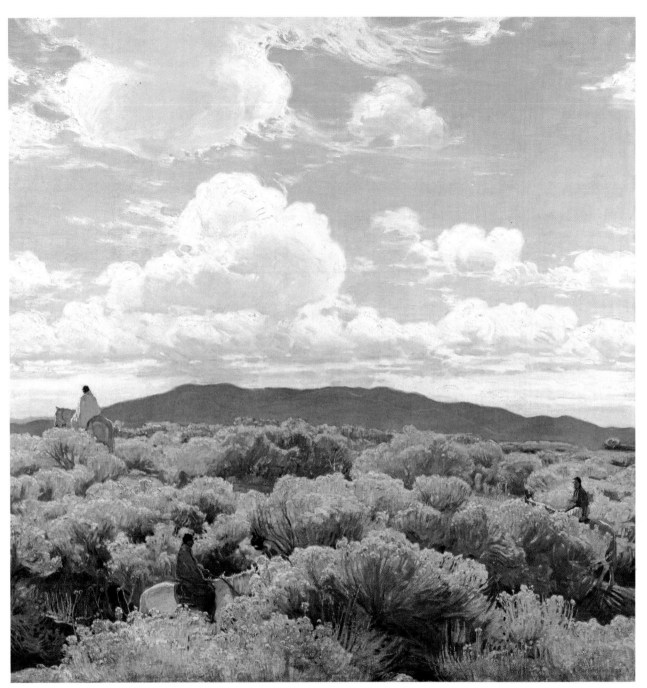

ERNEST MARTIN HENNINGS
Coming through the greasewood
Signed, 43in by 45in (109.2cm by 114.3cm)
New York $47,000(£25,405). 27.X.77
From the collection of the late Ronald Tree

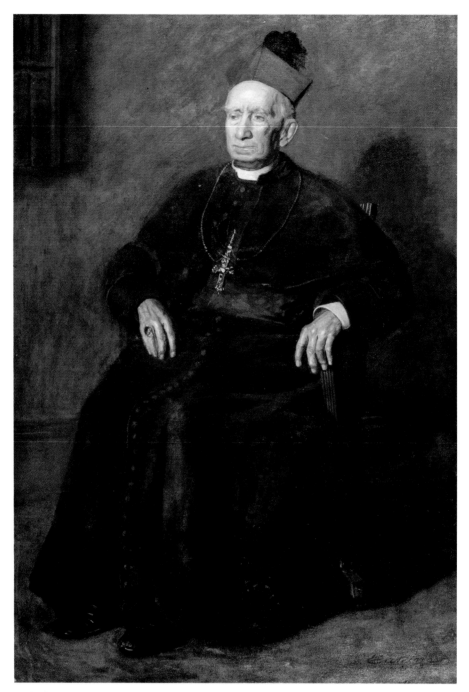

THOMAS EAKINS
Portrait of William Henry Elder, Archbishop of Cincinnati
Mounted on panel, signed and dated *1903*, 66½in by 45½in (168.9cm by 115.6cm)
New York $265,000(£143,243). 21.IV.78

JAMES WILSON MORRICE, RCA
La communiante
32¾in by 46½in (83.2cm by 118.1cm)
Toronto Can $98,000 (£47,343: $87,585). 15.V.78

DAVID BROWN MILNE
Maine Monument
Signed, titled on the reverse, 1914, 20in by 22in (50.8cm by 55.9cm)
Toronto Can $19,000 (£9,179: $16,981). 27.X.77

JACOB HENDRIK PIERNEEF
Saliena by Phalaborwa
Signed and dated '45, 23¾in by 29¾in (60.5cm by 75.5cm)
Johannesburg R9,200(£5,750:$10,638). 5.XII.77
From the collection of Mr and Mrs Leslie Derber

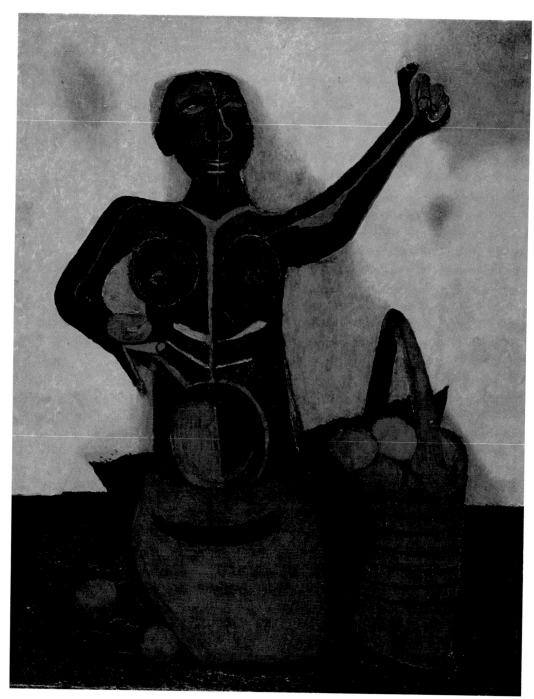

RUFINO TAMAYO
Mujer India
Signed and dated '42, 46½in by 36⅜in (118cm by 92.5cm)
New York $47,500(£25,676). 5.IV.78
From the collection of Nathan Cummings

Prints

JACQUES CALLOT
Le combat à la barrière
Etching, the set of ten plates (one illustrated) plus the four rare additional plates
London £1,800($3,330). 17.XI.77

ALBRECHT DÜRER
The landscape with the cannon
Etching on iron, 1518, 8½in by 12¾in (21.8cm by 32.3cm)
London £14,000($25,900). 26.IV.78

Because Dürer used iron instead of copper plates for his etchings, he was faced with the danger of the plates rusting. *The landscape with the cannon*, the last and largest of his six etchings, is rarely found in impressions such as this before the rust marks

ALBRECHT DÜRER
Knight, Death and the Devil
Engraving, 1513, 9⅜in by 7½in (23.7cm by 19cm)
New York $32,500(£17,568). 3.V.78

REMBRANDT HARMENSZ. VAN RIJN
Landscape with an obelisk
Etching and drypoint, second and final state, $3\frac{1}{4}$in by $6\frac{3}{8}$in (8.3cm by 16.2cm)
London £10,000($18,500). 17.XI.77

JOHN ROBERT COZENS
Studies of trees
Soft-ground etching with aquatint, the set of fourteen plates from the first edition,
published 1 February 1789
London £3,200($5,920). 2.XII.77

GEORGE STUBBS, ARA
A recumbent leopard by a tree
Mixed method engraving, published 1 May 1788, $9\frac{7}{8}$in by 13in (25.1cm by 33cm)
London £8,000($14,800). 26.IV.78

ANDERS ZORN
Fisherman at Saint Ives
Etching, the first state of two, 1891,
$10\frac{7}{8}$in by $7\frac{7}{8}$in (27.7cm by 20cm)
New York $1,800(£973). 12.I.78

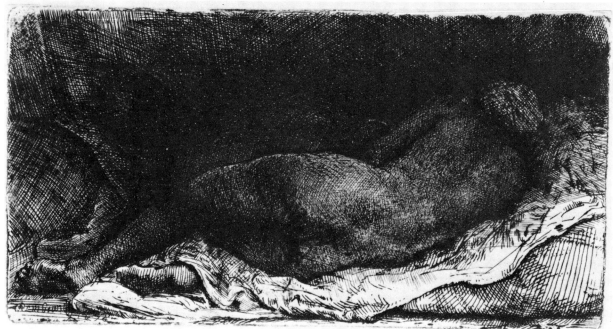

REMBRANDT HARMENSZ. VAN RIJN
Negress lying down
Etching, the second state of three, $3\frac{1}{4}$in by $6\frac{1}{4}$in (8.2cm by 15.8cm)
London £5,200($9,620). 26.IV.78

FRANCISCO JOSE DE GOYA Y LUCIENTES
A woman reading
Lithograph on laid paper, one of only eight or nine known proofs, $6\frac{5}{8}$in by $9\frac{5}{8}$in (17cm by 24.5cm)
London £16,000($29,600). 17.XI.77

Fig 1
HENRI DE TOULOUSE–LAUTREC
Idylle princière
A lithograph printed in colours on wove, a fine impression of a trial proof before the addition of the purple and rose stones, and before the edition of sixteen impressions, 1897, $14\frac{7}{8}$in by $11\frac{1}{4}$in
(37.7cm by 28.5cm)
London £37,000($68,450). 27.IV.78

Toulouse-Lautrec lithographs from the Charell Collection

Wolfgang Wittrock

In a dedication on one of his lithographs Toulouse-Lautrec acknowledges an important debt: *A Pellet l'intrépide éditeur.* Gustave Pellet (1859–1919), the Parisian art dealer, published almost all of Lautrec's most beautiful colour lithographs. Today it seems strange that it should need courage to publish what are now recognised as Lautrec's masterpieces, but we forget that at the end of the nineteenth century colour lithography was generally regarded as a commercial process and had no connection with serious graphic art.

Black-and-white lithography was invented by the Bavarian, Alois Senefelder, at the turn of the eighteenth century and the new technique was immediately applied to commercial fields, such as the printing of sheet music and maps. Interest in the technique spread and in the early nineteenth century the first acceptable colour lithograph was printed by Godefroy Engelmann in France. In turn, this 'chromolithography', as it was known, was also used commercially, largely for printed reproductions of paintings. A few artists, among them Goya, Géricault and Delacroix, recognised the creative possibilities of the technique, but these were exceptions. It was not until 1874 that Edouard Manet began to bring colour lithography into the world of the fine arts. For most of the century the technique remained in the hands of professional printers, where it underwent considerable refinement, reaching a peak of sophistication in the 1890s. From then on it was steadily replaced by photographic techniques. Only a few twentieth-century artists, such as Jasper Johns, have kept the technique alive and produced fine colour lithographs.

In the second half of the nineteenth century, lithography was used for almost all sheet printing where text and illustration needed to be reproduced together. Above all, colour lithography was used to print posters, the first of the mass media, which had a powerful effect on popular imagination and taste. The public's favourite designer between 1870 and 1890 was the Frenchman, Jules Chéret (1836–1932), who was not only a designer, but also head of the printing works Chaix and a highly accomplished lithographic technician in his own right.

Toulouse-Lautrec received his first commission for a colour poster in 1891 from the Moulin Rouge. Many more commissions followed and Lautrec's posters were recognised, even at the time, as the best designed and most influential ever produced, but they were never taken seriously as art. Although more and more artists used lithography, the art-buying public rejected it, just as photography has been largely rejected until very recently. Given these circumstances the reasons for Lautrec's dedication to Pellet become clearer. It needed a brave and imaginative publisher to support Lautrec in his attempt to take up what Manet had begun: to use colour lithography as a means of producing small-scale works with serious artistic claims.

Pellet may have been attracted to Lautrec's work through the subject-matter, the theatres, music-halls and prostitutes of Paris. He was already publishing specifically erotic material by Félicien Rops and Louis Legrand in large quantities. By comparison, the mere twenty works he published by Lautrec seem modest, in every sense.

Another bond between Lautrec and Pellet was their admiration for Edgar Degas who, in the 1870s and '80s, produced a group of etchings, lithographs and monotypes of crucial importance, many of the latter hand-coloured and finished with pastel. They were never published and were accessible only to the artist's friends. Lautrec met Degas through his cousin, Désiré Dihau, and he could then have seen these hand-coloured monotypes. He certainly must have seen them by 1896 when the estate of Gustave Caillebotte, who had owned several of the monotypes, was presented to the Musée Luxembourg in Paris. The delicate colouring and in some cases even the individual compositions are derived from Japanese woodcuts, which both Degas and Lautrec admired. In the colour lithograph *Femme qui se lave*, from the series *Elles*, Lautrec's style closely resembles Degas', in particular his pastel-coloured monotype *La toilette fillette* (Janis 150). But Lautrec achieves the effects which Degas attempted in the colour monotypes through the medium which he had made his own, colour lithography. The choice of medium was partly a matter of character. Degas lived and worked in quiet and solitude, Lautrec was in his element in the strident night life of Paris. He sought the widest currency for his work and cared nothing for academic definitions of an original work of art: his work was as well printed on the commercial presses as on the traditional ones, a fact which Madame Dortu recognises in her book *Lautrec by Lautrec* (Lausanne/Paris 1964) by including works which could be termed reproductions in the catalogue of original prints.

Until his relationship with Pellet, Lautrec gave most of his prints to the dealer Edouard Kleinmann, who took them on commission and only paid the artist for what he sold. Lautrec's income was very irregular and his needs increased as his life-style grew more extravagant. The allowance from his family was curtailed when their wine estates ran into difficulty. From 1896 onwards his requests for money in his letters to his mother grew more and more pressing. A rich publisher like Pellet, who commissioned Lautrec's lithographs himself and paid the artist for the work he did rather than for the work he sold, must have been very welcome. Lautrec's relationship with Pellet and with another dealer, André Marty, shows the crucial role which a committed and supportive dealer can play. It was commissions from these two men which stimulated Lautrec's greatest colour lithographs.

The first commission Lautrec received from Marty was for a lithograph of Loïe Fuller, the American dancer, in her famous Fire Dance (Fig 2). In this dance her floating drapery was illuminated by the newly-invented multi-coloured electric footlights. Colta Feller Yves describes the print:

'Lautrec's depiction of her is so unusual and daring, so foreign to anything in western art up to that time (and but a step away from twentieth-century abstract art) that the concept could only have come from the Japanese.'[1]

Fig 2   HENRI DE TOULOUSE–LAUTREC
Miss Loïe Fuller
A lithograph printed in colours on wove, 1892–93, 14$\frac{3}{8}$in by 10$\frac{1}{2}$in (36.5cm by 26.8cm)
London £14,500($26,825). 27.IV.78

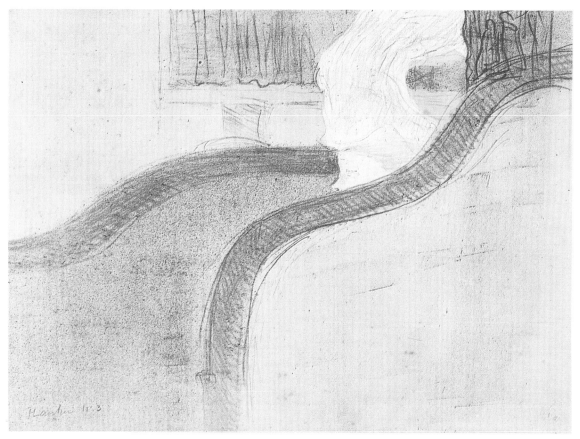

Fig 3   HENRI DE TOULOUSE-LAUTREC
La petite loge
A lithograph printed in colours, one of an edition of twelve, signed in pencil and inscribed *No 3*,
1897, $9\frac{1}{4}$in by $12\frac{1}{2}$in (23.5cm by 31.7cm)
London £10,000($18,500). 27.IV.78

The print has often been described as having watercolour applied to it because it has been assumed that colour lithography could not print the rainbow of light on the dancer's dress. This is to underestimate the range of the medium. Lautrec used a technique called 'Irisdruck' in which each band of colour merges delicately with the next without becoming blended, even though printed from the same stone at the same time. It has often also been claimed that the artist himself dusted each print with gold and silver, for metal colours cannot be printed directly from a stone, but close investigation reveals that the area to be covered by the metal powders was first printed in a neutral colour and then the gold and silver were dabbed onto the sheet where they adhered to the wet ink, a task which the printer could have performed himself. Naturally the areas treated in this way differ slightly from print to print but the differences cannot be attributed to deliberate intention on the artist's part.

In April 1896 Pellet published the series *Elles* in an edition of one hundred. Among the very few people who bought the series were Edvard Munch, the Norwegian painter who at this time was influenced by Lautrec, and Ambroise Vollard, the art

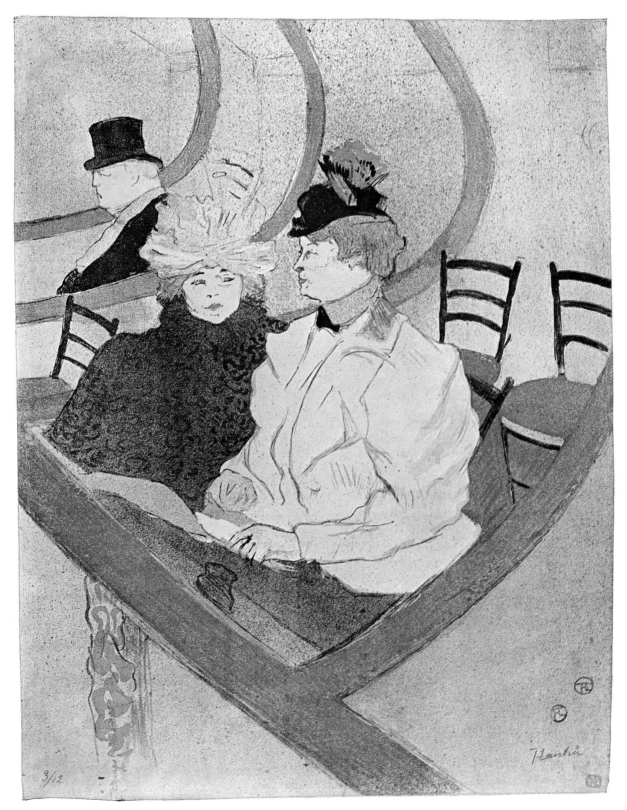

Fig 4   HENRI DE TOULOUSE-LAUTREC
La grande loge
A lithograph printed in colours, one of an edition of twelve, signed in pencil, stamped with the
monogram and inscribed 3/12, 1897, 20⅛in by 15⅝in (51cm by 39.8cm)
London £5,500. 6.X.66 (The first Charell sale)

Fig 5 HENRI DE TOULOUSE-LAUTREC
Elsa, dite la Viennoise
The fifth of a sequence of five lithographs printed in colours on wove and *chine*, signed, 1897,
approximately 22¼in by 14¾in (56.7cm by 37.5cm)
London £20,000($37,000). 27.IV.78

dealer, who showed them in June 1896 at his *Exposition des Peintres-Graveurs*, the exhibition which launched his career as one of the most important print publishers of the twentieth century. The price which Pellet fixed for the series, 300 francs, then rather high for Lautrec's work, shows that he did not mind if the prints did not sell at once and indeed sixty years later the Pellet family still had complete sets of the *Elles*. At the end of 1896 Pellet commissioned more colour lithographs, this time to be printed in very small editions, for collectors who were already interested in the artist's work.[2] Lautrec, working with the printer, Stern, produced several new masterpieces. The entire group of prints was not only signed by Lautrec but bore the editor's monogram and stamp, a sign of the new importance of his role.

The Charell Collection, which was sold at Sotheby's in two parts, in October 1966 and April 1978, included the entire *Elles* series and all these special works commissioned by Pellet. *La grande loge* (Fig 4), published in an edition of twelve impressions, was sold in 1966 before the great rise in Lautrec prices. The second sale included a rare proof of the *Idylle princière* (Fig 1) before the edition of sixteen impressions. It is printed on a larger sheet of paper than the edition giving the image more room to breathe. Also included was a fine impression of *La petite loge* (Fig 3).

However, the outstanding feature of the second sale was a group of five proofs, each different, of *Elsa, dite la Viennoise*, before the edition of seventeen impressions; it was the only group of working proofs of such importance to be found outside a museum. Lautrec usually tore up his working proofs but on this occasion someone, either the printer or Pellet himself, saved the precious documents and pieced them together. The sequence demonstrates Lautrec's working methods and mastery of technique, his repeated reworking of the subject to strengthen or weaken the intensity of the colours to achieve a balance between colour and composition of a subtlety and perfection unique in his work. The four trial proofs show the development of the drawing stone from grey through dark olive green to black. In the final version (Fig 5) the drawing stone is printed in black. The greyish mauve stone is only lightly inked, in marked contrast to the fourth state, and the blue and red stones are strongly inked producing a more brilliant tone.

The Charell brothers, Ludwig and Erik, began their collection in the early 1930s, founding it on their purchases from the auction of the collection of Heinrich Stinnes. They went on buying until the early 1950s by which date the collection was almost complete and was presented to the public in the form of a travelling exhibition. In turn it was sold in these two auctions, giving print collectors a new chance to acquire the rarest and the finest of Lautrec's lithographs.

---

[1] *The Great Wave: The Influence of Japanese Woodcuts on French Prints*, The Metropolitan Museum of Art, New York, 1974

[2] *La grande loge*, D. 204, A/W 205, edition of 12, 60 francs each
La clownesse au Moulin Rouge, D. 205, A/W 206, edition of 20, 50 francs each
Idylle princière, D. 206, A/W 207, edition of 16, 50 francs each
La danse au Moulin Rouge, D. 208, A/W 209, edition of 20, 50 francs each
La petite loge, D. 209, A/W 212, edition of 12, 50 francs each
Elsa, dite la Viennoise, D. 207, A/W 208, edition of 17, 50 francs each

PAUL GAUGUIN
Te faruru – ici on fait l'amour
Woodcut printed in black, ochre, and yellow on japan paper, 1894,
14in by 8in (35.6cm by 20.4cm)
£15,000($27,750)

PAUL GAUGUIN
Les cigales et les fourmis
One of the complete set of ten zincographs printed in black or sanguine on brilliant yellow wove
paper, 1889
£29,000 ($53,650)

The prints on these two pages are from the collection of the late Sir Rex de C. Nan Kivell, CMG and
were sold in London on 4 October 1977

EDVARD MUNCH
Frauen am Meeresufer
Woodcut printed in colours on wove, signed, 1898, 18in by 20in (45.7cm by 50.8cm)
London £40,000($74,000). 15.XII.77

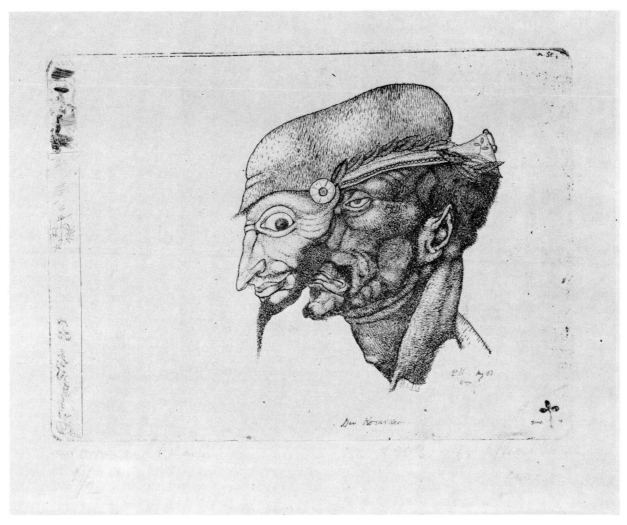

PAUL KLEE
Komiker – inv. 4 (the first version)
Etching printed in dark green on wove, signed and dated *1903*, 4⅝in by 6⅜in (11.8cm by 16.1cm)
London £15,500($28,675). 4.X.77
From the collection of the late Sir Rex de C. Nan Kivell, CMG

Only two other impressions of this print are recorded, one a trial proof, the other numbered 1/2.
This is the last impression taken from the plate as indicated by the inscription *Letzer drück, platten zerstört* (last print, plate destroyed)

PABLO PICASSO
La Minotauromachie
Etching, signed, 1935, 19½in by 27⅛in (49.5cm by 69cm)
New York $125,000 (£67,568). 4.V.78

FRANZ MARC
Ruhende Pferde
Woodcut printed in colours on japan paper, one of only about ten impressions, signed and inscribed
No 9, 1911–12, 6⅝in by 8⅞in (16.7cm by 22.7cm)
London £7,500($13,875). 26.IV.78

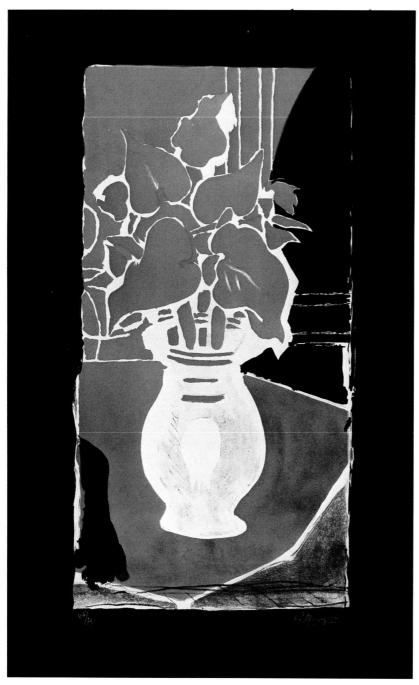

GEORGES BRAQUE
Feuilles, couleur, lumière
Lithograph printed in colours, signed, 1953
38¼in by 23¾in (97.1cm by 60.3cm)
New York $18,000 (£9,730): 10.II.78

Manuscripts and Printed Books

GABRIELE CAPODILISTA
Itinerario di Terra Santa
An Italian manuscript on vellum with two folding maps and a double-page miniature,
contemporary Italian binding, Padua, *circa* 1475
London £44,000 ($81,400). 11.VII.78

The Battle of the Lamb
A leaf from the Bibliothèque Nationale *Beatus* manuscript, Northern Spain, *circa* 1200
London £45,000($83,250). 20.VI.78
From the collection of the late Robert von Hirsch

The Crucifixion
One of a pair (with *St Anthony blessing the animals*) of illuminated leaves on vellum by the Veronica Master, Cologne, *circa* 1405
London £90,000($166,500). 20.VI.78
From the collection of the late Robert von Hirsch

The Hours of Raoul d'Ailly
A Latin manuscript on vellum with four large miniatures by the Luxembourg Master (possibly
identical with Simon Marmion), eighteenth-century French red morocco binding, Amiens,
circa 1430–40
London £130,000($240,500). 11.VII.78

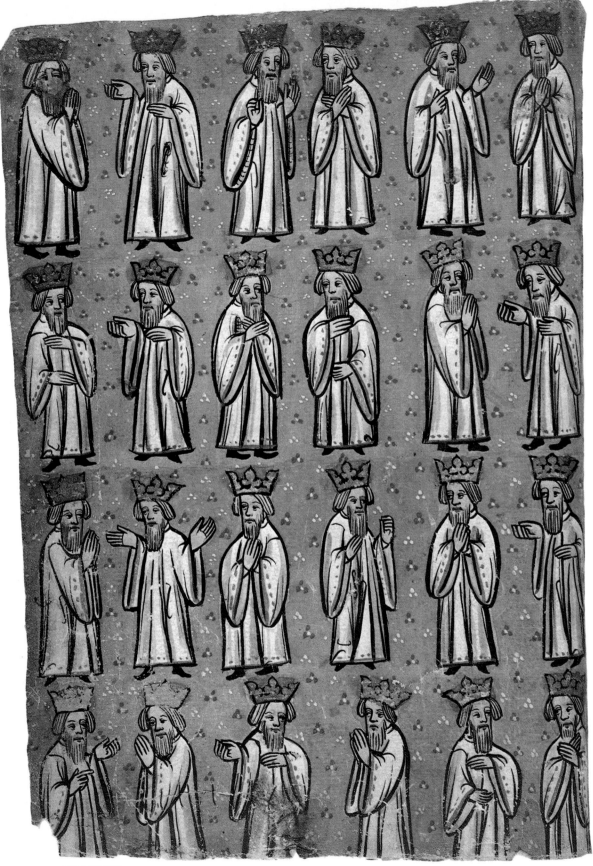

OTTO VON PASSAU
Die vierundzwanzig Alten
A German manuscript on vellum written by the scribe Heinrich Ebinger, one large and twenty-four
small miniatures, Switzerland, *circa* 1397
London £13,000 ($24,050). 20.VI.78
From the collection of the late Major J. R. Abbey

The Dall'Armi Hours
A Latin manuscript on vellum, written by the scribe Pierantonio Sallando of
Reggio, twelve historiated initials and four full-page miniatures in Venetian
style, Bologna, *circa* 1500
London £9,000 ($16,650). 11.VII.78

Megillat Esther (Scroll of Esther)
A Hebrew manuscript on vellum,
floral and foliate decoration, on a
wooden roller in a cylindrical
carved wooden case, Italy, mid
eighteenth century
London £2,200 ($4,070). 25.X.77

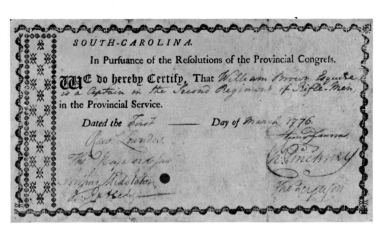

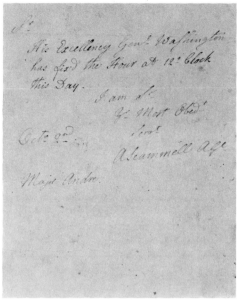

ARTHUR MIDDLETON
A signature on a military commission, part of a complete set of
signatures of the signers of the Declaration of Independence,
fifty-seven pieces, 1748–1825
$195,000(£105,405)

ALEXANDER SCAMMELL
An autograph note signed to Major André,
advising him that he was to be executed at
12 o'clock the same day, 2 October 1780
$11,000(£5,946)

PAUL REVERE
An autograph bill for expenses on his famous ride from Boston to New York and back
to alert New York and Pennsylvania of the events of the Boston Tea Party, 1774
$70,000(£37,838)

The items on this page are from the collection of the Elsie O. and Philip D. Sang Foundation and were sold in
New York on 26 April 1978

LUCRETIA BORGIA
An autograph letter to Ercole d'Este, Duke of Ferrara, written on the eve of her marriage to his son and sending a sword which the Pope, her father, had consecrated in honour of her consort, Rome, 1501
London £8,500($15,725). 16.V.78

EDWARD MONTAGU, EARL OF MANCHESTER
The marriage certificate of Charles II and Catherine
de Braganza retained by the Portuguese
Ambassador, Francisco de Melo e Torres, part of
the archive of the Ambassador's papers
London £33,000($61,050). 24.VII.78

Francisco de Melo e Torres, Conde da Ponte and
Marquis de Sande, was an outstanding military,
diplomatic and political figure at the time of the
Portuguese Restoration. He belonged to the group
of forty noblemen who in 1640 proclaimed
Portuguese independence from Spain and from
1657 to 1665 was Portuguese Ambassador to
England

NAPOLEON BONAPARTE
One from a series of 233 letters to Prince
Eugène de Beauharnais, his stepson,
adopted heir and Viceroy of Italy, June
1805 to July 1813
London £17,000($31,450). 16.V.78

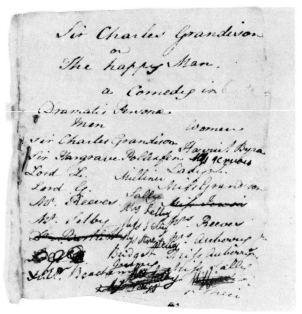

JANE AUSTEN
Sir Charles Grandison or The Happy Man
The autograph manuscript of a hitherto unknown play
on fifty-three small pages, 1799 or after
London £17,000 ($31,450). 13.XII.77
From the collection of great-great nephews of the
author

JANE AUSTEN
The Watsons
The autograph manuscript on seventy-six pages, with
extensive autograph revisions, Bath, 1804–5
London £38,000 ($70,300). 25.VII.78
From the collection of Joan Austen-Leigh

WILLIAM MORRIS
Pygmalion and the Image
A manuscript on vellum written and illuminated by Alberto and Raphael Sangorski, bound by them
in an elaborate jewelled binding, 1919
London £6,000 ($11,100). 23.VI.78

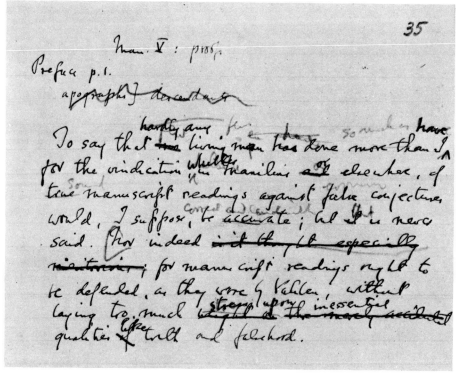

GEORGE CRUIKSHANK and **CHARLES DICKENS**
An autograph letter from the former, with Dickens'
autograph reply, 1839
New York $800 (£432). 11.IV.78
From the collection of David Borowitz

A. E. HOUSMAN
An autograph notebook containing drafts for his celebrated lecture *The Name and
Nature of Poetry*, delivered in 1933, and other material, *circa* 1930
London £5,500 ($10,175). 25.VII.78

6.

I am sorry that the Ice-bay of Forochel has not (so far) been cast for any significant part. It's just 'Elvish' for Northern Ice; and is a mere remnant of the colds of the North, the realm of the prime Dark Lord of earlier Ages. Arvedui, the last King of Arnor, is said, indeed, to have fled thither, and attempted to escape thence by ship, but to have been destroyed in the ice; and with him perished the last of the _palantíri_ of the North Kingdom.

I am afraid this is a preposterously long letter; and perhaps presumptuous in its length, though your kindness and interest offer some excuse.

Soon after your visit, as pleasant as unexpected, I had a copy made of the chronology of the Second and Third Ages, for your perusal — purely annalistic and unmotivated. If it would still interest you, I will send it.

I was sorry to find, when it was returned, that the sheet on 'languages' etc. had been sent uncorrected, and with lots of words and phrases unerased, so that parts were hardly intelligible.

You may be interested to hear that a reprint of The Fellowship seems already to be needed. But I do not suppose the first printing was very large.

Yours sincerely
JRRTolkien.

J. R. R. TOLKIEN
An autograph letter to Naomi Mitchison concerning her review of _The Lord of the Rings,_ 1954
London £700($1,295). 13.XII.77
From the collection of Naomi Mitchison

Fig 1   VIGERIUS DE LA ROVERE (CARDINAL MARCUS)
Decachordum Christianum, first edition,
ten full-page and thirty-three smaller woodcuts,
Hieronymus Soncinus, Fano, 10 August 1507
London £1,900($3,515). 14.XI.77

Movable types

J. C. T. Oates

'It is quite purposeless', wrote the late S. H. Steinberg in his *Five Hundred Years of Printing*, 'to enumerate the dozens of one-horse towns in the Abruzzi or Savoy which can boast of one or perhaps even two early presses or to trace the steps of these wandering printers in their quest for patrons and customers'. So magisterial a dismissal of so important an element in the history of Italian printing cannot but give the reader pause, while some may deplore as well the implicit disrespect for the horse, an essential partner (with his cousins the mule and donkey) without whose co-operation the proto-typographers of Germany could hardly have got their gear beyond the Rhine basin. And can 'dozens' be right? Let us consult the authorities[1] and at the same time salute in retrospect the Broxbourne Library formed by the late Mr Albert Ehrman to illustrate the spread of printing. It contained no fewer than thirty-five of the forty-six Italian printing places mentioned below and abundantly illustrated what is surely one of the most attractive and humane aspects of this field.

Before 1520 only two towns in the Abruzzi are known to have had presses, Aquila, lying west of the Gran Sasso d'Italia and Ortona, a town on the coast much troubled by Turks and earthquakes. To the former in 1482, at the invitation and with the financial support of a consortium of local men of letters, came one Adam de Rottweil, a German who had previously operated a small and undistinguished press at Venice, to print the translations into Italian by a scholar in neighbouring Rieti of some of Plutarch's *Lives* and the *Chronica* of St Isidore, together with two smaller works by a local Franciscan. This venture ended, Adam, it seems, took to the road again (he may be the Adam Alamanus who printed a *Fasciculus temporum* in 1486 somewhere in Piedmont or Southern France) to be replaced at Aquila in 1493 by Eusanius de Stella, a native of the place, whose small output included an *Aesopus moralisatus* in Latin and Italian reprinted from a famous Naples edition with copies, not very expert, of its woodcuts, and a *Storia di Santo Grisedio*, also with woodcuts, some derivative, the rest crudely original.

Thereafter there was no printing in the Abruzzi until 1518–19, when Hieronymus Soncinus (Gershon ben Moses of Soncino) visited Ortona. He was one of the most peripatetic of printers, his career taking him from his native town (east of Milan), where he partnered his father in a Hebrew press in 1488, to Brescia and Barco and then in 1502 to Fano (Fig 1), where his output became humanist rather than Hebrew, and so on to Pesaro in 1507, thence to Ortona, and then northwards into the

Fig 2   ALBERTANUS
De loquedi ac tacendi modo,
first edition, a single woodcut,
Viotus de Dulcis, Cuneo, 4 December 1507
London £1,000($1,850). 14.XI.77

This was the first book printed at Cuneo

Romagna at Rimini in 1521 and Cesena in 1527, reaching his last resting-place at Constantinople in 1530.

By 'Savoy' Dr Steinberg presumably refers to what is now Piedmont, from the consideration of which we may exclude Turin as being unquestionably multi-horse on the Steinberg Scale. The first city of the region to receive the new craft was Mondovì, whither in 1472 Balthasar Corderius, a member of an influential family there resident, transported a press which he had acquired in Genoa, taking into partnership one of its former owners. Their output included an edition of the *Confessionale Defecerunt* of Antoninus, Bishop of Florence, of which over seventy fifteenth-century editions are known, and an Ovid, *Heroides*, before the enterprise ended in acrimony with Corderius incarcerating his partner in the hope of adjusting their financial relationship to his own advantage. One other press operated at Mondovì before the century ended, a halting concern run by the De Vivaldis family, which produced five books between 1476 and 1495. There followed a gap until 1508–9, when Vincentius Berruerius, a native of the city, brought to it a press he had operated at Saluzzo and with it produced a number of illustrated works of popular devotion in Italian. This press continued as a family business until 1521, when its last owner moved on to Savona on the Ligurian coast.

Fig 3 JOHANNES LUDOVICUS VIVALDUS
Opus regale, two parts in one volume,
three woodcuts, Jacobus de Circhis and
Sixtus de Somaschis, Saluzzo,
25 January 1507
London £4,500($8,325). 9.V.78

As at Mondovì it was an important resident who brought printing to Savigliano, Saluzzo's near neighbour to the west, in about 1473, if indeed the press *sine loco* whose products were signed by Christoforus Beyamus (i.e. de' Beggiami, a noble family seated at Savigliano) and Johannes Glim is correctly assigned to it. They too produced an *Heroides* and, though signed by Glim alone, the first edition of one of the most influential of Western works, the *Consolatio philosophiae* of Boethius. Caselle, a paper-making town, appears, somewhat mysteriously, as the place of printing of two books signed by Johannes Fabri, who had a substantial business in Turin, a mere five miles away. Paper was likewise made at Pinerolo where Jacobus Rubeus, driven from Venice by the plague, printed five books in 1479–81, including the *Consolatio* and Ovid's *Metamorphoses.* He was followed to Piedmont in 1506 by yet another established Venetian printer Simon Bevilaqua, who in that year moved to Saluzzo, where he printed a Carthusian Breviary, before proceeding to Cuneo (Fig 2) (where his output included books against the Waldensians), Novi Ligure, Savona, and finally Lyons. He had been preceded at Saluzzo (Fig 3), at this period perhaps the most

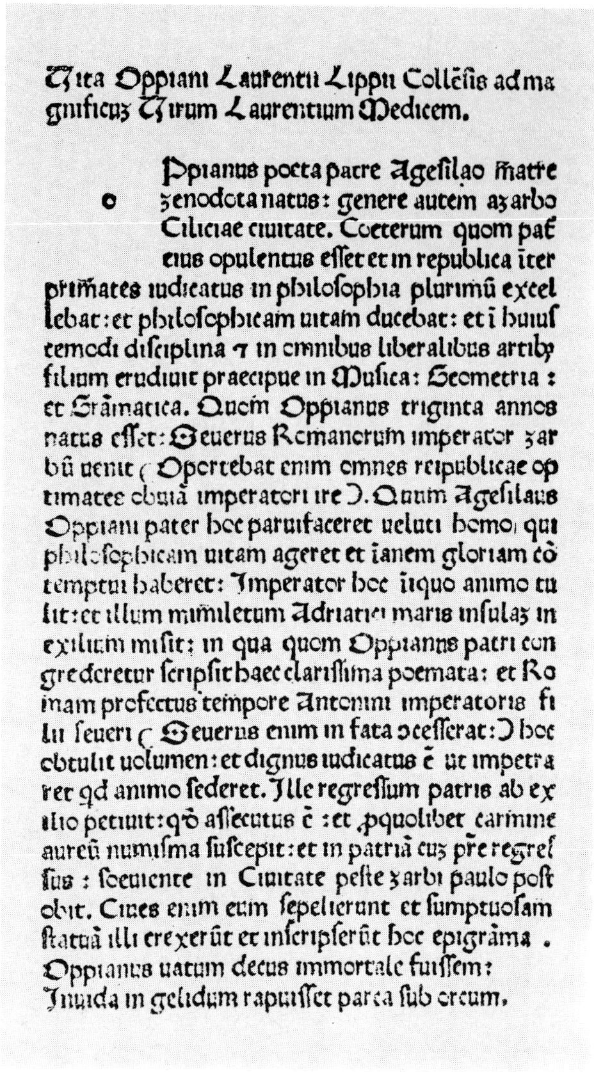

Vita Oppiani Laurentii Lippii Colleñis ad ma
gnificuz Virum Laurentium Medicem.

o Ppianus poeta patre Agefilao matre
zenodota natus: genere autem azarbo
Ciliciae ciuitate. Coeterum quom pat
eius opulentus effet et in republica iter
primates iudicatus in philofophia plurimu excel
lebat: et philofophicam uitam ducebat: et i huiuf
cemodi difciplina 7 in omnibus liberalibus artibz
filium erudiuit praecipue in Mufica: Geometria :
et Gramatica. Quom Oppianus triginta annos
natus effet: Seuerus Romanorum imperator zar
bu uenit (Oportebat enim omnes reipublicae op
timates obuia imperatori ire). Quum Agefilaus
Oppiani pater hoc paruifaceret ueluti homo, qui
philofophicam uitam ageret et ianem gloriam co
temptui haberet: Imperator hoc iiquo animo tu
lit: et illum mimiletum Adriatici maris infulaz in
exilium mifit: in qua quom Oppianus patri con
grederetur fcripfit haec clarifima poemata: et Ro
inam profectus tempore Antonini imperatoris fi
lii feueri (Seuerus enim in fata oceflerat) hoc
obtulit uolumen: et dignus iudicatus e ut impetra
ret qd animo federet. Ille regreffum patris ab ex
ilio petiuit: qd affecutus e : et pquolibet carmine
aureu numifma fufcepit: et in patriam cuz pre regref
fus : foeuiente in Ciuitate pefte zarbi paulo poft
obit. Ciues enim eum fepelierunt et fumptuofam
ftatuam illi erexerut et infcripferut hoc epigrama .
Oppianus uatum decus immortale fuiffem:
Inuida in gelidum rapuiffet parca fub orcum.

Fig 4   OPPIANUS
*Vita Oppiani Laurentii Lippii Collesis
admagnificu[m] Virum Laurentii Medicem,*
first edition, Bonus Gallus, Colle di
Valdelsa, 12 September 1478
London £3,500 ($6,475). 14.XI.77

This was the first printed book on
fishing and also contains recipes for
cooking by Lippius

important centre of cultural activity in Piedmont, in 1481 by Martinus de Lavalle
(who went on to Pavia) and at the turn of the century by the brothers Le Signerre,
whose main business was at Milan. Novi too had already seen printing, Nicolaus
Girardengus, a native of the town, having printed there in 1484 the first edition of the
Rosella by the local writer Baptista de Salis. Two presses were briefly located at Casale
di Monferrato north of Alessandria della Paglia (where however printing did not
begin until 1547–48); their known production numbers three items, of which one
was, once more, Ovid's *Heroides* and another an Italian translation of his *Ars amandi.*
Sangermano, Vercelli, and Chivasso successively (and with the encouragement of a
local patron of letters Pietro Cara) housed the press in 1484–86 of Jacobinus Suigus,
who printed at the first-named a Breviary for its house of Cistercians and at the last
the earliest of some two dozen fifteenth-century editions of the *Summa* of Angelus de
Clavasio, whose name proclaims his local connection. In the early years of the
sixteenth century printing came to Trino (in 1508) and to Asti (in 1518), both presses,
though there was no connection between them, specialising in legal folios.

S. Benedictus Cenobiti ce vitc inftitutor.   S. Romualdus Eremiti ce vite inftitutor.

Fig 5   *Proemialis epistola in qua de origine cenobitice [et] eremitice vite,*
a single woodcut, Monastery of San Salvatore, Fontebuono, 1520
London £1,000($1,850). 14.XI.77

This was the first book printed at Fontebuono

Fig 6   PAULUS DE MIDDELBURGO
De recta Paschae celebratione,
two parts in one volume, woodcut borders
and initials, Octavianus Petrutius,
Fossombrone, 1513
London £800 ($1,480). 15.XI.77

Although Steinberg's 'dozens' is thus seen to be a harmless hyperbole, other towns throughout Italy, most of them north of Florence, saw the same restless activity. Printers moved from one town to another to find a new and better market, often somewhere where paper was made and an overhead might be consequently reduced, as at Colle di Valdelsa (Fig 4) or Toscolano, or to escape some political upheaval or epidemic. They sought powerful and enlightened patrons, men like Ottaviano, brother of Federigo, Duke of Urbino (whose own antipathy to print is notorious) at Cagli, or the Boiardi at Scandiano, to promote or support their enterprises, or played upon the ambitions of local authors to see their works in print, as at Forlì, where Nicolaus Ferettus summoned printers from Cesena to print his guide to fine writing, disliked the result, and found another printer to do the job again, or San Gimignano, where the work of the printer Symeon Nicolai Nardi suffered grievous interruptions from the author Paolo Cortese, or Aversa, where one Lucas Prassicius was conducting a controversy with Augustinus Niphus. Sometimes the commission was official or institutional, to print the local laws at Udine or Palermo, or Camaldolensian texts at Fontebuono (Fig 5), or the works of the grave Scotists in their delectable Isola di Garda near Salò, or personal-official, as when Octavianus Petrutius, the pioneer of music printing, after twenty years at Venice moved his press to his birthplace Fossombrone (Fig 6), perhaps at the instance of its bishop, Paulus de Middelburgo, and stayed there

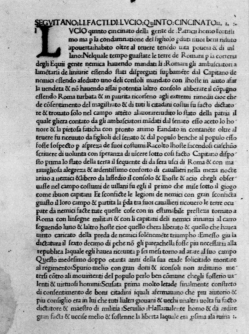

Fig 7   PETRARCH
Il libro degli homini famosi
Felix Antiquarius and Innocens Ziletus, Pojano, 1 October 1476
The Broxbourne copy presented to Cambridge University Library by Mr John Ehrman

Each biography has at its beginning a blank space within a woodcut border for the insertion of a portrait of its subject

for a decade. Some were simply amateurs, like Felix Antiquarius at Pojano (Fig 7) or the priest Giovanni Leonardo Longo at Vicenza, Torrebelvicino, and Trent. These itinerants printed many important books for the first time, and many that were unimportant, works of Italian literature as well as Latin grammars, and, no doubt, much that was ephemeral and has disappeared altogether. They pursued a craft which big business at Nuremberg, Basel, Venice, Paris and Lyons was busy organising into an industry decently demarcated into type-founding, printing and publishing and properly equipped with rules and codes of practice to suppress the enthusiasm of the human spirit. They were French and German as well as Italian, *ces goliards de la presse*, as Fumagalli called them. They made no fortunes, but the Italian sun shone on their journeyings, and the scenery was fair; and Italy, according to Robert Burton, was (*pace* Dr Steinberg) 'a paradise for horses'.

[1] S. Fumagalli, *Lexicon typographicum Italiae*, 1905; V. Scholderer, *Catalogue of books printed in the fifteenth century now in the British Museum*, 1966, Pt VII (General Introduction); F. J. Norton, *Italian Printers 1501–1520*, 1958

ROBERTUS VALTURIUS
De Re Militari, first edition, over 100 woodcuts,
Verona, 1472
London £24,000($44,400). 12.VI.78
From the collection of the Carl and Lily Pforzheimer
Foundation, Inc

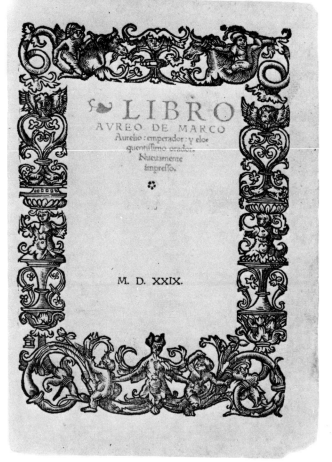

ANTONIO DE GUEVARA
Libro aureo de Marco Aurelio, one of only two copies
known of the first Antwerp edition, Antwerp, 1529
London £2,800($5,180). 22.V.78
From the collection of the late J. Peeters-Fontainas

Le voyage et na-
nigation/faict par les Espaignolz es
Isles de Mollucques/des isles quilz
ont trouue audict voyage/des Roys
dicelles/de leur gouuernement & ma-
niere de viure/auec plusieurs aultres
choses.

Cum priuilegio,

❡ On les vend a Paris en la maison de
Simon de Colines/libraire iure de lu
niuersite de Paris/demonrât en la rue
sainct Jehan de Beauluais/a lensei-
gne du Soleil Dor.

[NUMBER 11]

ANTONIO PIGAFETTA
Le Voyage et Navigation faict par les Espaignolz, first
edition, Paris, *circa* 1525
New York $130,000(£70,270). 6.XII.77

A fruteful/
and pleasaunt worke of the
beste state of a publpque weale, and
of the newe ple called Utopia:written
in Latine by Syr Thomas More
knyght, and translated into Englyshe
by Raphe Robynson Citizein and
Goldsmythe of London, at the
procurement,and earnest re-
quest of George Tadlowe
Citezein & Haberdassher
of the same Citie.
(. : .)

❡Imprinted at London
by Abraham Vele, dwelling in Pauls
churcheyarde at the sygne of
the Lambe. Anno.
1551.

THOMAS MORE
A fruteful and pleasaunt worke . . . called Utopia, first
English edition, London, 1551
New York $12,000(£6,486). 15.XI.77
From the collection of David Borowitz

The Apocalypse of St John
A block-book on forty-eight leaves, with contemporary colouring, seventeenth-century orange velvet
binding, Germany, *circa* 1465–70
London £180,000($333,000). 15.XI.77
From the Broxbourne Library, the collection of John Ehrman

STEPHAN FRIDOLIN
Schatzbehalter der wahren Reichtümer des Heils, ninety-six full-page woodcuts,
with contemporary colouring and binding, Nuremberg, 1491
New York $42,000 (£22,703). 23.V.78

GALILEO GALILEI
Sidereus nuncius, first edition, special copy on thick
paper, Venice, 1610
New York $39,000(£21,081). 2.XI.77
From the collection of the Library of the Franklin
Institute of Philadelphia

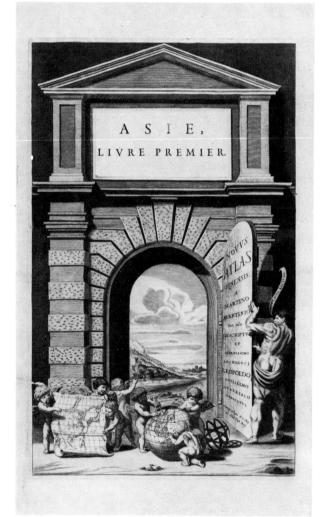

JOHANNES BLAEU
Le Grand Atlas, twelve volumes, over 600 engraved
maps and plans, contemporary vellum binding,
Amsterdam, 1667
London £38,000($70,300). 13.II.78
From the collection of the late Admiral Sir Frederick
H. G. Dalrymple-Hamilton, KCB

THOMAS GRAY
An Elegy wrote in a Country Church Yard, first
edition, bound with six other poems in
contemporary half calf, London, 1751
New York $22,000 (£11,892). 15.XI.77
From the collection of David Borowitz

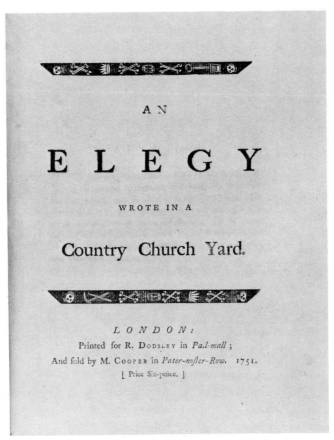

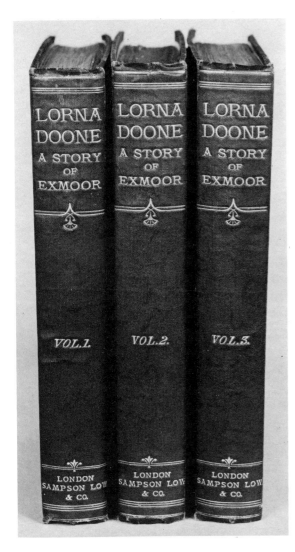

RICHARD D. BLACKMORE
Lorna Doone: a story of Exmoor, three volumes, first edition,
original cloth, London, 1869
New York $2,700 (£1,459). 15.XI.77
From the collection of David Borowitz

P. J. REDOUTE
Les Roses, three volumes, large paper copy of the first
edition, 169 coloured plates, contemporary half-
leather binding, Paris, 1817–24
London £28,000 ($51,800). 22.XI.77

The great Horologion, liturgies and prayers in parallel
texts of Greek and Arabic, contemporary Rumanian
red morocco binding, elaborately gilt, Snagov, near
Bucharest, 1701
London £5,000 ($9,250). 24.IV.78

A selection of books from the Toulouse-Philidor Collection of printed and manuscript music, sold en bloc
London £120,000($222,000). 26.VI.78
From the collection of St Michael's College, Tenbury Wells

EDWARD ORME
Collection of British Field Sports, twenty coloured plates, London, 1807–8
New York $14,500(£7,838). 26.X.77

ROBERT SCHUMANN
An autograph manuscript of *Fantasie for Piano and Orchestra, Op. 17,*
numerous additions and corrections, Leipzig, 1836
London £30,000($55,500). 23.XI.77

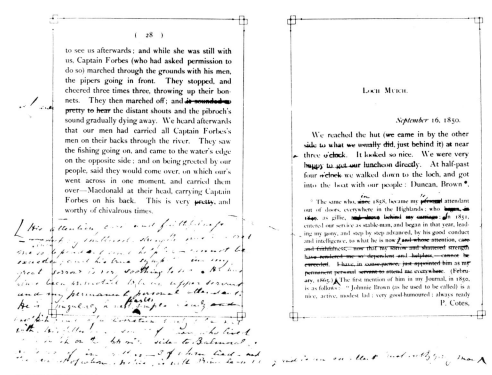

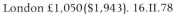

QUEEN VICTORIA
Leaves from the Journal of our Life in the Highlands, first edition, manuscript alterations and additions by Queen Victoria, Arthur Helps and his daughter, privately printed, 1865
London £1,050($1,943). 16.II.78

HONORE DE BALZAC
Le Chef d'oeuvre inconnu, limited to 340 copies, eighty-one illustrations by Pablo Picasso, Paris, Vollard, 1931
London £4,000($7,400). 5.V.78

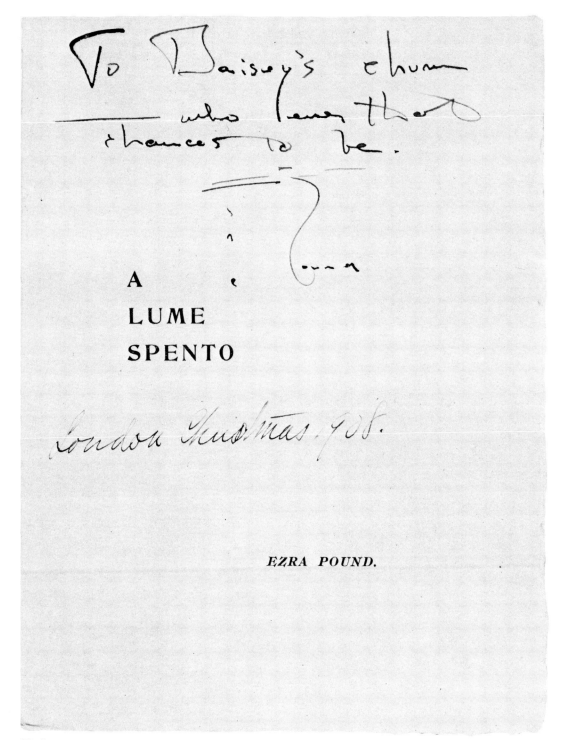

Fig 1
EZRA POUND
A lume spento
First edition, original printed wrappers, presentation copy, Venice, 1908
New York $18,000. 29.III.77

The Goodwin Collection of modern first editions

Robert Wilson

The sale of the Jonathan Goodwin Collection of modern first editions, held in three sessions, has already become recognised as a landmark in the history of twentieth-century book auctions. Indeed, one expert in the field has termed it 'the Streeter sale for moderns', thus ranking it with one of the greatest book sales of any century. In the field of English and American literature, only a handful of sales can be thought of in the same class, the Quinn sale in 1923–24, the Kern sale in 1929, the Guffey sale in 1958 and the Stockhausen sale in 1975, although none of these renowned sales are exactly comparable. The Quinn sale most closely approximated the Goodwin sale in its scope but was in actuality a financial disaster. The time was not yet ripe for full appreciation of the gems it included, not even the original holograph manuscript of James Joyce's *Ulysses*. It fetched only $1,950 and an outraged Joyce tried in vain to re-purchase it from Dr A. S. W. Rosenbach, who cannily refused to part with it. The Guffey sale, while it established Hemingway in the 'big time' insofar as interest by collectors is concerned, was limited solely to Hemingway. The Kern sale set prices that have seldom been surpassed but contained few moderns. Mr Stockhausen was also chiefly concerned with works by authors of the seventeenth to nineteenth centuries, although his collection of works by Robert Frost has yet to be bettered. Thus the Goodwin Collection was unique in its total concentration on moderns.

It was also unique in many other respects. Both the breadth and the depth were amazing. The entire field of twentieth-century literature in English was thoroughly covered, beginning with Ezra Pound and William Carlos Williams in the first decade of the century, continuing with Eliot, Joyce, Lawrence and Stein to Hemingway and Faulkner, then running on through Miller, Durrell, Shaw and Moore until right up to the present day with Kerouac, Ginsberg, and Duncan. Every major author was represented, usually by his first book, an especially difficult field. To list the names of the authors whose first books appeared would fill at least two pages but the collection cannot be discussed without mentioning the major names. Highlights from the list were the first book by Ezra Pound, *A lume spento* (Fig 1) published at Pound's expense in Venice in 1908 in an edition of one hundred copies and that by William Carlos Williams, whose *Poems* (Fig 2) was published in Rutherford a year later also at his own expense in an edition of one hundred copies. Only twenty-six copies of Pound's book are known and only twelve of Williams'. Probably no other private collection has ever been graced by both. However, with these were also the first

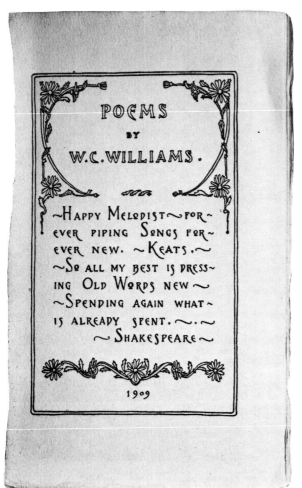

Fig 2
WILLIAM CARLOS WILLIAMS
Poems
First edition, original printed wrappers,
presentation copy, Rutherford N.J., 1909
New York $16,000. 29.III.77

books of seventy-three other twentieth-century writers, including Beerbohm, Benet, Betjeman, Conrad, Durrell, Eliot, Fitzgerald, Forster, Frost, Ginsberg, Greene, Hemingway, Huxley, Joyce, Lawrence, Shaw, and Steinbeck. These alone would have constituted a staggering collection.

But Mr Goodwin was not content just with first books. With the majority of these authors he also acquired the main body of their work and with some favourite authors he collected in depth, particularly with Hemingway and Frost. The collection of works by Hemingway was especially impressive, being one of the most extensive ever formed and housing a staggering amount of letters. These included his early letters to his parents and those to companions before his literary fame began, as well as important correspondence about his work with editors and critics (Fig 3) during the height of his career. It even included a complete set of *Trapeze* for Hemingway's senior year in high school. It was to this magazine that he contributed his earliest work and this set may well be the only complete one extant. The $7,000 (£3,784) it fetched is a tribute to its rarity.

Mr Goodwin is obviously a scholar who knows the field and the content of the books, something that cannot always be said of every collector. This is shown by the

Fig 3
ERNEST HEMINGWAY
One of forty-three letters
to the critic Malcolm
Cowley, Cuba, Idaho and
Italy, 1940–52
New York $32,500 (£17,568).
25.X.77

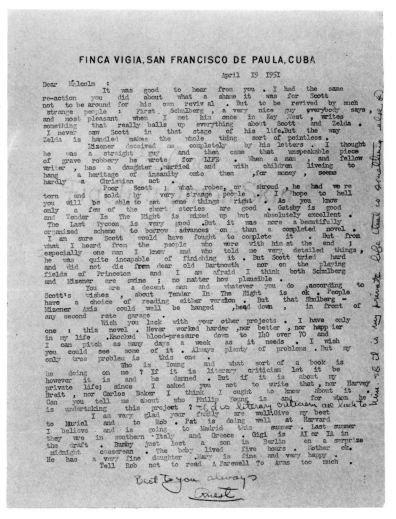

care with which he filled in the background of the giants, particularly from the '20s and '30s. Included was the work of many writers who are now beginning to be appreciated such as Robert McAlmon, Djuna Barnes and Harry Crosby and, to epitomise the period with one item, there was an inscribed presentation copy of the score of George Gershwin's *An American in Paris* (Fig 4). Also helping to fill in the background of the period, the Goodwin Collection included complete or near-complete sets of seminal periodicals of the period, magazines in which much of the important work of the '20s and '30s appeared prior to book appearance. These included *The Little Review, transition, The Transatlantic Review, Blast, Broom, The Exile, The Egoist, Others, The Double Dealer, Navire d'Argent, Contact,* and *Secession.*

Finally, Mr Goodwin anticipated the current rage for original photographs by many years, having collected numerous superb examples of literary portraits by such important photographers as Giselle Freund and Berenice Abbott.

However, over and above the tremendous scope one over-riding factor was dominant and that was Mr Goodwin's strict adherence to one of the cardinal rules of collecting in any field, the insistence on fine condition. With very few exceptions, his books were the best possible examples to be found. Dust jackets were always present,

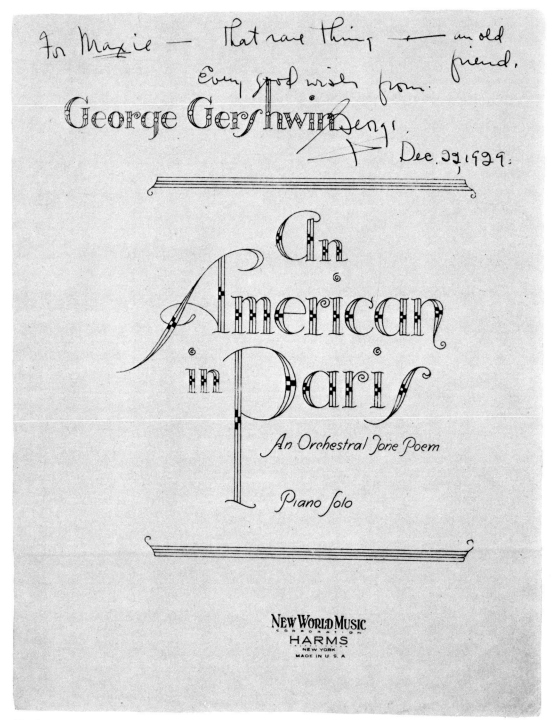

Fig 4
GEORGE GERSHWIN
An American in Paris
First edition of the piano version, presentation copy, New York, 1929
New York $1,900. 29.III.77

Fig 5
EDGAR RICE BURROUGHS
Tarzan of the Apes
First edition, original cloth,
with pictorial dust jacket,
Chicago, 1914
New York $2,500 (£1,351).
25.X.77

and almost always in unbelievably fresh condition (Fig 5). On occasion the rule about condition would be relaxed slightly but only in favour of an astounding association copy such as Sherwood Anderson to Gertrude Stein or Scott Fitzgerald presenting *The Great Gatsby* to Zelda's sister.

The collection was comparatively recent. One of the first books Mr Goodwin bought for it was purchased as late as the autumn of 1957, a copy of *Ulysses*, which later appeared as lot 443 in the second session of the sale. Mr Goodwin has said of this purchase 'at that time $85 really did seem like an awful lot of money'! The sale has, most certainly, eradicated any lingering doubts about the strength and popularity of modern first editions as a collecting field. The collection, comprising 867 lots, totalled over $1,000,000, a figure rarely matched by a book sale in any period and certainly unmatched as far as moderns go. Even very modern authors such as Ginsberg and Kerouac, still looked down on by many collectors, fetched impressively high prices; Kerouac's *The Town and the City*, his first book, inscribed by him and Ginsberg, brought a cool $2,500 (£1,350) a considerable appreciation over the $125 the same copy was priced at in a dealer's catalogue only ten years ago. The prices for almost every lot set new records, which will remain touchstones for many years to come. With this sale the moderns have taken a commanding place in the field of book-collecting thanks to Mr Goodwin's taste and perspicacity.

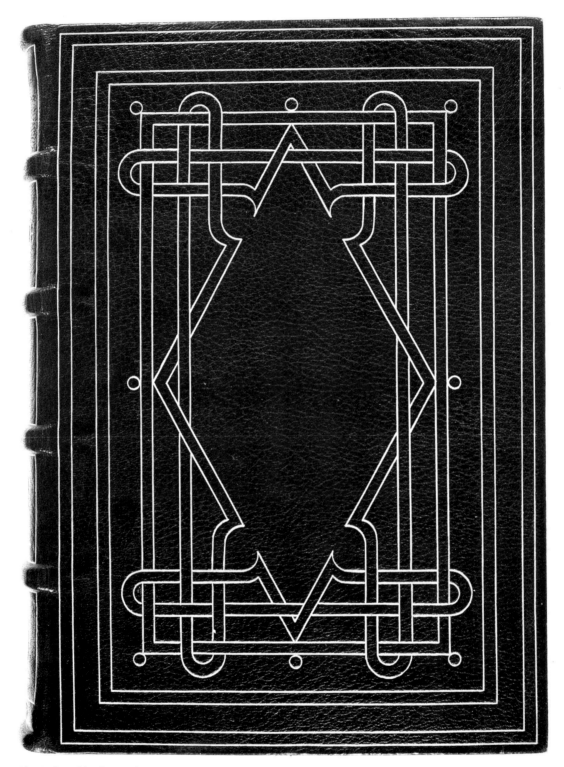

The Holy Bible, five volumes, one of only two copies printed on vellum, bound by the printer in
dark blue morocco, gilt, Doves Press, 1903–5
London £62,000 ($114,700). 23.VI.78
From the collection of the late Robert von Hirsch

Robert von Hirsch owned an almost complete collection of Doves Press books

92   TEA-TABLE

fhould return, he might find the objeĉt of his foul married to his fon.

The parting of the two lovers is a fcene too tender to be defcribed. Arietta fears every thing from the dangers of the fea, and the rude winds; while Polydore attempts to comfort her, and takes his leave, in obedience to the commands of his uncle.

No fooner had Polydore failed, than Avarus wrote down to his fon, to order him up to London immediately. Robin, for fuch was his name, received the letter in the evening, as they were celebrating harveft home; they were dancing on the grafs, to the found of the tabor and the pipe.

Hogarth. See, ladies and gentlemen, the picture of rural amufements.

RICHARD JOHNSON
Tea-table Dialogues, first edition, twelve wood-engraved illustrations, the first recorded copy (hitherto known only from advertisements), T. Carnan, 1771
London £310($574). 13.X.77

JOHANN DAVID WYSS
The Family Robinson Crusoe, first English edition, three engraved illustrations, M. J. Godwin & Co, 1814
London £700($1,295). 14.X.77

KATE GREENAWAY
A young lady reclining on a chaise-longue, watercolour on paper, signed with initials, for *Language of Flowers* published in 1884
London £420($777). 23.XI.77

EDMUND DULAC
Morgiana pouring oil on the forty thieves, watercolour on paper, signed, for *Stories from the Arabian Nights* published in 1907
London £1,450($2,682). 3.III.78

GEOFFREY CHAUCER
Troilus and Criseyde, one of 225 copies, wood-engraved illustrations by Eric Gill,
Golden Cockerel Press, 1927
London £700($1,295). 26.X.77

Works of Art

A Limoges enamel eucharistic dove, from the Marienstift of Erfurt (Thuringia), *circa* 1200, height 7½in (19cm)
London £100,000 ($185,000). 22.VI.78
From the collection of the late Robert von Hirsch

Fig 1
Two views of a North Italian bronze figure of a naked kneeling woman, inscribed *STEF N S LAGER P:*(?) *ME FECIT*, *circa* 1100, height 12$\frac{5}{8}$in (32cm)
London £100,000($185,000). 22.VI.78

Medieval bronzes and enamels from the Robert von Hirsch Collection

Richard Camber

The medieval bronzes and enamels in the Robert von Hirsch Collection were the most important to have appeared on the market since the end of the last war. Originally acquired during the 1920s and '30s, at a time when major medieval objects, particularly in Germany, were more easily obtainable, they owed their outstanding place in the collection to the fact that there were among them a number which were of consuming interest to the art historian, quite apart from their undeniable rarity and beauty. Frequently of only modest dimensions, but originating in commissions from those who held power in medieval Europe, these pieces were almost inevitably the work of master craftsmen. Moreover, such evidence as is now available clearly indicates that many of these craftsmen stood in the very forefront of stylistic innovation and were not merely the slavish followers of artists working in other media.

Something of the importance of the medieval bronzes may be gauged from the celebrated Romanesque figure of a naked woman (Fig 1). Closely related in form to the aeolipiles or fire-blowers of the Middle Ages which were always human-shaped, its precise function remains uncertain, although it seems probable that it was originally intended as a support for a candlestick or baptismal font. Its interest, however, is due not so much to its form as to the inscription which appears on the circlet around the forehead. This reads *STEF N S LAGER P:(?) ME FECIT* and may be expanded, according to Albert Boeckler, as reading *Stefanus Lagerensis Pictor Me Fecit*. Boeckler identified the place-name referred to in the term *Lagerensis* with the Valle Lagarina, a valley in the Italian Tirol situated between Verona and Trento. These arguments, which Boeckler advanced in the course of his fundamental study on the Romanesque bronze doors of the church of San Zeno in Verona, were of more than merely parochial interest since it was observed that there was a very close stylistic connection between this figure and certain of the relief panels on the doors. Boeckler concluded from this that there was no obvious reason why the doors could not also have been the product of a local workshop, an opinion which previous scholars had been reluctant to accept, believing them to be the work of northern craftsmen working in Italy. Robert von Hirsch's kneeling woman was thus directly responsible for the recognition of an indigenous tradition in medieval North Italian bronze-casting.

Fig 2   An English bronze-gilt base from a candlestick or altar-cross, early twelfth century, height 4in (10.1cm)
London £550,000($1,017,500). 22.VI.78

The figure of a man extracting a thorn from his foot can be seen in the centre of this view

Another area of Europe in which the existence of an indigenous bronze-casting tradition has frequently been regarded as somewhat uncertain is England. Even the Gloucester Candlestick, which today is one of the glories of the Victoria and Albert Museum, was once considered by Otto von Falke as an imported work. Although this conclusion is now almost universally considered mistaken, largely on the grounds that ample parallels for the decorative details on the candlestick can be found in late eleventh-century English manuscript illumination, the fact remains that it is the only complete example of what we know from documentary evidence to have been a not uncommon object in English medieval churches. The large bronze-gilt base from a candlestick or altar-cross in the von Hirsch Collection (Fig 2) was thus an object of supreme importance in this context since, although von Falke also considered it as being of continental manufacture, its points of contact with the Gloucester Candlestick, particularly as regards the handling of the foliage, the winged dragons which form its feet and the six little figures distributed around it, make it probable that it was a product of the same indigenous tradition. An amusing sidelight on the iconographical sources available to craftsmen working within this tradition is provided by one of these figures, which shows a man extracting a thorn from his foot, a motif well-known both in antiquity, and later in the Renaissance, in the celebrated figure of the *Spinario*.

The von Hirsch Collection provided a further indication that the English contribution to medieval metal-work and enamelling, particularly in the twelfth century, should not be underestimated. The set of three translucent and opaque *champlevé* enamel plaques (Fig 3) was completely unknown before its appearance at Sotheby's in

Fig 3   Three English translucent and opaque *champlevé* enamel plaques from a casket, late twelfth century, width 6½in (16.5cm)
London £260,000($481,000). 22.VI.78

Fig 4
A Mosan copper-gilt and *champlevé* enamel medallion of an angel representing *Operatio* (Charity)
from a spandrel of the Stavelot Retable, *circa* 1150, diameter 5¾in (14.6cm)
London £1,200,000($2,220,000). 22.VI.78

1935, when it was sold by an English collector and acquired shortly afterwards by Robert von Hirsch. Although catalogued at that time as being of Mosan manufacture, i.e. from the valley of the Meuse, the decorative features on these plaques, particularly the acanthus on the borders and the plant forms linking the roundels, can be closely paralleled to a very small group of late twelfth-century enamelled caskets and liturgical ciboria which has long been recognised as being of English origin. The place of origin of the von Hirsch plaques is therefore no longer in doubt, nor is the fact that they came from a casket, but their iconography, which has clear baptismal connotations, remains largely obscure.

Turning from England and Italy to those areas of northern Europe where bronze-casting and enamelling attained a degree of perfection which has rarely been surpassed, the valleys of the Rhine and Meuse, the von Hirsch Collection was chiefly renowned for its inclusion of a number of pieces which are at one and the same time of rare documentary importance as well as of outstanding beauty. The first of these was the copper-gilt medallion with the *champlevé* enamel figure of *Operatio* (Charity) from the Stavelot Retable (Fig 4). This medallion, together with its companion piece in the Museum für Kunsthandwerk in Frankfurt am Main and two strips with inscriptions, is all that remains of one of the major ecclesiastical commissions of the twelfth century, the silver-gilt and *champlevé* enamelled shrine and retable ordered by Abbot Wibald of Stavelot (1130–1158) in honour of Saint Remaclus, the founder of the Abbey. Of greater importance than its rarity, however, is its sheer perfection of execution. So accomplished is it, indeed, that it has sometimes been attributed to Godefroid de Claire, the almost legendary craftsman who is conventionally regarded as having brought the indigenous tradition of metal-working and enamelling in the valley of the Meuse to the very summit of its achievement. However tempting such a conclusion may be, and it is known that Wibald actually employed a goldsmith whose name began with 'G' in the period around 1148, there is no evidence that Godefroid himself ever worked on the Saint Remaclus shrine, nor is it likely that he personally would have been responsible for two such comparatively minor details as the surviving pair of medallions, which were originally placed high up in the spandrels over the central arch of the retable. All that can be said, but it cannot be said too emphatically, is that whoever it was who made them was an artist of outstanding skill and sensitivity.

The second of the two medieval objects for which the von Hirsch Collection was chiefly renowned was the *armilla* (Fig 6), a copper-gilt bracelet or shoulder-piece superlatively embellished in *champlevé* enamel with a depiction of the Crucifixion. The precise date of this piece is still disputed by scholars, although in general terms it is agreed that it must have been made by a Rhenish or Mosan craftsman between about 1160 and 1180. One very curious circumstance suggests, however, that, together with its companion piece in the Louvre showing the Resurrection, it may have been produced shortly before 1165. Both objects were discovered in the last century at Vladimir near Moscow and, thus far, the only hypothesis which satisfactorily explains their discovery in Russia is that they were taken back by the embassy which is known to have been sent in 1165 by Grand Prince Andrew Bogoloubski of Vladimir to negotiate with the Emperor Frederick I Barbarossa at Aachen. *Armillae* were certainly part of the coronation regalia of the Holy Roman Emperors and they could have reached Russia only as a personal gift from the Emperor himself. More-

Fig 5
A detail from the lid of a Lower Saxon wood reliquary casket showing a Cologne *champlevé* enamel plaque of Saint Matthew, *circa* 1150–75, width of plaque 3¼in (8.2cm) London £150,000($277,500). 22.VI.78

Fig 6
A Rhenish or Mosan copper-gilt and *champlevé* enamel *armilla*, *circa* 1165, height 4½in (11.5cm) London £1,100,000($2,035,000). 22.VI.78

Fig 7
An Upper Rhine copper-gilt and
champlevé enamel medallion of *The*
Visitation, early fourteenth century,
diameter 2½in (6.3cm)
London £130,000($240,500). 22.VI.78

over, although the von Hirsch and Louvre *armillae* are the only surviving examples of this regalia, a slightly later pair is known to have survived in the Treasury of the Holy Roman Emperors in Nuremberg until around 1796 and these could conceivably have been made as replacements after the original pair had been given away.

A link with Germany's medieval past was also provided by the chest-shaped wood reliquary casket with a *champlevé* enamel plaque of Saint Matthew on the cover (Fig 5). On stylistic grounds, it seems certain that the enamel, which is one of the finest of its type, was produced at Cologne during the third quarter of the twelfth century, but the casket itself must be regarded as Saxon work of the same period, since it is known to have formed part of the so-called Guelph Treasure in the Cathedral of Saint Blaise in Brunswick, where it was recorded as early as 1482. This treasure, a collection of some one hundred and forty precious objects donated by the rulers of Brunswick between the eleventh and fifteenth centuries, was dispersed as recently as 1930, but the von Hirsch casket was the most important item from it still remaining in private hands, the greater part of it now being in museums in Germany and the United States.

Although Robert von Hirsch's natural preference was for metal-work and enamelling of the Romanesque period, his unerring eye for quality led him to acquire, shortly before the last war, one of the minor masterpieces of Gothic enamelling. This was the copper-gilt medallion embellished in *champlevé* enamel with a representation of the Visitation (Fig 7), in all probability the work of a craftsman active in the Upper Rhine region during the first quarter of the fourteenth century. Despite its modest dimensions, this medallion, in which the enamelling on the figures serves to emphasise the shadows the greater part being left unenamelled, displays to perfection that concern for sculptural form which was so characteristic a feature of Gothic art. That Robert von Hirsch should have wanted it for his own collection, where it remained an almost isolated example of the enamelling of this period, is an indication that the guiding principle behind his activities as a collector was a continuing search for works of art which were supremely representative of the periods in which they were created. No historian of medieval art could ask for more from a collector.

A Byzantine ivory relief of Christ in Majesty, Constantinople, mid eleventh century, height $9\frac{5}{8}$in (24.5cm) London £630,000 ($1,165,500). 22.VI.78
From the collection of the late Robert von Hirsch

This ivory belongs to the so-called *Romanos* group in Adolph Goldschmidt's standard classification of the Byzantine ivories of the tenth to thirteenth centuries. The group is named after an ivory in the Cabinet des Médailles, Paris, which shows Christ crowning an imperial couple identified as *Romanos Emperor of the Romans* and *Eudokia Empress of the Romans*. This could refer to the six-year-old Romanos II and his four-year-old bride Eudokia, which would mean the entire Romanos group would date from the mid tenth century. Recent research has tended to support an alternative identification of the couple as Romanos IV and Eudokia Makrembolitissa, which entails re-dating the whole group, including this ivory, to the middle of the eleventh century

A Carolingian ivory relief with a figure of St John the Evangelist, from the cover of a manuscript gospel, inscribed *MORE VOLANS AQUILA VERBVM PETIT ASTRA IOHANNIS* (Just like a flying eagle the word of John seeks the stars), Aachen, Palace School, early ninth century,
height 7½in (19cm)
London £255,000 ($471,750).
15.XII.77

This important and unrecorded ivory carving was probably one of a set of four made at Aachen around the year 800 to decorate the cover of a now lost manuscript of the Gospels. The three other plaques are now also lost. The inscription along the upper border is a quotation from the *Carmen Paschale* of the Latin poet Sedulius and was probably added very shortly afterwards at Tours in the Loire valley. The complete cover was subsequently copied in another Carolingian ivory which was formerly at Bourges but is now in the Cabinet des Médailles, Paris

A South Italian Romanesque ivory relief of the Journey to Bethlehem, *circa* 1100,
height 6½in (16.5cm)
London £190,000 ($351,500). 22.VI.78
From the collection of the late Robert von Hirsch

An ivory relief with scenes from the Life of David, probably from the cover of
a psalter, North Italian or St Gall, mid tenth century, height 6⅛in (15.5cm)
London £460,000 ($851,000). 22.VI.78
From the collection of the late Robert von Hirsch

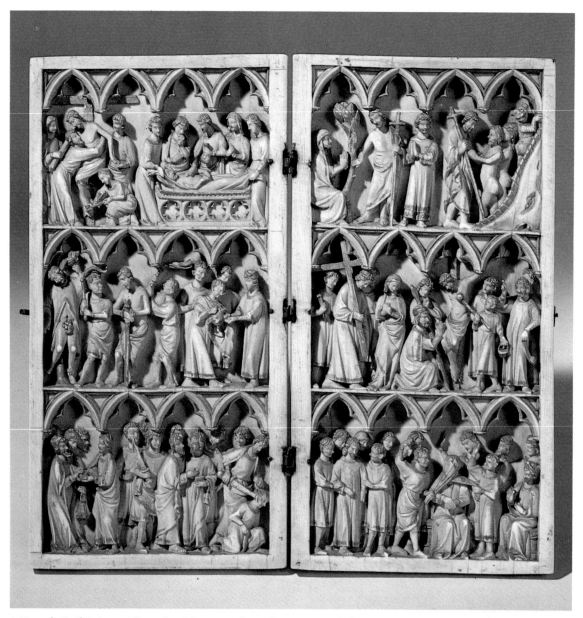

A French Gothic ivory diptych with scenes from the Passion of Christ, *circa* 1300, height 7¼in (18.5cm)
London £58,000 ($107,300). 22.VI.78
From the collection of the late Robert von Hirsch

A Flemish ivory relief of the Deposition, *circa* 1600, height 5¼in (13.3cm)
London £9,600 ($17,760). 15.XII.77

A Sienese polychrome wood figure of the Virgin, *circa* 1450, height 24¾in (63cm)
London £75,000 ($138,750). 22.VI.78
From the collection of the late Robert von Hirsch

A Ferrarese walnut polychrome group of the Virgin and Child, *circa* 1470, height 26¾in (68cm)
London £110,000 ($203,500). 22.VI.78
From the collection of the late Robert von Hirsch

A Florentine bronze figure of the young
Hercules, early sixteenth century,
height 13⅜in (34cm)
£42,000 ($77,700)

A Venetian bronze figure of a negress with
a mirror, mid sixteenth century,
height 13in (33cm)
£62,000 ($114,700)

The bronzes on this page are from the collection of the late Robert von Hirsch and were sold in London on 22 June 1978

A Lombard terracotta bust of a prelate, *circa* 1600, height 27⅜in (69.5cm)
Florence L6,500,000 (£4,088:$7,563). 18.X.77

A Malines polychrome wood group of the
Virgin and Child, *circa* 1515–20,
height 13¾in (35cm)
New York $10,000 (£5,405). 1.VI.78
From the collection of Lawrence Downer Buhrer

An Upper Rhine limewood figure of a bishop saint,
circa 1510, height 52¾in (134cm)
Munich DM58,000 (£14,684:$27,165). 29.IX.77

A South Netherlandish alabaster group of the Pietà, from the circle of the Master of Rimini, *circa* 1430, height 9¾in (25cm)
London £25,000 ($46,250). 22.VI.78
From the collection of the late Robert von Hirsch

A South Netherlandish walnut relief plaque of the Flight into Egypt, late sixteenth
century, height $39\frac{1}{2}$in (100.3cm)
New York $19,000 (£10,270). 16.II.78

A Franconian limewood relief plaque of the Annunciation, workshop of Tilman
Riemenschneider, *circa* 1515, height 36¾in (93.5cm)
London £30,000 ($55,500). 13.IV.78

A German engraved crown of antlers, signed with the monogram of Thomas Boos, with the arms of
Lang von Wellenburg and of von Kuenburg and allegorical figures of the Wise and Foolish Virgins,
dated *1563*, width 48in (122cm)
New York $52,000 (£28,108). 22.X.77
From the collection of Kenneth Jay Lane

An ebony and engraved horn veneered games board, Augsburg, *circa* 1600, width 16in (45cm)
London £12,000 ($22,200). 13.IV.78

The top and bottom of the games board when closed, are designed for chess and nine men's morris
and are inlaid with the heads of Emperors and Kings and with figures of the seasons, angels and
owls respectively. At each corner of the backgammon board inside is a figure of a soldier in
contemporary dress

A French enamelled gold reliquary pendant, early fifteenth century, diameter 1¼in (3cm) £20,000 ($37,000)

A German gold amatory locket brooch, fourteenth century, height 1¼in (3cm) £21,000 ($38,850)

These objects are from the collection of the late Robert von Hirsch and were sold in London on 22 June 1978

A French gold and enamel pendent jewel, mid sixteenth century, height 2½in (6.4cm)
New York $11,000 (£5,946). 5.X.77

A Florentine *pietra dura* and ebony tray, made by the Tuscan court workshops, early eighteenth century, width 23in (58.5cm)
London £7,500 ($13,875). 15.XII.77

A North German amber and ivory casket with ivory lion couchant feet, mid seventeenth century,
height 11in (28cm)
New York $24,000 (£12,973). 1.VI.78
From the collection of Vladimir Wassilieff

A French equestrian statuette of the Dauphin dressed in classical armour, bronze
with ebony base, made in the studio of Martin Van Der Bogaert,
eighteenth century, height $17\frac{3}{4}$in (45cm)
Monte Carlo FF60,000 (£6,857:$12,686). 5.II.78

A bronze equestrian group by Pierre
Jules Mêne, French, signed and dated
1869, height 24in (61cm)
London £5,100 ($9,435). 21.VI.78

A pair of bronze centaurs by J. de Luca, signed and inscribed *Fond Delmar*, Italian, *circa* 1860,
heights 63in and 54in (160cm and 137.2cm)
London £10,500 ($19,425). 21.VI.78.

A white marble figure of Cleopatra by William Wetmore Story, signed and dated *Rome 1858*, height 55in (140cm)
New York $40,000 (£21,620). 21.IV.78
From the collection of the Right Hon. Lord Iliffe

Story's *Cleopatra*, with its companion piece *The Lybian Sibyl* was sent by Pope Pius IX, one of the artist's patrons, to the London Universal Exhibition of 1862. They were highly acclaimed in England even before the exhibition opened and they were bought by Mr Morrison for his collection at Basildon Park, Berkshire, where they remained until this year

A pair of Venetian marble blackamoor busts, eighteenth century, height 26½in (67.3cm)
London £22,000 ($40,700). 2.XI.77

The Resurrection, probably Moscow, late seventeenth century, 58in by 41½in (147.5cm by 105cm)
London £13,500($24,975). 13.II.78

St John the Baptist in the wilderness, seventeenth century, 10in by 8in (26cm by 20.5cm)
New York $6,250(£3,378). 9.VI.78

The Vladimir Mother of God, late sixteenth century, 11in by 9in (28cm by 23cm)
New York $6,400(£3,459). 9.VI.78

A silver-gilt and shaded enamel *kovsh* in the form of a peacock, maker's mark of *P. Ovchinnikov* stamped under Imperial warrant, Moscow, 1899–1908, width 9½in (24.1cm)
$14,000 (£7,568)
From the collection of Mrs Tatiana Chaliapin Chernoff

From left to right
A silver-gilt and enamel photograph frame by Fabergé, containing a photograph of the Grand Duke Boris Vladimirovitch, workmaster Michael Perchin, St Petersburg, late nineteenth century, height 4½in (11.4cm), $5,000 (£2,703)
A silver and black *champlevé* enamel casket painted *en plein* with a seventeenth-century scene showing the Tzar's falconers being drawn by Europeans, Moscow, *circa* 1910, width 6⅜in (16.2cm), $9,000 (£4,865)
A nephrite, silver and gold photograph frame by Fabergé, workmaster Michael Perchin, St Petersburg, late nineteenth century, height 3½in (8.9cm), $2,500 (£1,351)

The objects on this page were sold in New York on 13 December 1977

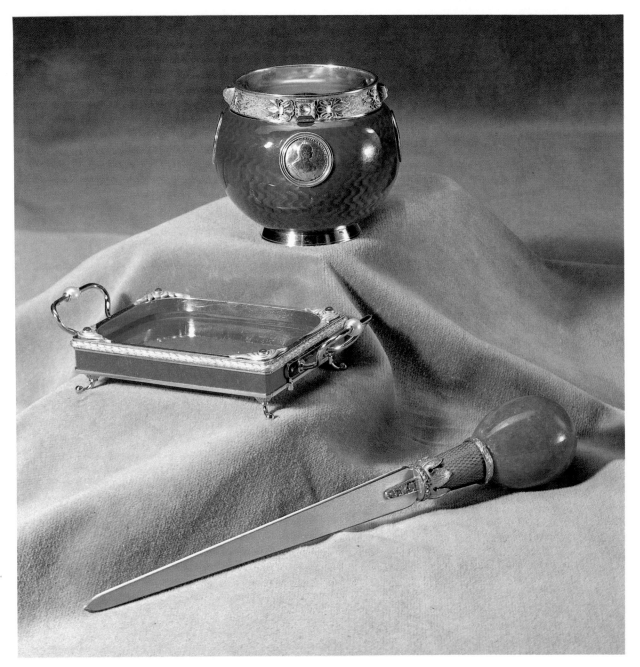

Three Fabergé objects all made in St Petersburg, *circa* 1900:

From top to bottom
A silver and enamel *bratina*, workmaster Anders Nevalainen, height 2⅜in (6cm), $5,250(£2,838)
A gold-mounted purpurine tray, workmaster Henrik Wigström, width 4⅞in (12.4cm)
$12,000(£6,486)
A gold, silver, enamel and rhodenite paper knife, workmaster Henrik Wigström, length 8in (20.3cm)
$4,750(£2,568)

The objects on this page are from the Forbes Magazine Collection and were sold in New York on
13 December 1977

A silver-gilt and niello snuff box, late eighteenth century, width 3¾in (9.2cm)
London £1,800($3,330). 19.VI.78

A silver-gilt and niello salt, maker's mark *V.A.*, Moscow, 1792, height 4½in (11.5cm)
London £920($1,702). 19.VI.78

A silver-gilt and niello Imperial presentation *kovsh*, with an inscription from Catherine the Great to the commander of the Don cossacks, maker's mark *M.Tz.S.*, Moscow, 1793, width 10¼in (26cm)
New York $5,750(£3,108). 13.XII.77

A silver-gilt and shaded *cloisonné* enamel vase, maker's mark of Maria Semyonova, Moscow,
circa 1900, height 8in (20.4cm)
New York $15,000(£8,108). 13.XII.77

A *cloisonné* enamel clock garniture flanked by a pair of *cloisonné* enamel four-light candelabra by Christofle et Cie, Paris, 1874, height of each 16¼in (41.5cm), 18in (46cm)
London £2,000($3,700). 2.XI.77

Nineteenth-century experiments in enamelling

Julia Clarke

An anonymous enthusiast writing in the *Art Journal* in 1871 deplored the current lack of interest in enamelling in England: 'The *cloisonné* enamels of China and Japan form elegant articles of dress and ornament which might be very advantageously imitated by our workmen. Is there no manufacturer who will secure the lead in this favourite branch of industry, by a bold and enlightened application of his capital to its development? He would no doubt reap a rich reward'. In fact, commercial firms of silversmiths had been showing increasing interest in the use of enamels since the time of the Great Exhibition in 1851. In particular, the firms of Elkington & Co of Birmingham and Christofle et Cie of Paris had each already perfected the simpler art of *champlevé* enamelling (the colours flooded into hollows dug into the surface of the metal ground) and were experimenting with the more complex skills necessary for *cloisonné* enamelling (the colours divided by wires applied onto the surface of the metal ground).

Since 1842, when the young Charles Christofle had been licensed to use Elkington's patent for electroplating in France, the two companies had expanded into roughly comparable positions as mass-producers of both electroplated and silver wares in their own countries. It was, however, in the highly competitive arena of the universal exhibitions of the second half of the nineteenth century that they were to become rivals, each able to channel a large portion of their profits into the employment of superior workmen and designers and into the production of magnificent, if esoteric, works of art, largely for the sake of prestige and, of course, advertisement. The field of enamelling is symbolic of their neck-and-neck adventures. At every stage, marked by the objects being shown at an exhibition, each firm claimed total innovation and superiority whereas both, with similar flair and production facilities, often displayed almost identical items.

In his *Masterpieces of Industrial Art*, dealing with works shown at the 1862 London Exhibition, J. B. Waring illustrates several *champlevé* enamelled electrotypes in the Moresque manner by Christofle and a *champlevé* enamelled dessert service in the Pompeian style by Elkington. More enamelled objects in these styles were shown at the 1867 Paris Exhibition although by this date there is evidence of the awakening interest in *cloisonné* enamelling. This had been aroused by the impact of the first groups of Japanese wares to be exhibited in Europe shown at the 1853 Dublin Exhibition and others shown at the 1862 International Exhibition (which had already influenced porcelain manufacturers in England and France). Another influence had been the very first experiments in European *cloisonné* enamelling by the Parisian bronze founders, Barbedienne. Alfred Darcel wrote in 1868 in the *Gazette des Beaux-Arts:*

'MM. Christofle et Cie se sont . . . inspirés des émaux cloisonnés sur cuivre qui nous arrivent de l'empire du Milieu . . . Si le dessin de ces pièces a été inspiré par celui des porcelaines et des émaux de la Chine, la disposition générale et parfois la composition en sont tout à fait européennes' . . . 'M. Elkington, en Angleterre, s'est mis à fabriquer des émaux dans le genre de ceux de M. Barbedienne: l'imitation est flagrante, mais la forme des pièces est moins étudiée et les bronzes qui leur servent de monture . . . offrent des bizarreries que nous n'approuvons point'.[1]

It was, however, at the Vienna Exhibition of 1873 that the two firms first unveiled genuine *cloisonné* enamels in Oriental and European styles, with their slightly more commercial substitutes, enamels finished by hand but on an electrotype ground. The Vienna Exhibition made a disastrous financial loss but it had a great influence on the manufacturers who showed there and the art and trade critics who attended. These were at pains to explain the different techniques to their readers in order that they could fully admire the effects achieved. As Frank G. Jackson of *The Jeweller and Metalworker* explains: 'The champ leve (sic) differs from the [*cloisonné*] in that the cells are *cut or carved out* instead of being formed by *partitions laid in*, this is done generally upon a "pattern" and copies reproduced by casting or by electro-

An electrogilt electrotype *jardinière* with *champlevé* enamel decoration, Elkington & Co, Birmingham, 1875, width 15¾in (40cm)
London £340. 2.VIII.72

An electrogilt electrotype pot-pourri vase and cover with *champlevé* enamel decoration, Elkington & Co, Birmingham, 1875, height 8¾in (22.2cm) London £160. 24.I.74

deposition'. Professor Archer of *The Art Journal* adds: 'The repetition of desirable patterns is very easy, because a design once produced can be reproduced by electro-deposit as often as required . . . the firing [is] easy and the liability to injure very small; hence such works are comparatively cheap'. Frank Jackson disagrees: 'Of the champ leve (sic) varieties the enamelling on deposited metal is the most difficult, from the peculiar character of its texture. The advantages to be derived from this mode of reproduction (i.e. electro-deposition) being fully appreciated by Messrs Elkington, led them to combat the difficulties they at first encountered; the result has justified their endeavours'. Both reserve their highest praise for *cloisonné* enamelling which 'is by far the most ingenious and artistic of the two methods, as requiring greater care and patience on the part of the producer',[2] '*cloisonné* enamels can never be cheap; they are therefore limited in their use, and can only be in demand among those who seek for costly decorative Art'.[3] Commenting on Christofle's splendid group of enamels designed by Emile Reiber, who was later called, 'le grand-prêtre du japonisme'[4] and who had made use of long hours sketching at Baron Cernuschi's exhibition of treasures from the Orient revealed to Paris in 1871, Jackson wrote: 'the enamels are exquisite . . ., based for the most part upon Oriental types, but not slavishly copied — not mere reproductions, but fruits of an intelligent study of recognised authorities in this truly beautiful and ancient art'.[5] The French jury, however, reported sourly:[6] 'Tout le bruit fait autour de ces pièces est plutôt une affaire de mode, d'envie de faire du nouveau avec du vieux, qu'un progrès véritable',[7] unpalatable words, but soon to be proved correct.

A pair of *cloisonné* enamel vases after a design by Auguste Adolphe Willms, Elkington & Co, Birmingham, 1874, height 9½in (24cm) London £480($888). 15.XII.77

Elkington's had a certain *succès d'estime* with their enamels at Philadelphia in 1876 (the French did not show) but were overshadowed by the rich and extravagant 'japanese' works of Tiffany and Gorham. Both Christofle and Elkington showed enamels in Paris in 1878 but by this time Christofle were also using Japanese combinations of hammered and encrusted metals and textures, moving towards the naturalism of Art Nouveau. Elkington's, on the other hand, hampered by the strict British laws forbidding mixtures of precious and base metals and already tainted by the sickness in the British silver industry which led to their eventual decline, compromised with the mixed surfaces of engraving, parcel-gilding and frosting in the Aesthetic manner. In 1880, *The Jeweller and Metalworker* tersely wrote the obituary: '[Elkington's have] virtually abandoned the production of *cloisonné* enamel owing to the impossibility of successfully competing in this costly work with the Japanese producers but they are still large importers of Japanese enamel for which there is a large and growing market in this country'.[8]

[1] 'Messrs Christofle have been . . . inspired by the *cloisonné* enamels on copper sent to us from Cathay . . . if the design of their objects has been inspired by Chinese porcelain and enamels, the general arrangement and sometimes the composition are totally European' . . . 'In England, Elkington's have begun to manufacture enamels in the style of Barbedienne: the imitation is flagrant, but the shape of their objects is less well-considered and the bronze mounts reveal peculiarities of which we cannot approve'
[2] *The Jeweller and Metalworker*, 15 October 1874, p 257
[3] *The Art Journal*, 1874, pp 275–76
[4] H. Bouilhet, *L'Orfèvrerie Française aux XVIII et XIX Siècles*, 1912, vol III, p 144
[5] *The Jeweller and Metalworker*, 15 August 1874, p 212
[6] *Rapports de la Délégation Française à l'Exposition Universelle de Vienne 1873*, p 22
[7] 'All the fuss made about these objects is rather a matter of fashion, a desire to create something new out of something old, than a true advance'
[8] *The Jeweller and Metalworker*, 15 February 1880, p 49

Left
A Swiss gold snuff box the lid set with a Roman mosaic, signed *A.D.*, maker's mark *FJ*, nineteenth century, width 3½in (9cm) £5,200 ($9,620)
Right
A Roman gold, hardstone and mosaic snuff box, *circa* 1820, width 3½in (9cm) £3,400 ($6,290)

These objects were sold in London on 8 May 1978

From left to right
A Birmingham enamel snuff box, *circa* 1760–65, width 3½in (9cm) £480 ($888)
An English enamel snuff box, the lid painted with the arms of the Worshipful Company of Distillers and its motto *Insignia: Distillatorum/Deut:32V.2:Drop as rain:Distill as:Dew*, *circa* 1765, width 3¼in (8.3cm) £900 ($1,665)
A Birmingham enamel snuff box, *circa* 1750–60, width 2½in (6.5cm) £1,100 ($2,035)

These objects were sold in London on 22 November 1977

A gold, enamel and lapis lazuli charger by Charles Duron, Paris, signed and dated *1867*, diameter 17¾in (45cm)
New York $47,000(£25,405). 14.VI.78

An English gold-handled cane, maker's mark *WH* a pellet between, possibly for William Hopkins or William Hunt, London, 1761, height of handle 2½in (6.5cm)
London £1,300($2,405). 12.XII.77

An English gold, enamel and glass scent bottle, maker's mark of A. J. Strachan, *circa* 1835, height 3¼in (8.3cm)
London £3,000($5,500). 8.V.78

A diamond and emerald zarf with gold and silver mounts, nineteenth century, height 2½in (6.5cm)
London £14,500($26,825). 8.V.78

A French gold, diamond, emerald and enamel presentation snuff box, maker's mark *LT*, *circa* 1860, width 3¾in (9.5cm)
Zurich SFr 34,000(£9,164:$16,954). 16.XI.77

A Swiss gold and enamel *nécessaire* the inside and outside of the lid set with enamel landscapes,
signed *Moulinie Bautte et Moynier a Geneve, circa* 1820, width 5¾in (14.5cm)
Zurich SFr 64,000 (£17,250:$31,912). 16.XI.77

A Swiss four-colour gold and enamel musical automaton box, maker's mark *M&P* crowned, *circa* 1780, width $3\frac{1}{8}$in (7.8cm) $72,500(£39,189)

A gold and agate automaton snuff box by *James Cox*, London, *circa* 1760, width $3\frac{1}{8}$in (8cm) $47,500(£25,676)

The interior of this box is fitted with a watch. There is also a concealed compartment with an ivory miniature depicting a group of women and children watching a magic lantern show. The lantern is mechanical and has a shutter-form series of three erotic scenes, the third of which is automated

The objects on this page are from the collection of Henry Ford II and were sold in New York on 25 February 1978

A Swiss four-colour gold and enamel snuff box, the enamels set in the top and base after paintings by Jean-François de Troy, *circa* 1760, width 3½in (9cm) $30,000 (£16,216)

A Swiss gold and enamel automaton box, *circa* 1800, width 3⅜in (8.5cm) $100,000 (£54,054)

The cover of this box is in three separate sections. The centre lifts to reveal a singing bird with automated beak, crest and tail and the two outside panels reveal erotic scenes

The objects on this page are from the collection of Henry Ford II and were sold in New York on 25 February 1978

A gold and shell snuff box, Paris, *circa* 1755, width 3¼in (8.3cm)
Zurich SFr98,000 (£26,415:$48,868). 16.XI.77

A gold and hardstone snuff box by Johann Christian Neuber, signed and
dated *Dresde 1777*, width 3½in (9cm)
London £35,000 ($64,750). 8.V.78

The base of this box has a second compartment which contains a booklet
listing the stones used and the exact locality in which they were found

Fig 1

Above A Spanish gold and enamel pendant, early seventeenth century, height 2⅛in (4.8cm), $3,100

A French gold and enamel portrait pendant, *circa* 1600, height 2⅝in (6.7cm), $6,250

Centre An Italian gold and enamel necklace and pendant, seventeenth century, length 17½in (44.4cm), $4,000

A German or Flemish gold, diamond and enamel pendant, *circa* 1620, height 2⅞in (7.4cm), $19,000

Below A silver-gilt and enamel medal bearing the profile of William II of Bavaria, *circa* 1626, height 2½in (6.4cm), $650

A gold and enamel medal bearing the profile of Christian, Margrave of Brandenburg, *circa* 1600, $4,500

These objects were sold in New York on 17 February 1977

Portrait of a collection

Eric F. Heckett

Although the instincts of a collector derive from special character traits, his range develops from erudition and connoisseurship. Yet more often than not, the collection itself is conceived by chance: an inherited nucleus, a sudden passion for a particular style or period or just simple opportunism. While both my parents had the innate character traits in full measure, the collection itself began accidentally, by an insignificant inheritance from my father's parents.

Before the First World War, my grandmother had formed, in a desultory way, a collection which included about one hundred nondescript continental miniatures and sixty seventeenth- and eighteenth-century needlework pictures. My grandfather, her husband had, in turn, amassed a large though diffuse conglomeration of coins and medals which later my father disciplined into cohesion during his youth. My own mother, for her part, was in her youth an avid amateur archaeologist digging in Yucatan in 1922–23 and in Peru two years later. She was also enthralled by early Chinese pottery when this was disdained on aesthetic grounds (her T'ang and Han collection disappeared during the war – I never knew it). Development inevitably stopped during the Depression and when our family transplanted itself from Europe to America in 1939–40 it left all impedimenta, including art works, behind. Alas, the end of the Second World War found our family's accumulations scattered to the European winds. Only my grandmother's miniatures and needlework, a few bronzes and my mother's archaeological finds (presumably none considered worth looting) remained as a basis for the Heckett Collection as it ultimately became.

From about 1948 onwards the urge and opportunity to collect overtook my parents again. Acquisitions included Coptic textiles, Egyptian and classical bronzes, Oriental ceramics, Roman cameos. Additionally, my father made a deliberate decision to 'round out', as it then seemed, his mother's collection of miniatures.

The mainspring of any serious collector, especially in the modern, faster world, must be a strong competitive spirit and this my mother, more than my father, had in generous measure. Furthermore, she had time and tremendous energy. She always claimed that her gift for languages was also a major asset. During the period 1948 to 1955, all these tremendous energies were devoted to developing the collections. (Although I write 'all these tremendous energies' I must note in passing that single-handed she simultaneously built one of the half-dozen most famous breeding herds of Aberdeen Angus in the world.) At first her acquisitions were based on historical knowledge rather than connoisseurship, though she always remained a maverick, tempted perversely to the temporarily unfashionable – if she liked it – feeding her own acquisitive and intellectual appetites behind my father's more formal aesthetic judgment. By 1952, as her confidence and judgment matured, she began also to tackle

Fig 2
MRS ANNE MEE
Colonel Thomas Grosvenor, *circa* 1796,
$2\frac{7}{8}$in (7.4cm)
New York $3,200(£1,730). 5.X.77

Fig 3
LAWRENCE CROSSE
A nobleman, signed with
monogram, *circa* 1690, $3\frac{1}{8}$in (8cm)
London £3,400($6,290). 24.IV.78

Fig 4
JOHN HOSKINS
A gentleman with long brown hair,
signed and dated *1646*, $2\frac{1}{2}$in (6.5cm)
London £3,000($5,550). 24.IV.78

Fig 5
RICHARD COSWAY
Anne, Countess of Mountnorris, *circa* 1790,
3in (7.7cm)
London £7,200. 11.VII.77

Fig 6
HEINRICH FRIEDRICH FÜGER
Count Franz Joseph Johann Fries, 3in (7.7cm)
Monte Carlo FF13,000(£1,486:$2,749). 4.V.78

my father's more austere field of coins, medals and manuscripts, all of which she saw as being allied to portrait miniatures.

In 1952 also, with the purchase of the collection of Baron Reitzes of Vienna, her collection became substantially more important. Twenty-eight major English miniatures, all with detailed provenance had been accumulated most carefully by Baron Reitzes in 1910–12, the majority from Duveen and other well-known collections. Mostly reframed by Baron Reitzes in specially designed silver-gilt frames, they were exhibited *en masse* at the Albertina in Vienna in 1924 and singly elsewhere. Seven of them are to be found illustrated in Jean de Bourgoing's *English Miniatures* and others in other publications. This group included seven miniatures by Cosway, six by Samuel Cooper, five by Lawrence Crosse (Fig 3), four by Flatman, several by Dixon, and one each by Hoskins and Gibson. With considerable detective work ten of them have been subsequently reattributed to other equally-ranked artists and six sitters reidentified. This acquisition was a watershed in my mother's collection, its uniform quality made her much more particular afterwards, the solid provenance and bibliography disciplined her both intellectually and with regard to quality. It also unbalanced, almost over-powered, the pre-1952 collection, so that henceforth she inevitably broadened still further this English section both by period and by artist (Figs 4 and 5). Although it is outside the scope of this article, it is fascinating to study the changes in identification since 1914; also to analyse the prices – first, those paid by Reitzes in 1910–12 (£5,600), then the price my mother paid in 1952 (£2,100) and, lastly, the dispersal results for all twenty-eight items, £56,300, in 1977–78. By 1952 the miniatures (and also the classical bronzes) had become well enough known to attract peripatetic museum curators and collectors to the wilds of Western Pennsylvania; thus the Heckett Collection began to signify to the outside world, if not to my parents, specifically one of portrait miniatures.

My father at that period made habitual rounds of the dealers, especially in London, Amsterdam, New York and Chicago, all cities he visited regularly on business. He, for instance, purchased the Füger (Fig 6) himself in 1952, from an emigrant out of what was then the Eastern Zone of Germany. It had a considerable pedigree, the Gutmann Collection and before 1910 the Backstitz Collection in Berlin. Also it had been published in *Deutsches Barock und Rokoko* by G. Biermann and exhibited at the Carnegie Museum and elsewhere. This was the collection's first major continental miniature and always remained a favourite of my father's.

Fig 7
FRANCISZEK SMIADECKI
Called James Posten, signed
with monogram, 2⅛in (5.4cm)
London £4,400($8,140).
24.IV.78

Fig 8
NICHOLAS HILLIARD
Called Anne, Lady Hunsdon,
circa 1585, 2¼in (5.8cm)
New York $13,000(£7,027).
5.X.77

Mother, meanwhile, carried out impressive correspondence with curators, dealers and collectors around the world (many very witty examples remain to me) and pored over every available auction catalogue. She would commission some friend or relation, often myself, to bid on any lots she fancied. She would never, or could never, explain why she wanted one lot instead of another, nor why she would give me strict price limits on one object yet give me carte-blanche on what appeared to me to be a similar example from another sale. She was never satisfied with my voluntary help; either I paid too much or stopped too soon, I should have either shied off because the item was cracked or I should *not* have shied *although* the item was cracked, the question of an original frame mattered sometimes, sometimes not. Above all, she would insist that I used my eyes and my heart and never trust a catalogue completely. Although occasionally she was wrong, she could not bear to part with her mistakes. She liked them as objects or she would not have bought them, that was the essence. After 1953 she almost never worried about obtaining formal expert opinion although the famous Leo Schlidoff became a valued adviser as well as a balancing mechanism for her enthusiasm. The miniature by Smiadecki (Fig 7) was obtained from him directly in 1955 for £62, a generous price which reflects his gentlemanly behaviour.

Quickly during the 1950s the collection grew: a cascade of miniatures, Stuart relics, German memento mori and commemorative medals. My father would come back from Paris with an underglaze portrait of Catherine the Great on porcelain and the next week, my mother would just 'have to have', from an auction sale, an Elizabethan medal engraved by Crispin or Simon de Passe. The medal by de Passe, incidentally, was her personal favourite (see *Art at Auction 1976–77*, p 389). Cameos, Persian miniatures, illuminated charters, all fitted into the Design and the Design kept expanding. 1955 was the great year – for instance, the radiant little Hilliard (Fig 8) was acquired for £500 in October from Agnew, London, at a time when my mother's appetite and knowledge was reaching its peak. During the same trip to England my parents acquired, all with good provenances, two magnificent Corneille de Lyons portraits, the smallest Hilliard in existence (at Sotheby's, 5 October 1955), a lovely series of small seventeenth-century Dutch and French flower paintings and superb Elizabethan jewellery. After that spree, the miniature collection had just about matured and the collection began more and more to spread into complementary areas.

It is worth noting that although for dispersal purposes, Sotheby's broke down the Heckett Collection into logical components (European portrait miniatures, jewellery, classic coins, commemorative medals, Classical and Renaissance bronzes and objects of vertu) each group of objects had been lovingly and judiciously planned to balance in depth as well as breadth, to make, as my mother described it, a Platonic Unity. To her, as indeed in logic, all these arbitrarily separated components made one whole, the individual private symbols of great European and small family events or as she thought of it, history in microcosm (Fig 1).

Meanwhile, the more esoteric field of coins and medals had been more my father's interest but as he was much more possessive and secretive, that collection never became as recognised as my mother's. Despite this, the sale on 25 May 1977 was considered a milestone in its own right (see *Art at Auction 1976–77*, pp 390–91). The fun went out of mother's 'hunt' during my father's serious illness in 1957, after which she concentrated on filling gaps rather than expanding. Significantly, her own interest in coins and medals only dates from his illness and dominates her interests after my father's death in 1962. By then she was looking for a new intellectual challenge which, in her last ten years, she found in Greek and Roman coins. Simultaneously, the miniatures were losing their interest, she knew that field too well. Mere fastidiousness should have filled the minor gaps but as she would not sell anything she ever acquired, there was no point in 'purifying' the collection.

Both my parents had always been drawn to the small, the portable, and the tactile and they favoured the period between 1550 and 1650. While for my father this period meant the Renaissance, my mother's romantic nature responded to Elizabethan England and especially vividly to the Jacobite tragedy. The result of this was a voracious, though open-ended conglomeration of Maundy purses, gaming counters, patch boxes, Jacobean relics, and Tudor laundry lists, the 'objects of vertu' in the sale catalogues, which served the miniature collection like harmony accompanies a lyric.

As I write, the dispersal is complete and looking through my mother's inventory it is interesting to compare results with the pattern of her acquisition. Not only has the balance of taste changed (particularly notable is the ascension of Persian miniatures and gold coins) but twenty-five years ago the Hilliards cost no more than the Hoskins; the Smarts much less than the Cosways and the rarities such as her Rosalba Carriera and Anne Mee (Fig 2) held no special value. Also, many of her canniest acquisitions came not from uninformed sources, but from well-regarded art dealers and at auction.

Although the miniature collection was more or less complete by 1956 the number of total objects in the entire collection doubled between then and 1969, when she withdrew from active life, largely in the field of Greek and Roman coins as outlined above. However, the very last inventory number, 1460, was connected with miniatures and therewith goes a story. In the summer of 1969, at a Dublin antique shop, I had bought myself a pair of gold cuff-links with four very banal, badly painted nineteenth-century Indian miniatures on ivory inset under glass. When my mother saw me wearing them, she insisted they belonged to the collection as a type of miniature that she did not yet possess. I protested that they were worthless as miniatures and pointed out that I had no other cuff-links with me but nothing would swerve her. To keep her happy, I relinquished them and went home with sleeves rolled up. Ironically, in the dispersal they fetched eight times what I had paid for them ten years previously.

RICHARD GIBSON
Sir Thomas Wolryche, signed,
circa 1690, 3in (7.5cm)
New York $4,400(£2,378). 5.X.77
From the collection of Edward Gatacre

NICHOLAS HILLIARD
A lady of the court, *circa* 1590,
2in (5cm)
London £12,000($22,200). 26.VI.78

JOHN HOSKINS
A nobleman, signed with
monogram, *circa* 1625, 2in (5cm)
London £3,200($5,920).
19.XII.77

NICHOLAS HILLIARD
King James I, *circa* 1610,
1⅝in (4.1cm)
London £5,500($10,185).
20.III.78

NICHOLAS HILLIARD
Called George Clifford, 3rd Earl
of Cumberland, dated *1594*,
1¾in (4.3cm)
London £7,000($12,950).
19.XII.77

JOHN SMART
A pair of miniatures of William and Maria Burroughs, signed and dated *1797* on the reverse, $2\frac{5}{8}$in (6.6cm)
£16,000 ($29,600)
From the collection of E. A. Elgar

GEORGE ENGLEHEART
A young girl, *circa* 1780,
$2\frac{3}{8}$in (6cm)
£4,200 ($7,770)

GEORGE ENGLEHEART
Captain Aeneas Mackay, 1798, 3in (7.5cm)
£2,400 ($4,440)
From the collection of A. G. A. Mackay

The miniatures on this page were sold in London on 19 December 1977

JEAN BAPTISTE ISABEY
General Apraxin, on paper, signed, *circa* 1815,
5½in (14cm)
Zurich SFr22,000(£5,930:$10,971). 15.XI.77

FRIEDRICH JOHANN GOTTLIEB LIEDER
A nobleman, on card, signed and dated *1820*,
5¼in (13.5cm)
London £2,600($4,810). 19.XII.77

JEAN BAPTISTE AUGUSTIN
A lady, signed and dated *1793*, 3in (7.5cm)
New York $3,400(£1,838). 25.IV.78

FRIEDRICH JOHANN GOTTLIEB LIEDER
An officer, on card, signed and dated *Prag,
1818*, 5¼in (13.5cm)
London £1,900($3,515). 19.XII.77

RICHARD COSWAY
Thomas Postlethwaite D.D., signed and
dated *1794* on the reverse, $2\frac{7}{8}$in (7.2cm)
£1,400($2,590)

HORACE HONE
Mrs Chamberlain, signed and dated *1788*,
$2\frac{3}{4}$in (7cm)
£1,550($2,868)

Above Attributed to ANTOINE VESTIER
Two sisters with a bouquet of roses, *circa* 1775,
3in (7.5cm)
£1,200($2,220)

Left PETER PAILLOU
A family group, signed and dated *November 1788*,
$3\frac{1}{2}$in (9cm)
£1,700($3,145)

The miniatures on this page were sold in London on 26 June 1978

LOUIS FRANÇOIS AUBRY
Self portrait of the artist as a young man, 5⅝in (14.3cm)
Zurich SFr23,000(£6,200:$11,470). 15.XI.77

Coins and Medals

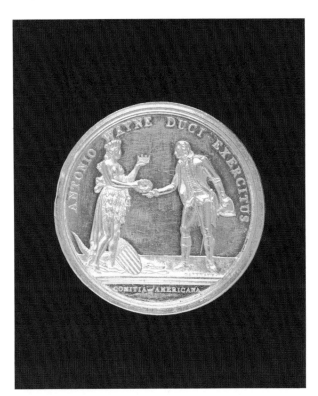 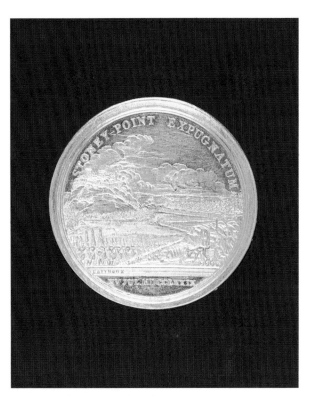

An extremely rare *Comitia Americana* medal in gold, awarded to Brigadier-General Anthony
Wayne for the taking of Stony Point, New York, 15 July 1779
New York $51,000(£27,568). 15.VI.78
From the collection of Anthony Wayne Ridgway

General 'Mad' Anthony Wayne was born at Waynesborough, Chester County, Pennsylvania, on 1
January 1745. He was one of the most distinguished officers in the American army and won a
number of important engagements, including a victory over the Miami tribe of Indians in 1794 and
the taking of Stony Point, New York, on 15 July 1779. In 1792 he was appointed Major-General and
Commander-in-Chief in the war against the Western Indians and he died at Presque Isle, on Lake
Erie, on 14 December 1796. The storming of Stony Point took place at midday and the troops under
General Wayne's command were instructed to leave their muskets unloaded '... with the most
pointed orders not to fire on any account, but place their whole dependence on the bayonet, which
order was literally and faithfully obeyed.' Upon his receipt of General Wayne's letter of 17 July
1779, recounting the events of the successful assault, General Washington wrote to the President of
the Continental Congress transmitting '... the particulars of this interesting event'. In writing of
General Wayne's attack he adds with pleasure '... that his own conduct (General Wayne)
throughout the whole of this arduous enterprise merits the warmest approbation of Congress. He
improved upon the plan recommended by me and executed it in a manner that does signal honour
to his judgement and to his bravery'

BYZANTINE, solidus of Tiberius III
(698–705 AD)
London £440 ($814). 14.VI.78

ANCIENT GREEK, gold
octodrachm of
Arsinoe II of Egypt,
circa 270 BC
London
£2,300 ($4,255).
16.XII.77

SASANIAN, dinar of Xusro II
(591–628 AD)
London £2,100 ($3,885). 10.V.78

ARAB-SASANIAN,
dirhem of the
Omayyad governor
Bishr ibn Marwan,
circa 690 AD
London £1,300 ($2,405).
26.X.77

ISLAMIC, Omayyad dinar dated
AH102, of the Spanish mint of
Al Andalus (Andalusia)
London £3,600 ($6,660). 6.IV.78

ENGLAND, London
mint, noble of
Edward III (1327–77)
London £920 ($1,702).
19.VII.78

ANGLO-SAXON, portrait-type penny
of Eadmund (939–946)
London £950 ($1,758). 14.VI.78

ROMAN, sestertius of Nero,
(54–68 AD)
London £1,200 ($2,220).
26.X.77

SPAIN, Visigothic tremissis of
Reccesvinth (649–672 AD)
London £620($1,147). 10.V.78

GERMANY, ducat of Wismar under
Charles XI of Sweden, 1676, the third
known example of this date
London £3,000($5,550). 8.III.78

Left
ENGLAND, George III, gilt-bronze medal
commemorating Captain Cook's second
voyage in 1772
London £680($1,258). 8.III.78

Right
HOLY ROMAN EMPIRE, Albrecht von
Wallenstein, Duke of Friedland and
Mecklenburg, 10 ducats, 1631
London £7,000($12,950). 8.III.78

Below
BRAZIL, gold bar issued at Serro Frio under
Peter I
London £2,100($3,885). 19.VII.78

ISLE OF MAN, card money for 5 shillings,
1812
London £680($1,258). 14.VI.78

GERMANY, Westphalia,
Order of the Crown of
Westphalia, Commander's
badge
London £6,000($11,100).
23.XI.77

The Most Illustrious Order of St Patrick, breast
star, *circa* 1820
London £950($1,757). 23.XI.77

East and West Africa medal,
1887–1900, 1 clasp, Dawkita
1897, awarded to Lieutenant
F. B. Henderson, RN, the only
British officer present
London £2,400($4,440).
22.XI.77

IMPERIAL RUSSIA, Order of St Anne,
presentation badge for
distinguished service
London £560($1,036). 12.IV.78

Gold, Silver and Pewter

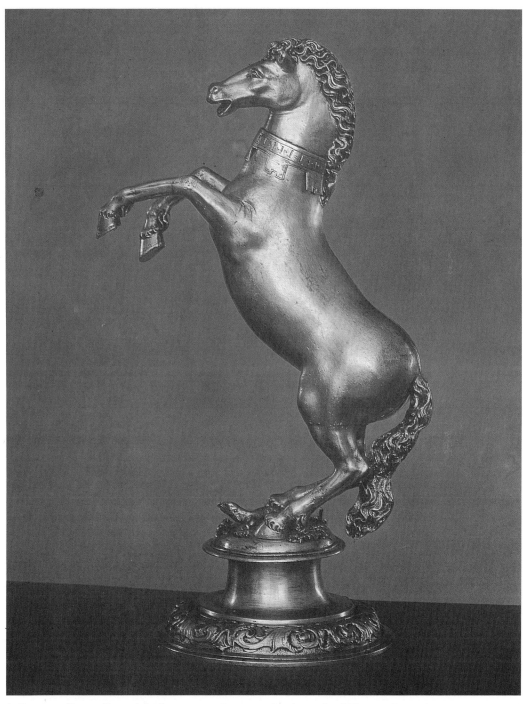

A German silver-gilt model of a rampant horse, maker's mark of Thomas Stoer the younger, Nuremberg, *circa* 1635, height 11in (28cm)
Zurich SFr72,000(£19,407:$35,903). 18.XI.77

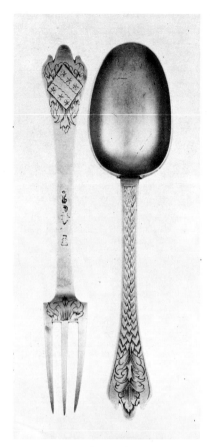

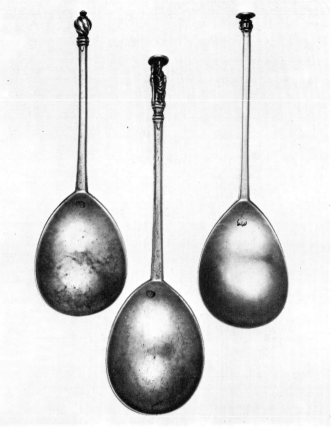

A Louis XIV silver-gilt spoon and
fork, maker's mark of Marin
Marie, Paris, 1681
Zurich SFr15,000(£4,043:$7,480).
18.XI.77
From the collection of D. David-
Weill, Président du Conseil des
Musées Nationaux

From left to right
A Henry VIII 'Wrythen' knop spoon, London, 1533,
£2,600($4,810)
A Henry VIII Apostle spoon, St Thomas, London, 1537,
£2,400($4,440)
An Edward VI seal top spoon, London, 1552, £750($1,388)

These spoons were sold in London on 15 June 1978

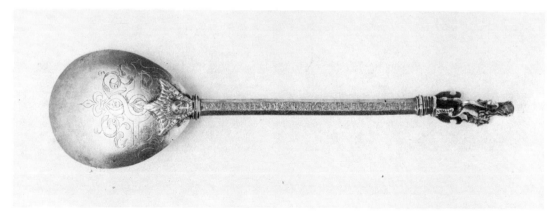

A German parcel-gilt spoon, unmarked, late sixteenth century
New York $2,200(£1,189). 15.VI.78

One of a pair of George III soup tureens with covers and stands, maker's mark of Paul Storr, London, 1807, width of stand 21in (53.3cm)
Los Angeles $37,000(£20,000). 8.VI.78

The tureens are engraved with the arms of Cavendish with Compton in pretence for George Augustus Henry, third son of 4th Duke of Devonshire, who was created Earl of Burlington in 1831. He married Elizabeth, daughter and heir of 7th Earl of Northampton

A pair of George III sauce tureens with covers, maker's mark of Paul Storr, London, 1804, height 6½in (16.5cm)
Johannesburg R5,800(£3,625:$6,706). 29.X.77

One of a pair of George III silver-gilt four-light candelabra, maker's mark of Digby Scott and Benjamin Smith, London, 1804, height 25⅝in (65.1cm)
New York $25,000(£13,514). 6.X.77

A Queen Anne silver-gilt toilet service, maker's mark of Benjamin Pyne, London, 1711, comprising:
    A pair of large rectangular caskets with hinged covers, width $10\frac{1}{4}$in (26cm)
    Two pairs of circular boxes with slip-on covers, diameter of each $5\frac{1}{2}$in (14cm) and $3\frac{3}{4}$in (9.5cm)
    A pair of octagonal candlesticks, height $7\frac{1}{4}$in (18.4cm)
    A pair of scent bottles, height $6\frac{1}{4}$in (15.9cm)
    A snuffer's stand, height $5\frac{1}{8}$in (13cm)
    A chamber candlestick with three bun feet
New York $32,000(£17,297). 29.X.77
From the collection of the late Edith Kane Baker

A George II silver-gilt cream jug, attributed to Paul de Lamerie, *circa* 1740, width 4⅜in (11.2cm)
New York $7,000(£3,784). 2.III.78
From the collection of Enid A. Haupt

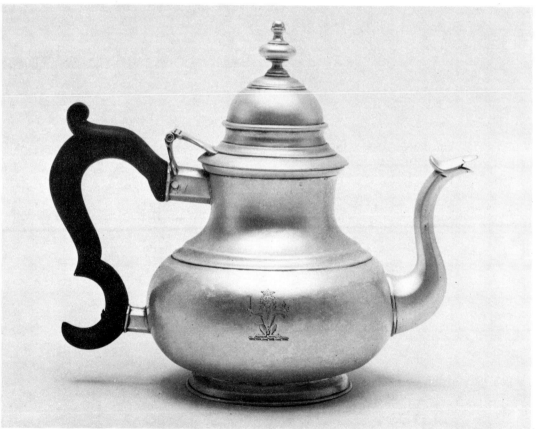

An American teapot, maker's mark of Peter Van Dyck, New York, *circa* 1720–40, height 7½in (19cm)
New York $47,000(£25,405). 2.II.78
From the collection of Robert Lenox Dwight

A George II tapered cylindrical coffee pot, maker's mark of Paul de Lamerie, London, 1738, height 8¾in (22.2cm)
London £11,000($20,350). 4.V.78

A George III circular gold salver 'The Rutland Salver', maker's mark of Paul Storr, engraved with
the arms of Manners, Duke of Rutland and the arms of the sixteen towns and cities copied from the
gold freedom boxes which were melted down to make this salver, London, 1801, diameter 12in (30.5cm)
London £60,000 ($111,000). 4.V.78

A German travelling service in silver-gilt, porcelain and glass, contained in a velvet-lined tooled leather case, the majority of the silver-gilt objects with the maker's mark of Joh. Erhard Heuglin II, Augsburg, *circa* 1730; the Meissen porcelain gilt at Augsburg in Chinoiserie style, *circa* 1730, width of case 19½in (49.5cm)
Zurich SFr70,000 (£18,868:$34,906). 18.XI.77

A George IV silver-gilt bowl, maker's mark of Edward Farrell, London, 1820, the base stamped *Lewis Silversmith to HRH The Duke of York St James's St* for the retailer Kensington Lewis, width over handles 17in (43.2cm) London £3,200 ($5,920). 15.VI.78

The Queen's cup, Ascot Races, 1883, a three-handled cup and cover, maker's mark of James Garrard of R. & S. Garrard and Co, London, 1882, height 19½in (49.5cm) London £2,600 ($4,810). 15.XII.77

An American ewer, maker's mark of Tiffany & Co, New York, *circa* 1900, height 21¾in (55.2cm) New York $3,600 (£1,946). 2.II.78 From the collection of Mrs John Bergen

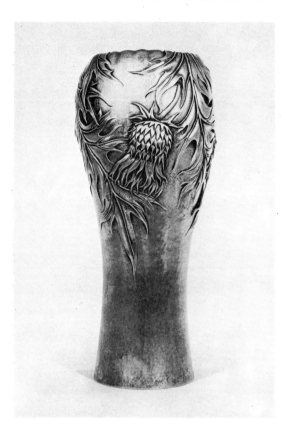

A flower vase, maker's mark of Gilbert Marks,
London, 1898, height 10½in (26.7cm)
London £900($1,665). 29.IX.77

A rose bowl and cover, maker's mark of R. E. Stone, London, 1954, the underside engraved *Designer
A.G. Styles, Maker R.E. Stone – for Garrard & Co Ltd London*, width 15¾in (40cm)
London £360($666). 29.IX.77

A Swiss silver-gilt four-piece tea set, maker's mark of Johann Karl Bossard,
Lucern, *circa* 1890
£1,750 ($3,238)

A German oval soup tureen, cover and mirror plateau, *circa* 1860, width of
plateau 19½ in (49.5cm)
£1,700 ($3,145)

The silver on this page was sold in London on 13 July 1978

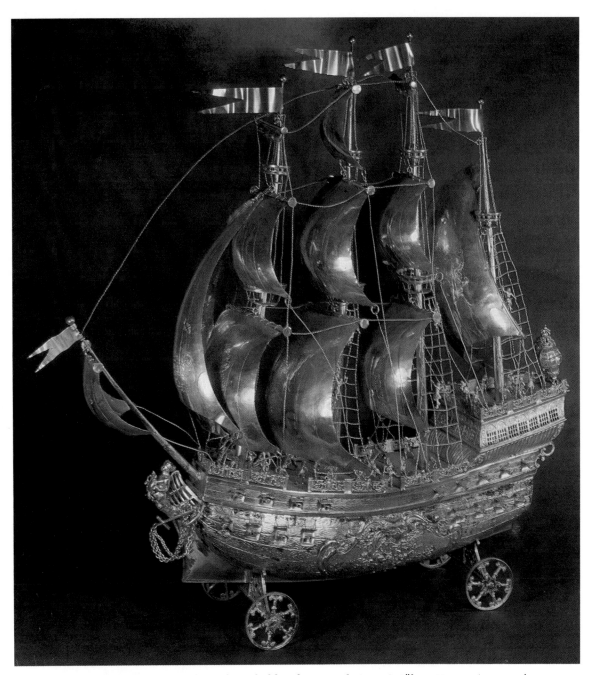

A German four-masted nef, maker's mark probably of B. Neresheimer & Söhne, Hanau, importer's mark of Berthold Müller of B. Müller & Son, Chester, 1910, height 37⅜in (95cm)
London £6,500 ($12,025). 13.VII.78

A German ewer and basin by Iohan Georg Klingling,
eighteenth century, height of ewer $7\frac{3}{4}$in (19.7cm)
London £620($1,147). 11.V.78
From the collection of the late Mrs Z.M. Gyerey

A Charles I flagon, *circa* 1640, height $11\frac{7}{8}$in (30.2cm)
London £950($1,758). 9.II.78

An English wriggled-work plate, *circa* 1695,
diameter $8\frac{1}{2}$in (21.6cm)
London £800($1,480). 9.II.78

A Swiss flagon by Pierre Machin, late seventeenth century,
height $13\frac{3}{4}$in (35cm)
New York $3,250(£1,757). 16.II.78

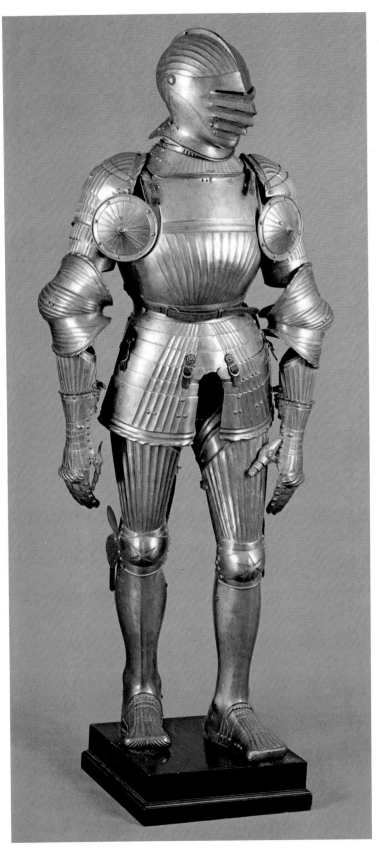

Arms
and Armour

A suit of Maximillian-style fluted armour,
height 72in (182.5cm)
Los Angeles $6,000(£3,243). 9.IV.78

This suit was probably constructed *circa*
1870–80, using portions of original armour

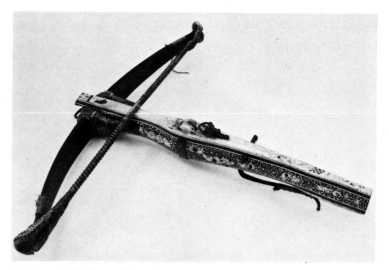

An ivory inlaid crossbow, late sixteenth century, length of iron bow 34in (86.4cm)
Los Angeles $6,200(£3,351). 9.IV.78

An Austrian etched halberd, the fluke inscribed *FR, circa* 1556–64, length overall 83in (211cm)
London £2,200($4,070). 14.III.78

A German bronze cannon, weight *W.59½PT*, signed and dated *Oswaldus Baldnerus, Normberge Me Fecit 1550*, length 24⅜in (62cm)
London £3,800($7,030). 14.III.78

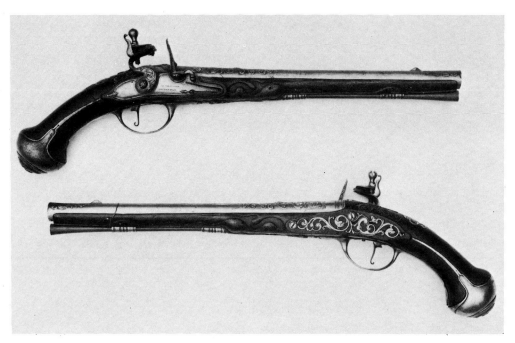

A pair of Dutch flintlock holster pistols, signed *Jan Van Suilen, Amsterdam*, late seventeenth century, length 20½in (52cm)
London £11,000($20,350). 14.III.78

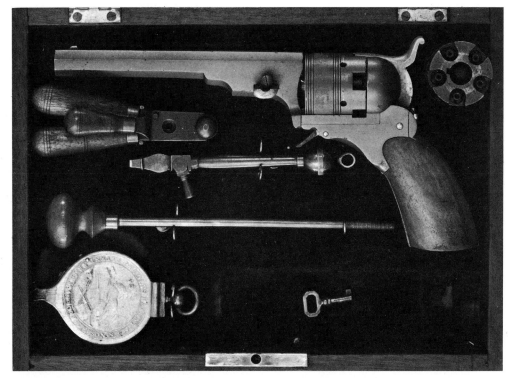

A Colt Paterson Belt model revolver in a velvet-lined mahogany case with loading tool, cleaning rod and cap dispenser, length of barrel 4⅞in (12.3cm)
Los Angeles $17,000(£9,190). 9.IV.78

A silver-mounted flintlock fowling piece, signed *H. Hadley*, maker's mark of P. Esteva on barrel, heel plate numbered *2*, London hallmark for 1764, length 55in (139.7cm)
London £3,900($7,215). 20.XII.77

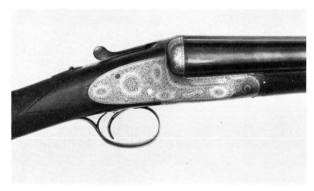

One of a pair of D.B. 12-bore round-action side-lock single-trigger semi self-opening ejector sporting guns by Boss & Co, serial numbers 5157/5158, length 46¼in (117.5cm)
Gleneagles £6,000($11,100). 29.VIII.77

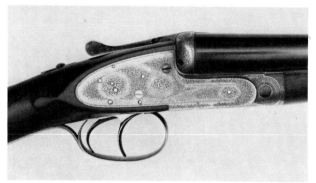

One of a pair of D.B. 12-bore side-lock self-opening ejector sporting guns by J. Purdey & Sons, serial numbers 25509/25510, length 45in (114.3cm)
Scone Palace £8,500($15,725). 10.IV.78

A Kentucky flintlock rifle, signed *J. Brooks*, early nineteenth century, length 57in (144.8cm)
Los Angeles $10,000(£5,405). 9.IV.78

Antiquities, Asian and Primitive Art

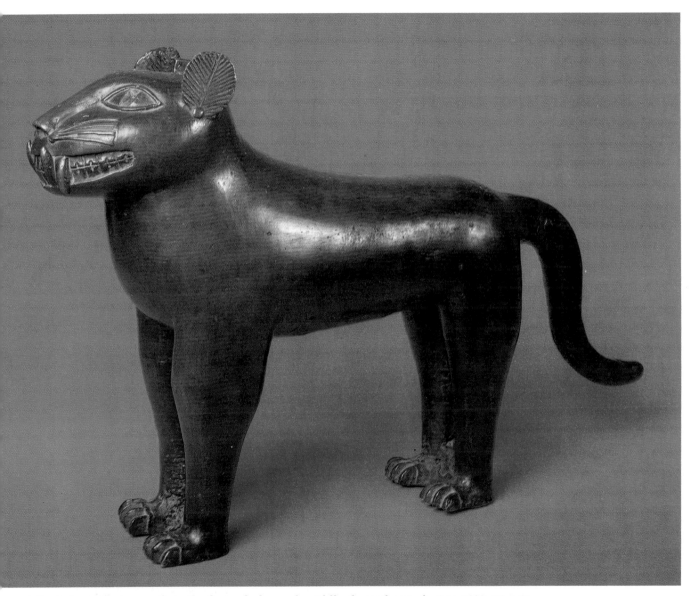

A Benin bronze aquamanile in the form of a leopard, middle classical period, *circa* 1600, Nigeria, height 12⅛in (30.8cm)
London £150,000($277,500). 29.VI.78
From the collection of George Ortiz

A Lower Niger bronze female figure holding a vessel, height 8¼in (20.6cm)
London £120,000($222,000). 29.VI.78
From the collection of George Ortiz

A Lower Niger figure from the George Ortiz Collection

Robert Bleakley

The sale of a remarkable Lower Niger bronze figure for £120,000 marked an exciting recognition by the art market of a field relatively neglected until recent years. Twenty-six years earlier, another figure, subsequently recognised by George Ortiz as being the work of the same master, was sold at Sotheby's for only £650 and was later bought by the British Museum (see over). Both bronzes display an extraordinary degree of artistic licence, apparent in the massively exaggerated hands of the present figure and in the omission of part of the right leg of that in the British Museum. In spite of the great diversity of bronzes encompassed by the Lower Niger rubric, these pieces are clearly the work of one founder. Several other works attributable to this artist survive, including a pair of magnificent bronze heads, described by William Fagg as being in the 'hunter style', one in the Museum für Völkerkunde, Berlin and the other in the British Museum.

The term 'Lower Niger' was originated by William Fagg in 1963 to distinguish a large body of uncategorised bronzes from the region between the confluence of the Niger and the Delta in the south, from works of the Benin and Ife court styles further north. Although much work has recently been undertaken in an attempt to give more specific attributions, there is no consensus of opinion and suggested places of origin range across a wide area of Southern Nigeria.

One of these places may have been the large Igbo town of Akwa which lies to the east of the Delta and across the Niger river. Akwa was renowned as a traditional metal-working centre and its smiths had a long established history of forging and casting which was of sufficient complexity to sustain a guild system comparable to that of the Benin smiths. Travelling widely outside their own Igbo homeland, they supplied utilitarian metal implements and to a lesser extent, ceremonial bronzes, throughout a large region. Most notable amongst their works are small bronze ritual objects, *ofo*, (such as lot 41 from the George Ortiz Collection) supplied to Western Igbo patrons. The existence of these *ofo*, produced through a lost-wax process and often displaying a high level of technical accomplishment, suggests the possibility that Akwa smiths could also have produced the other types of bronzes found in Southern Nigeria. Interestingly, two tribes in Southern Nigeria, the Urhobo and Isoko, both record Igbo influences in their past and it may be that the Akwa smiths fulfilled a dual role in the supply of bronzes to these and neighbouring tribes by distributing bronzes made in other centres as well as their own.

Attempts to define precise sources of origin have been based on studies of historical and cultural traditions but they are severely restricted by the lack of supporting data. Recent analysis of stylistic attributions bearing affinities with Yoruba artistic traditions has suggested Old Owo, Ijebu-Ode and Owo as casting sites for some of the more imposing of these Lower Niger bronzes; Benin city itself has also been proposed as

A Lower Niger bronze figure of a hunter carrying
an antelope, height 14⅛in (35.8cm)
London £650. 16.I.52
This figure is now in the British Museum, London

a centre of multiple styles. However, this method is restricted by the fact that throughout the entire region metal-casters followed the traditional African practice of
recycling old bronzes. Another limitation is the extensive inter-tribal trading that
was carried out prior to European contact, especially along the Niger river, although
exact routes have yet to be determined.

Traditionally, the centres to the north are considered to be the greater manufacturers and users of bronzes. The southern tribes lacked a rich ceremonial life such as
that of the royal court of Benin, which sustained an extensive metal-working
tradition. Little is known of the extent of Benin bronze-casting for neighbouring
patrons and it may be that the Oba (or king) allowed a certain degree of latitude in
sanctioning commissions for works which combined provincial elements with the
rigid style of Benin court bronzes. William Fagg asserts however, that the Benin court
style was insulated from provincial influences by a royal prohibition on the casting of
bronzes for anyone other than the Oba. Of the large number of bronzes found in
Southern Nigeria, some are evidently direct Benin imports. Others display a wide
variety of styles, perhaps reflecting the pragmatic approach of visiting smiths adjusting their works to the tastes of successive patrons.

Regardless of the inability of scholars to achieve a consensus of opinion in
determining geographic sources, the outstanding artistic quality of some Lower Niger
bronzes remains uncontested. It was George Ortiz's recognition of the figure with the
bowl as representing one of the highest achievements of a master bronze-caster which
led him on a search lasting twenty years. He originally saw a photograph of it whilst
with Charles Ratton in Paris, shortly after the last war. Almost obsessed with the
desire to possess the figure, he eventually traced it through another photograph seen
in the album of Louis Carré some twenty-five years later. Ironically George Ortiz
enjoyed ownership of the figure for only a few years before being forced to part with
it together with the remainder of his outstanding collection of tribal art.

A Benin bronze plaque with a warrior wearing full regalia, *circa* 1600, Nigeria,
height 19½in (49.7cm)
London £72,000 ($133,200). 29.VI.78
From the collection of George Ortiz

Above left
A Lake Sentani wood lime spatula or fly-whisk handle, New Guinea, height 8½in (21.6cm)
£6,000($11,100)
Above right
A Lake Sentani wood knife-handle, New Guinea, height 8in (20.3cm)
£6,500($12,025)

A royal Bakuba ivory sceptre, Zaire, sixteenth to eighteenth century, height 15⅞in (40.3cm)
£46,000($85,100)

A Pentecost Island wood face mask,
New Hebrides, height 13½in
(34.3cm)
£180,000 ($333,000)

Masks such as this one were used in
religious rites in relation to the cult
of the ancestors

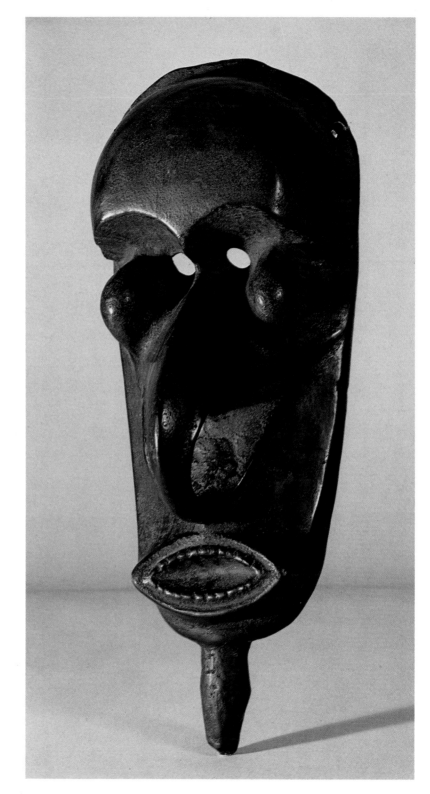

The objects on these two pages are
from the collection of George Ortiz
and were sold in London on
29 June 1978

A Maori wood door lintel (*pare*), New Zealand, probably *circa* 1810, width 37¾in (96cm)
£40,000($74,000)

The objects on these two pages are from the collection of George Ortiz and were sold in London on 29 June 1978

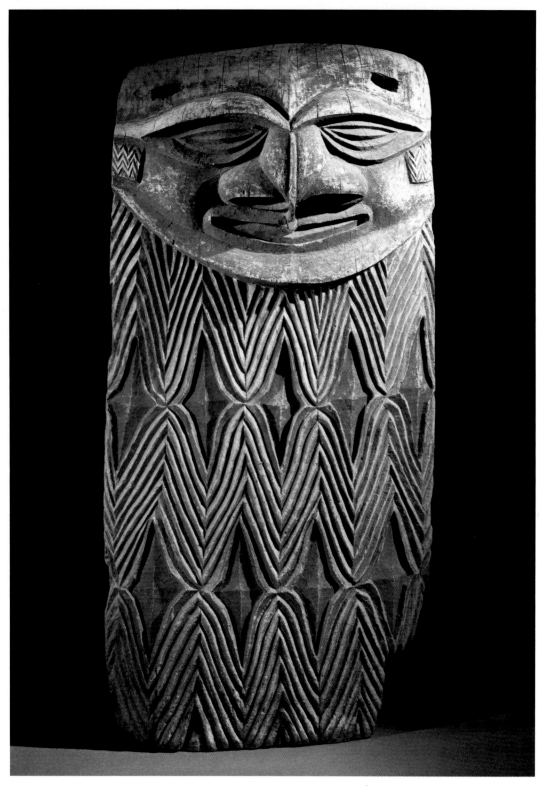

One of a pair of New Caledonian wood door-jambs (*jovo*), height 71¼in (181cm)
£44,000($81,400)

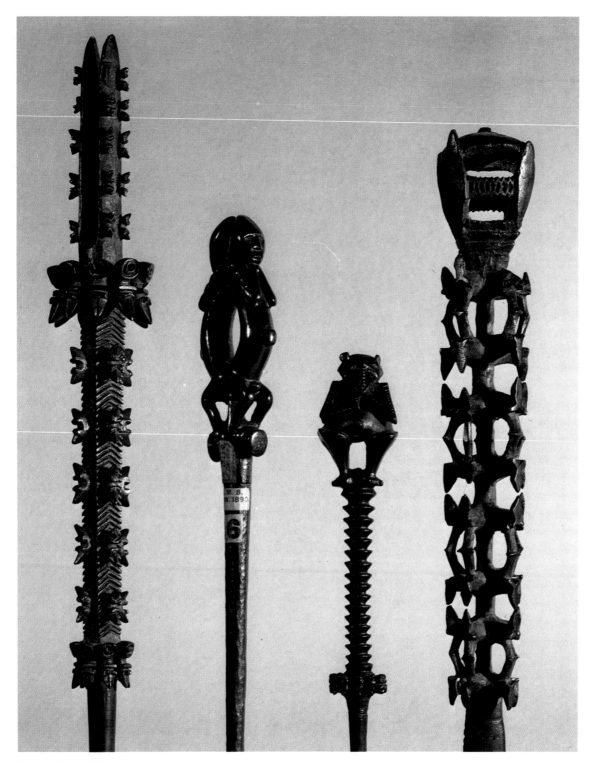

From left to right
A Rurutu casuarina wood god-staff, Austral Islands, Polynesia, height 21⅞in (55.6cm), £26,000($48,100)
A Tahitian wood fly-whisk handle, height 17in (43.2cm), £33,000($61,050)
A Rurutu wood fly-whisk handle, Austral Islands, Polynesia, height 10⅞in (27.8cm), £12,000($22,200)
A Mitiaro *toa*-wood god-staff, Cook Islands, Polynesia, height 16½in (42cm), £22,000($40,700)

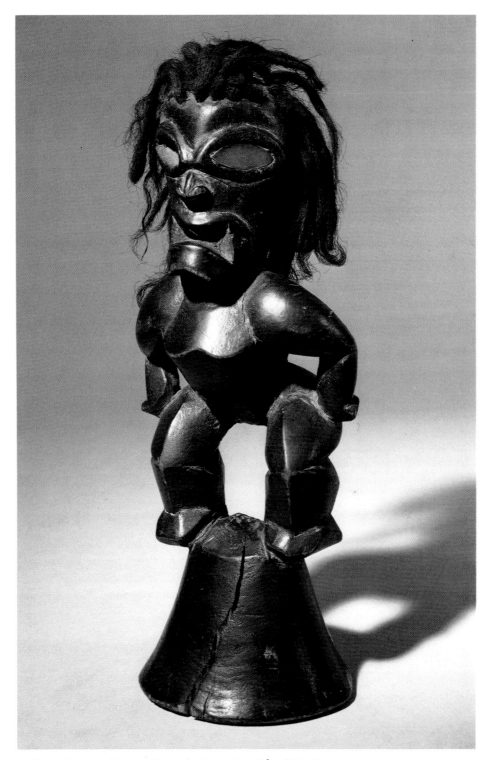

A Hawaiian wood image (*Aumakua*), height 10¼in (26cm)
£250,000($462,500)

This image and the Rurutu casuarina wood god-staff (far left) were probably acquired by Captain Cook during one of his expeditions

The objects on these two pages are from the collection of George Ortiz and were sold in London on 29 June 1978

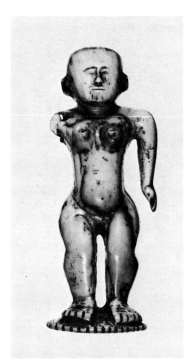

A Tongan ivory female figure,
Polynesia, height 5in (12.7cm)
London £27,000 ($49,950).
3.VII.78

An Olmec pottery figure of a seated baby, Las
Bocas, middle pre-classical period, *circa*
1150–550 BC, height 10½in (26.7cm)
New York $11,000 (£5,946). 14.X.77
From the collection of the late Dalton Trumbo

An Eskimo-Aleut stone lamp, Kodiak tradition, Kachemak stage,
first millennium AD, width 13⅜in (34cm)
New York $26,000 (£14,054). 3.III.78
From the collection of Mrs Mary Ghilardi

From left to right
A Babembe female fetish figure, Congo-Brazzaville, height $7\frac{1}{4}$in (18.4cm)
$6,000 (£3,243)

A Babembe male fetish figure, Congo-Brazzaville, height $8\frac{3}{4}$in (22.2cm)
$4,000 (£2,162)
From the collection of the late Malvina Hoffman

A Babembe male fetish figure, Congo-Brazzaville, height $5\frac{1}{4}$in (13.3cm)
$3,250 (£1,757)

A Babembe male fetish figure, Congo-Brazzaville, height $7\frac{1}{2}$in (19cm)
$2,750 (£1,486)

These figures were sold in New York on 15 October 1977

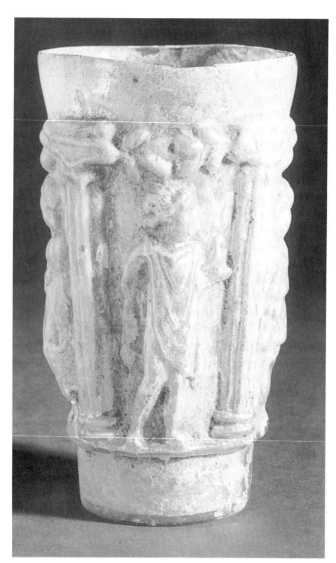

A Roman glass mould-blown beaker, first century AD, height $4\frac{7}{8}$in (12.5cm)
London £13,000($24,050). 3.VII.78

An Egypto-Phoenician blue faience cup, later Middle Kingdom, *circa* 1900–1700 BC, height $3\frac{7}{8}$in (9.8cm)
New York $17,500(£9,459). 17.II.78

An Egyptian glass paste royal male head,
eighteenth/nineteenth Dynasty,
height 1¾in (4.5cm)
London £30,000($55,500). 3.VII.78
From the collection of F. Nichols

A Cycladic marble figure of a goddess,
circa 2700–2500 BC, height 26½in (67.3cm)
New York $65,000(£35,135). 17.II.78

A Cycladic marble votive vessel, *circa* 2500 BC,
height 5in(12.6cm)
London £2,600($4,810). 7.XI.77
From the collection of Henri E. Smeets

An Egyptian bronze figure of Wadjet,
Ptolemaic or early Roman period,
height 19in (48.3cm)
London £20,000($37,000). 3.VII.78

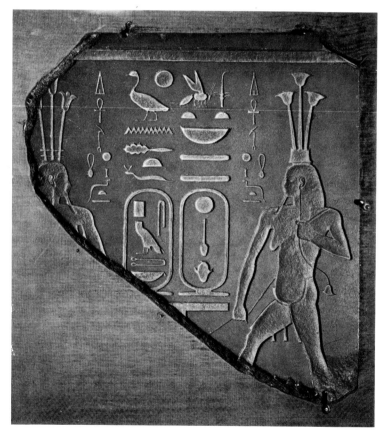

An Egyptian dark-grey schist fragment showing two Nile gods,
twenty-sixth Dynasty, height 11½in (29.3cm)
London £12,000($22,200). 10.IV.78

An Egyptian bronze figure of a reclining cat, Saite period, length 4¼in (10.8cm)
London £3,400($6,290). 10.IV.78

An Umbrian bronze figure of a warrior, fifth century BC, height 9in(22.9cm)
London £20,000($37,000). 7.XI.77
From the collection of Henri E. Smeets

A Cypriot terracotta female head, sixth century BC, height 8¼in (21cm)
London £4,500($8,325). 7.XI.77
From the collection of Henri E. Smeets

A Gandhara grey schist architectural relief carved with
the figure of Buddha, Pakistan, third/fourth century AD,
38½in by 14¼in (97.8cm by 36.2cm)
London £21,000($38,850). 4.VII.78

A Gandhara grey schist figure of Buddha, Pakistan,
fourth century AD, height 28in (71.1cm)
New York $18,000(£9,730). 3.XI.77
From the collection of John D. Rockefeller III

Islamic Works of Art

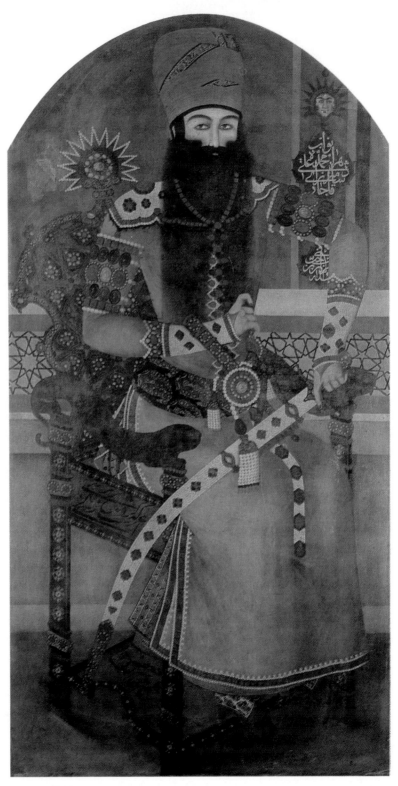

JAFAR
Portrait of Nawwab Shahzada
Muhammad 'Ali Mirza Qajar
On canvas, Qajar, 1230 AH/1814 AD,
82in by 42⅛in (208cm by 107cm)
London £60,000($111,000). 4.IV.78

FIRDAUSI

Shahnama, a Persian manuscript by the scribe 'Alijan ibn Haydar Quli al-Harawi, with 62 miniatures, the majority by Kazim Quli, Qajar lacquer binding, Khurusan, possibly Herat, dated *Rabi' 1011*/September 1602
London £310,000($573,500). 3.IV.78
From the collection of the Hagop Kevorkian Fund

الجعبة وتخرج الماء
من الطرف الآخر
من الانبوب وعليه
به الى كفة ق
وقد استرخت السلسلة
ونزل ذكر وكذ
باب كذ فانسد
وصعد الماء في باب
ه وجرى في انبوب
ح وارتفع وفار طولانا
وقدار تفع الماء ايضا
في انبوب السلسلة
ولم يبلغ اعلاه الا الفوارة
انزل منه وعند
مضى نصف ساعة
يمتلى الكفة وميل
فيرفع الانبوب والجعبة معا وينصب
الماء الى الكفة الاخرى وقد انسد
باب ه وانفتح باب كذ وكذلك ما
دام الماء يجرى لا المحوض منى اجكم العمل واتقن ما
اردت ايضاحه جليا واصف ما صنعته وهو آلة الزمر الدايم

IBN AL-RAZZAZ AL-JAZARI
Kitab fi ma 'rifat al-Hiyal al-Handasiyya (The Book of Knowledge of Ingenious Mechanical Devices), Arabic manuscript, by the scribe Farkh ibn 'Abd al-Latif, with an illuminated page and 107 miniatures and diagrams, Mamluk (Egypt or Syria), dated *Ramadan 715*/December 1315
London £160,000 ($296,000). 3.IV.78
From the collection of the Hagop Kevorkian Fund

Bahram Gur sends Narsi as Viceroy to Khurusan, a leaf from the Demotte *Shahnama*, Tabriz,
circa 1330–50
London £100,000($185,000). 3.IV.78
From the collection of the Hagop Kevorkian Fund

Hamza cutting the arm of a Byzantine Princess with his dagger, a leaf from the Emperor Akbar's copy of the *Hamza-nama*, painted on cotton, Mughal, *circa* 1570
London £32,000 ($59,200). 17.VII.78

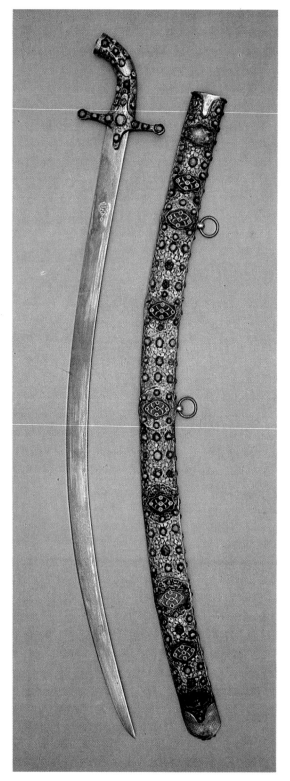

A Seljuk lustre pottery bowl, Syria, late twelfth
century/early thirteenth century, diameter 14in (35.5cm)
New York $3,300(£1,784). 13.V.78

A silver-gilt Turkish/Persian shamshir, with a Persian
watered steel blade by Kalb Ali, signed, late seventeenth
century, length 41¾in (106cm)
London £8,200($15,170). 3.IV.78

A Chinese carpet woven for the Islamic market, nineteenth century,
16ft 2in by 10ft 2in (493cm by 310cm)
London £15,000($27,750). 29.III.78

A Kashan carpet, *circa* 1590, 19ft 1in by 9ft 10in (582cm by 302cm)
Sold privately to the Iranian Carpet Museum, Tehran

A Mamluk carpet, *circa* 1500, 12ft 5in by 7ft 3in (378cm by 221cm)
London £110,000($203,500). 29.III.78

A Kazak rug, 8ft 4in by 5ft 8in (254cm by 173cm)
New York $15,000(£8,108). 10.XII.77

An antique Turkman Yomut bird *asmalik*, *circa* 1800, 4ft 4in by 2ft 5in (132cm by 74cm)
London £11,000($20,350). 29.III.78

A Bidjar carpet, *circa* 1860, 13ft 10in by 6ft 6in (422cm by 198cm)
London £4,000($7,400). 29.III.78

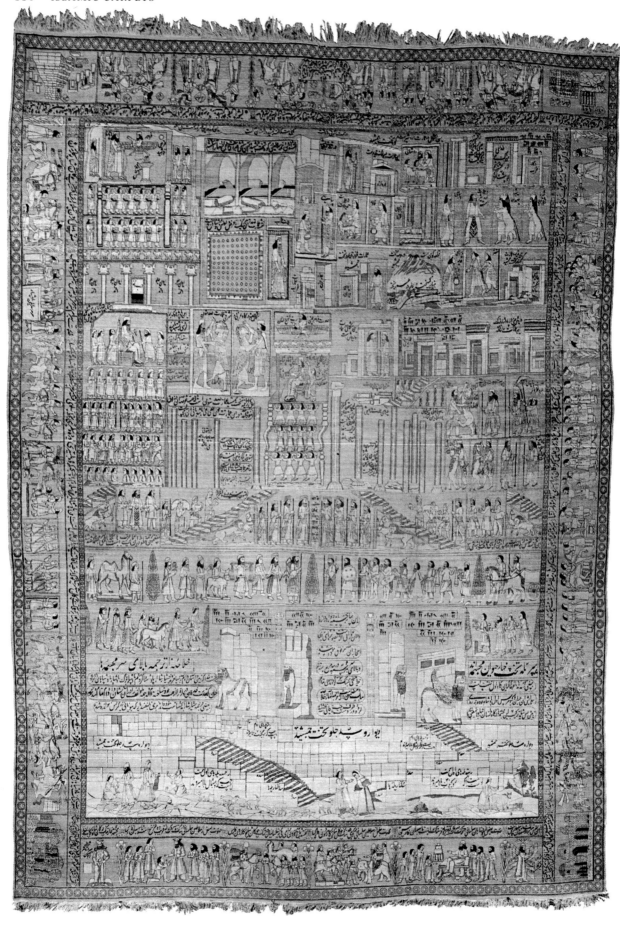

A Kashan silk Art Deco pictorial rug depicting a cartoon from the series *Bringing up Father*, designed by George McManus, *circa* 1925, 5ft 10in by 5ft (178cm by 152cm)
London £13,500($24,975). 29.III.78

Left
A Tabriz carpet depicting Persepolis during the Achaemenid period, *circa* 1896, 20ft 6in by 16ft 6in (625cm by 503cm)
Los Angeles $57,500(£31,081). 6.III.78

An Ushak rug, sixteenth century, 5ft by 3ft 7in (152cm by 109cm)
London £18,000($33,300). 29.III.78

Japanese Ceramics and Works of Art

A polychrome figure of a priest, possibly of the Patriarch Ryumyo, late Kamakura period, height 24in (61cm)
New York $22,000(£11,892). 3.XI.77

MASAKAZU
An ivory study of a *kappa* on a
turtle, Tamba, nineteenth
century
London £6,200 ($11,470).
29.XI.77

OYO IKKWAN
A wood model of a
mermaid, Nagoya,
nineteenth century
New York $4,200 (£2,270).
27.I.78

A wood model of an owl,
Nagoya, nineteenth century,
unsigned
London £1,700 ($3,145).
29.XI.77

TOYOMASA
A wood model of a tortoise,
Tamba, early nineteenth century
New York $13,000 (£7,027). 27.I.78

TADAYOSHI
A wood model of a
namazu, Nagoya,
nineteenth century
New York $2,000 (£1,081).
27.I.78

An ivory figure of a
foreigner, nineteenth
century, unsigned
London £2,100 ($3,885).
22.II.78

A wood study of a *shishi*,
Kyoto, late
eighteenth/early
nineteenth century,
unsigned
New York $4,000 (£2,162).
27.I.78

OKATORI
An ivory study of a rat,
Kyoto, late eighteenth
century
£10,500($19,425)

UNSHO HAKURYU
An ivory study of a tigress with three cubs, Kyoto, nineteenth century
£11,500($21,275)

MASATOSHI (attributed to)
A wood study of a goat, Nagoya,
unsigned, nineteenth century
£3,200($5,920)
From the collection of Professor and
Mrs J. Hull Grundy

KANO TOMOKAZU
A wood group of three rats,
Gifu, nineteenth century
£11,500($21,275)

RYUKOSAI JUGYOKU
An ivory group of seven
fish (*Shira-uwo*), Edo,
nineteenth century
£8,500($15,725)

HOGEN RANTEI
An ivory group of two hares, Kyoto, nineteenth century
£11,000($20,350)

The *netsuke* on this page were sold in London on 28 June 1978

Left
A gold lacquer box decorated with a figure of Seibo admiring herself in a mirror, nineteenth century, unsigned, length 4¾in (12cm)
New York $6,250(£3,378).
27.I.78

Right
SHIBAYAMA
A gold lacquer *inro* decorated with a *kendo* bout and with a hunter on the reverse, nineteenth century
New York $3,700(£2,000).
27.I.78

A *suzuribako*, late Edo/Meiji period, width 9⅝in (24.5cm)
London £3,400($6,290). 22.II.78

YASUMO
An ivory table screen inlaid with mother of pearl and stained ivory, late nineteenth century, height 8⅝in (22cm)
London £1,500($2,775). 3.VII.78

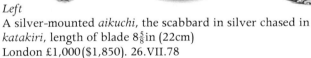

Left
A silver-mounted *aikuchi*, the scabbard in silver chased in *katakiri*, length of blade 8⅝in (22cm)
London £1,000($1,850). 26.VII.78

Centre
KAJIMA MITSUYOSHI
A gold, silver and *shibuichi* pipe case, late nineteenth century, length 8½in (21.6cm)
New York $3,000(£1,622). 27.I.78

Right
A silver-mounted *aikuchi*, the blade signed *Oite Hirado Munekazu tan* and dated *Meiji 3rd year* (1870) *spring month*, the scabbard decorated with cranes in gold and red *takamakie* on black lacquer, length of blade 8¾in (22.2cm)
London £1,800($3,330). 29.III.78

A *koto tachi*, the scabbard decorated with swallows flying over waves, signed *Denryusai Yoshiyuki*, length of blade 22in (56cm)
London £2,800($5,180). 29.III.78

Fig 1
Two views of a *shibuichi tsuba* by Seiryoken Katsuhei, signed, diameter 3⅜in (8.6cm)
London £4,200($7,770). 13.X.77

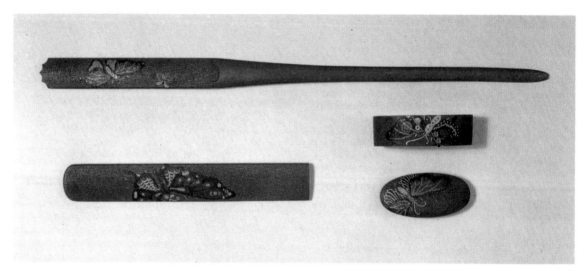

Fig 2
A copper *nanako* set by Wada Isshin comprising *kozuka, kogai* and *fuchi-kashira*, signed and dated
Ansei, winter of the dragon year (1856)
London £1,500($2,775). 13.X.77

Japanese sword-fittings from the Peter Hawkins Collection

Graham Gemmell

The heart of Japan lay in the sword and however admirable the prints, paintings, lacquer, *netsuke* or ceramics of the Japanese masters may be, the supreme artistic achievements of Japan were the blades by such swordsmiths as Masamune, Sadamune, Naotane, Muramasa and Sadakazu. The sword was considered to be the soul of the Samurai (the only class to be allowed the privilege of wearing two swords or *daisho*) and the decorative fittings that adorned it symbolized the personality, ideals, aspirations and strength of the warrior as well as indicating his aesthetic perception.

The Japanese sword was worn as often for ceremony and display as drawn for fighting and the most eye-catching feature was the *tsuba* or hand-guard, the purpose of which was to protect the hand whilst parrying the cut of an opponent. As well as having a centre aperture to house the blade of the sword, one or two holes were sometimes added to accommodate a *kozuka* (small dagger) or *kogai* (skewer or bodkin). When worn correctly the *tsuba* came almost to the centre of the body and as a result became an important detail of the warrior's dignified appearance. Yamamoto Tsunetomo, the eighteenth-century author of a book entitled *Hagakure*, states that all facets of the warrior's life, his actions, language, writings, apparel and accoutrements should demonstrate a 'quiet strength', a phrase which suggests a great deal about the Samurai's nature and his understanding of beauty and refutes the boorish and fierce image with which he is traditionally credited in Western mythology. However, it should be remembered that the Samurai were not the sole arbiters of taste nor the dominant market force upon what was after all a purely commercial craft-industry.

The story of the *tsuba* is largely the story of the sword and despite the independence of the makers of *tsuba* and fittings from the swordsmiths the development of the two arts is closely associated. The earliest recorded hand-guards are largely bronze or copper and were discovered in the burial dolmens constructed all over Japan during the period between the second century BC and the sixth century AD. With the upsurge of Buddhism in the sixth century came the introduction of the Chinese sword with its comparatively insignificant type of guard. This so-called *shitogi* guard was little more than a short quillon or cross-bar decorated, if at all, on the outer face alone. The ninth century brought with it a rise in the power of the warrior class, the celebrated Samurai, and at the same time a reversion to the discoid form of *tsuba* to provide sturdier hand protection. These *tsuba* were predominantly made of iron, although a surprisingly adequate alternative was found in the use of lacquered leather reinforced with multiple plates of thin iron or an iron rim. The decoration was rather spartan but the textural qualities were superb.

The Mongol invasion of Japan in the late thirteenth century and the accompanying switch from the use of mounted cavalry to armoured foot-soldiers created the need for hand-guards proportionately greater in size and strength. Made of the finest wrought iron and steel these were often forged by swordsmiths and armour-makers as well as the specialist *tsuba* craftsmen. The fourteenth and fifteenth centuries saw the addition of primitive copper and brass inlay as decoration on the flat iron plate.

From the end of the fifteenth century onwards the attitude towards the minor crafts, in particular metal-work, altered under the influence of the thought and idealism of the Zen Buddhist sect whose impetus elevated the sword blade and its fittings to the realm of the higher arts. The artist became freer to execute his *tsuba* with much more complex designs and to elaborate them with inlays and the application of softer metals, in particular two alloys of muted colours which are peculiar to Japan called *shakudo* (gold and copper) and *shibuichi* (silver and copper).

Following the centuries of internal strife and civil war, the regime of the Tokugawa clan commenced in 1601 and saw the beginning of a dynasty which ruled Japan until 1868. It was an era of almost uninterrupted peace and with it the necessity for strictly functional sword-mounts diminished thus giving artistic inspiration scope to flourish. Indeed, within a very short time the role of the sword changed from that of a deadly fighting weapon into a decorative adjunct of the already flamboyant dress of the seventeenth and eighteenth centuries. Many fine and attractive blades were made during this *Shinto* or 'new sword' period but the emphasis in assessing the quality of a sword was increasingly moving away from the blade alone. Now the shape and appearance of the *tsuba* and other mounts and the quality of the lacquer work on the *saya* or scabbard were all taken into consideration, as can be seen on the fine copper set by Wada Isshin (Fig 2).

In 1876, eight years after the restoration of the emperor Meiji, what became known as the 'Haotori Edict' was issued, thus bringing to a virtual close the history of the craft. This Imperial proclamation prohibited the wearing of the sword, in an attempt to bring 'medieval' Japan into step with modern Europe and its effects were far-reaching and quite devastating. Not only did it deprive the ancient warrior class of the sole instrument of its profession but thousands of swordsmiths, *tsuba* and fitting makers were thrown out of work and forced to turn their hands to other aspects of metal-work such as the making of snuff and cigarette boxes, *netsuke* and *inro*. There are those who claim that the disintegration of the *tsuba* industry came only just in time to forestall the approaching descent into decadence and over-elaboration but examples from the Hawkins Collection show that even in the 1870s and '80s superb craftsmanship was still in evidence even if these objects were never actually intended for use as protective guards. The splendid depiction of *The Three Sake Tasters* by Seiryoken Katsuhei (Fig 1) is a *tour de force* of metal technique. The subject is that of Buddha, Confucius and Lao-tse, the founder of Taoism, drinking from a single large sake jar, demonstrating the maxim that there is but one source of truth but many ways of interpreting it. The beauty of this work is such that it realised the highest price of the day.

Peter Hawkins' attitude towards the development of his collection of sword-fittings was almost hedonistic. He was not interested in the completionist's driving compulsion to have representative examples of the work of each major artist, each school, every style, all materials and periods but sought out and purchased those

Fig 3
A *shakudo tsuba* by a master of the Hirata school,
diameter 2⅞in (7.5cm)
London £1,900($3,515). 13.X.77

Fig 4
An iron *tsuba* by a master of the Hiragiya school,
diameter 3⅛in (7.8cm)
London £600($1,110). 13.X.77

pieces that appealed aesthetically rather than intellectually. As a consequence the collection included works that are almost exclusively by artists of the eighteenth and nineteenth centuries, the period when the sword-fitting maker's craft had reached a zenith in skill of execution as well as artistic conception. He had an eye for the finest examples of the metal-worker's craft and exercised it ruthlessly, rejecting rare artists or important schools if the quality of the piece was not of the highest. He visited the auction houses and dealers regularly but at times a year or more would pass by without any additions being made. Yet even throughout the frustrations of such a 'drought' he would steadfastly maintain his high standards.

Unlike many of his fellow collectors he was perfectly happy to acquire, purely for their aesthetic merits, unsigned and unattributed pieces such as the splendid example of the work of the eighteenth-century Hirata school of enamellers (Fig 3). The *shakudo* plate is enlivened with a stylised yet vivid floral design in *cloisonné* enamels. An iron *tsuba* of the nineteenth century (Fig 4), perhaps not so sumptuous or immediate in impact as the aforementioned piece, is nevertheless quite equal in quality. The texture and patina of the iron is a joy to touch and the skill with which the artist, who surprisingly did not sign this masterpiece, has employed the highly un-oriental technique of perspective is superlative. The balance of the design within the limitations of the circle, the raging movement of the waters beneath the bridge, the power and menace of the two protagonists, all combine to render this one of the finest objects in the collection.

Hawkins took particular delight in the supremacy of metal-working techniques as evinced by Japanese sword-fitting masters and no technique is more representative of far eastern art than that known as *katakiri* which reached its summit in the first half of the nineteenth century. The metal plate is cut or gouged at an angle thus producing an

Fig 5
A copper *tsuba* decorated in *katakiri* by Yokoya
Somin III, signed, diameter 3in (7.6cm)
London £1,000($1,850). 13.X.77

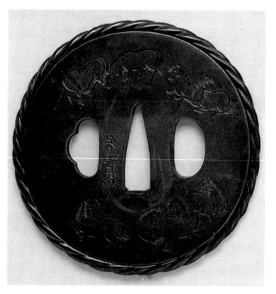

Fig 6
One of a pair of *shibuichi tsuba* for a *daisho*
decorated in *katakiri* by Katsura Eiju, signed,
diameter 2⅞in (7.5cm)
London £1,900($3,515). 13.X.77

Fig 7
A *sentoku tsuba* by Otsuki Mitsuhiro, signed,
diameter 3in (7.6cm)
London £800($1,480). 13.X.77

Fig 8
A *shakudo tsuba* by Juryusai Yoshinari, signed,
diameter 2⅝in (6.7cm)
London £600($1,110). 13.X.77

Fig 9
A modern copper *tsuba* by Ichiyoshi Morihei,
signed, diameter 3⅜in (8.5cm)
London £900($1,665). 13.X.77

uneven V-shaped trench, one side being at a much shallower angle to the surface than the other. This produces an effect akin to the *sumi-e* paintings of the Kano school, in their turn derived from Chinese scholar paintings. This can be seen in the beautiful copper *tsuba* by Yokoya Somin III (Fig 5) representing the two muscle-bound participants in a *sumo* wrestling bout and in the foreground their referee. It is also seen in the *daisho* set (literally meaning large and small but in this context referring to a pair of swords of equal size) of *shibuichi tsuba* by Katsura Eiju (Fig 6), the 'resident' *tsuba*-maker to the Daimyo (or local baron) of Kurume during the latter part of the eighteenth century.

With a joint mastery of technique and artistry, one of the great accomplishments of Japanese artists is the creation of atmosphere, which is well demonstrated by superb examples from both the late eighteenth and the early nineteenth centuries. The earlier fine brass *tsuba* by Otsuki Mitsuhiro (Fig 7) emanates the chill of an autumn evening. The full moon is only partially seen through breaks in the banks of cloud that scud overhead and the night winds have risen to bend the grasses in the foreground. By contrast the later one (Fig 8) depicts a summer evening with swallows swooping low over a meandering stream between banks of flowering irises. One can almost hear the hum of insects and feel the last rays of a setting sun.

It would be a disservice to leave the subject without paying tribute to Peter Hawkins' taste and judgement, which led him to acquire the fine copper *tsuba* by Ichiyoshi Morihei (Fig 9). This piece bears comparison with any in the collection for its qualities of balance and contrast and for its technical brilliance. However its particular significance is that it is one of the last of its kind. Morihei was and is regarded as the best and the last of the modern *tsuba* makers. He died in the early 1970s and left no pupils to carry on his work. Whilst there are tsuba-makers still working in iron, there is no-one of the standard of Morihei producing soft-metal *tsuba*. One may therefore look at this *tsuba* and see the last product of a tradition that has developed and refined over half a millennium.

An inlaid silver *koro* and cover, inset with panels of the seven gods of good fortune, signed by various masters, 1882, height 14¼in (36.2cm)
London £6,700($12,395). 10.XI.77
From the collection of R. Jenkins

An early Arita bottle, late
seventeenth century, height
10⅞in (27.6cm)
London £4,000 ($7,400). 5.VII.78

A Kakiemon bowl, early
eighteenth century, diameter
8⅜in (21.4cm)
London £3,800 ($7,030).
5.VII.78

An Oribe style green-glazed dish by Kitaoji
Rosanjin, signed *Ro*, width 8in (20.3cm)
New York $3,800 (£2,054). 9.V.78
From the collection of the late Dr Harold P.
Stern

A *nezumi* Shino dish, Momoyama/early Edo
period, width 7⅜in (18.7cm)
London £5,100 ($9,435). 22.II.78

A Takatori *chaire*, from
Chikuzen province, mid/late
Edo period, height 3¾in (9.4cm)
London £650 ($1,203). 5.VII.78

A *ko-imari* bottle with Kutani enamels, late seventeenth century, height 10¼in (26cm)
New York $12,000(£6,486). 10.V.78

KITAGAWA UTAMARO
Oban: The Niwaka Festival of Green Houses: Geisha
Signed
London £7,000($12,950). 31.V.78

UTAGAWA TOYOKUNI
*Oban: An O-kubi-e of the actor Nakamura
Noshio in a female role*
Signed, £2,100 ($3,885)

ICHIRAKUTEI EISUI
*Oban: An O-kubi-e of the courtesan Kisegawa
of Matsubaya*
Signed, £2,800 ($5,180)

HIROSHIGE
Oban yoko-e: White rain (Evening shower), from the series *The fifty-three stations of the Tokaido*
Signed, £2,100 ($3,885)

The prints on this page were sold in London on 31 May 1978

One of a set of paintings depicting
*The eight patriarchs of the Shingon
sect, Sumi, gofun,* colour and gilt on
silk, unsigned, late Muromachi/
Momoyama period, 39¾in by 22¾in
(101cm by 57.8cm)
New York $17,000(£9,189). 3.XI.77

Chinese Ceramics and
Works of Art

A glazed pottery figure of a harnessed Fereghan horse, T'ang Dynasty, height 25½in (64.8cm)
London £110,000($203,500). 11.VII.78

A pair of painted pottery covered jars, Han Dynasty, height 12¾in (32.4cm)
New York $19,000(£10,270). 11.V.78

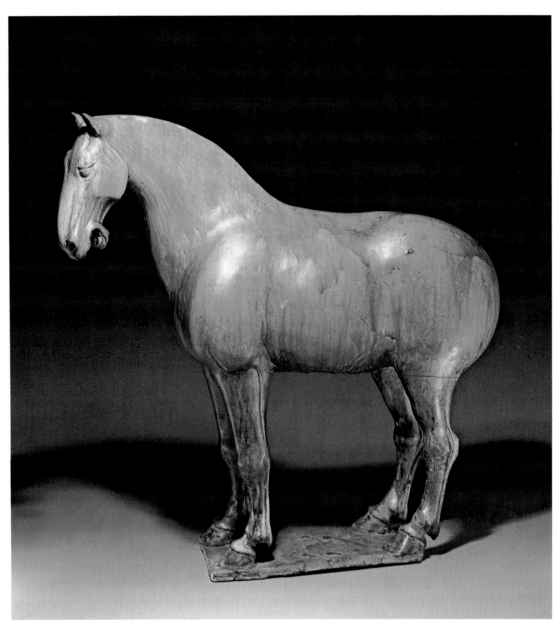

A chestnut-glazed pottery figure of a horse, T'ang Dynasty, height 23in (58.4cm)
Los Angeles $32,000 (£17,297). 26.X.77

An incised and painted Tz'ŭ Chou jar, Northern Sung Dynasty, height 7⅝in (19.4cm)
London £78,000 ($144,300). 11.VII.78

A Tz'ŭ Chou *sgraffiato* vase, late
tenth/early eleventh century,
height 16⅛in (41cm)
London £140,000 ($259,000). 11.VII.78

A leaf-decorated Chi Chou *temmoku* teabowl, Sung Dynasty, diameter 6in (15.2cm)
Hong Kong HK$260,000(£30,058:$55,607). 29.XI.77

A carved Ting-yao dish, Chin Dynasty, diameter 10⅜in (26.4cm)
New York $80,000(£43,243). 5.XI.77

A Yüan blue and white dish, mid fourteenth century, diameter 18⅝in (47.3cm)
London £150,000 ($277,500). 11.VII.78
From the collection of Mrs E. M. Hutton

A Yüan blue and white dish, mid fourteenth century, diameter 15⅝in (39.7cm)
Hong Kong HK$340,000 (£39,306:$72,717). 23.V.78

A *Hundred Deer* vase, seal mark of Ch'ien Lung, and of the period, height 17¼in (43.8cm)
Hong Kong HK$430,000(£49,711:$91,965). 29.XI.77

A Ming polychrome *Hundred Deer* vase, six character mark of Wan Li within a double circle, and of the period, height 13in (33cm)
London £80,000($148,000). 11.VII.78

Left One of a pair of *famille verte* shallow bowls, six character marks of K'ang Hsi in underglaze-blue within double circles, and of the period, diameter $5\frac{1}{4}$in (13.3cm) Hong Kong HK$180,000(£20,809:$38,497). 23.V.78

Right A *famille verte* bowl, period of K'ang Hsi, diameter $3\frac{7}{8}$in (9.9cm) Hong Kong HK$65,000(£7,514:$13,902). 23.V.78

A pair of Ch'ing black-ground saucer dishes, six character marks of Yung Chêng in underglaze-blue within double circles, and of the period, diameter 6in (15.2cm) Hong Kong HK$110,000(£12,717:$23,526). 23.V.78

A *famille rose* jar, four character hallmark, *ch'ing i t'ang chih* (made for the Ch'ing-i Hall) in iron red, period of Yung Chêng, height 12½in (31.8cm)
Hong Kong HK$370,000 (£42,775:$79,133). 29.XI.77

A pair of *famille rose* peach bowls, six character marks of Yung Chêng in underglaze-blue within double circles, and of the period, diameter 5⅜in (13.7cm)
Hong Kong HK$440,000(£50,867:$94,104). 23.V.78
From the collection of John M. Crawford, Jnr

A *famille verte* dish, six character mark of K'ang Hsi within a double circle, and of the period, diameter 20$\frac{7}{8}$in (53cm)
Hong Kong HK$260,000 (£30,058:$55,607). 23.V.78

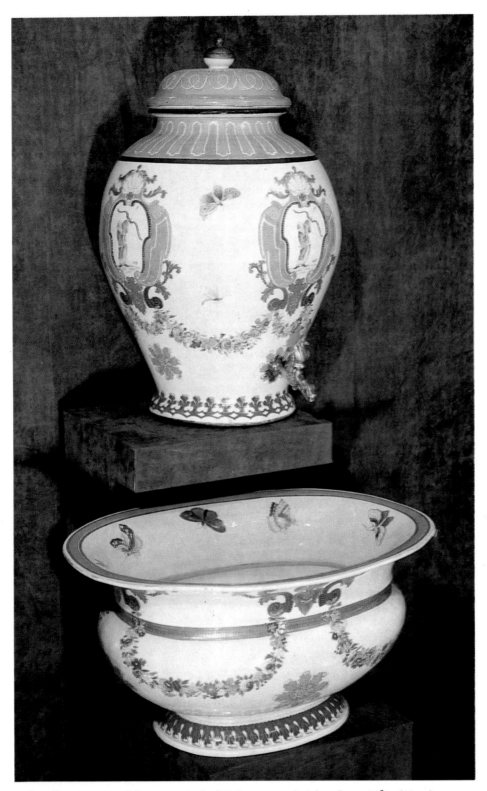

A *famille rose* urn and basin, period of Ch'ien Lung, height of urn 26¾in (68cm)
Monte Carlo FF120,000(£13,793;$25,517). 5.II.78

An early teapot and cover, signed
Kung Ch'un and dated *1513*, incised
mark *ta Ming Chêng-tê pa-nien Kung
Ch'un* (eighth year of the Chêng Tê
reign of the great Ming Dynasty,
Kung Ch'un), height 3¾in (9.5cm)
HK$60,000(£6,936:$12,831)

From left to right
A fish-head waterpot, impressed seal *Hsü Ling-yin chih* (made by Hsü Ling-yin),
width 3⅛in (8.2cm)
HK$12,000(£1,387:$2,566)

A toad and hollow log waterpot, impressed seal *Ch'ên Chung-mei chih* (made by Ch'ên Chung-mei),
length 2⅞in (7.3cm)
HK$12,000(£1,387:$2,566)

A double pomegranate waterpot, incised mark *Ming-yüan* and seals *Ch'ên* and *Ming-yüan,* and
incised mark *chên ts'ang* (precious treasure collected by the Meng family),
length 4¼in (10.8cm)
HK$20,000(£2,312:$4,277)

The I-Hsing wares on this page were sold in Hong Kong on 24 May 1978

A bronze covered wine vessel, Shang Dynasty, height 7½in (19cm) £16,000($29,600)

A bronze covered wine vessel, Shang Dynasty, height 7⅝in (19.4cm) £36,000($66,600)

The bronzes on this page are from the collection of the late Dr A. F. Philips and were sold in London on 30 March 1978

A bronze cauldron, late Shang Dynasty, height 8¼in (21cm)
London £30,000($55,500). 30.III.78
From the collection of the late Dr A. F. Philips

A Warring States bronze bell, fifth century BC, height 11½in (29.2cm)
London £32,000 ($59,200). 30.III.78
From the collection of the late Dr A. F. Philips

A wood figure of Kuan Yin, Sung/early Yüan Dynasty, height 68in (172.7cm)
New York $72,500 (£39,189). 11.V.78

A pair of wood figures of insignia bearers, period of Ch'ien Lung,
height 29⅛in (74cm)
Monte Carlo FF165,000 (£18,857:$34,886). 5.II.78

A pair of Canton vases with Buddhist lion handles, late nineteenth century, height 52¼in (132.7cm) London £5,800 ($10,730). 19.X.77

European Ceramics

A Vincennes polychrome figure of a naiad mounted in ormolu as a clock, *circa* 1756, height $21\frac{5}{8}$ in (55cm)
Monte Carlo FF750,000 (£85,714:$158,571). 5.II.78

An early Höchst group of *The fencing lesson*, wheel mark in red, *circa* 1755, height 6¾in (17.1cm)
New York $13,000(£7,027). 24.II.78
From the collection of Ilse Bischoff

A Meissen figure of Harlequin with a jug, modelled by Johann Joachim Kaendler, crossed swords
mark in underglaze-blue, *circa* 1738, height 6½in (16.5cm)
New York $23,000(£12,432). 24.II.78
From the collection of Ilse Bischoff

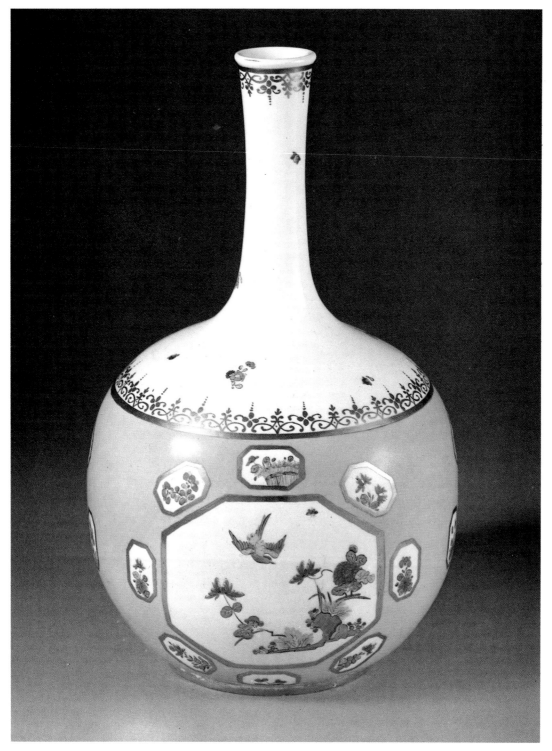

A Meissen *Augustus Rex* Johanneum vase, with *AR* mark in underglaze-blue and Johanneum mark,
circa 1725–30, height 11⅜in (29cm)
London £9,000($16,650). 27.VI.78

Both this vase and the macaw opposite were intended for the Japanese Palace at Dresden which was
to be entirely furnished in Oriental Meissen porcelain. The scheme, devised by Friedrich
Augustus III, Elector of Saxony, was never completed

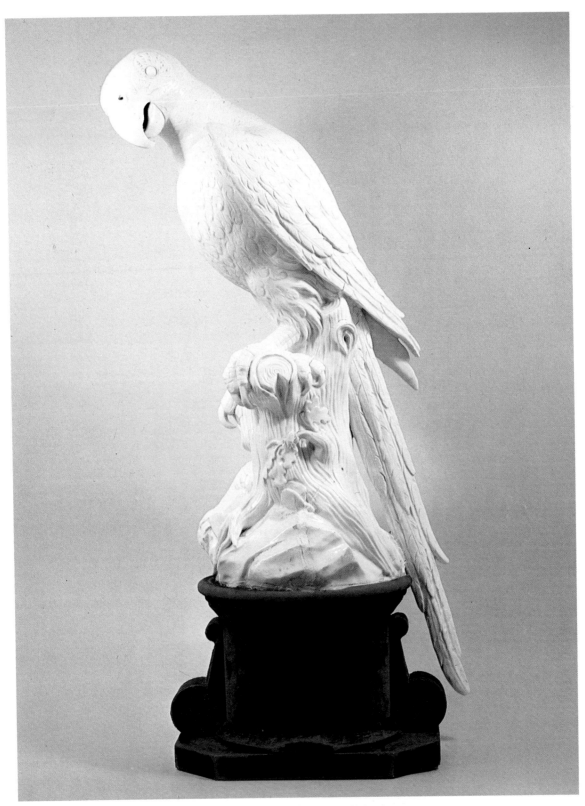

A Meissen white figure of a macaw, modelled by Johann Joachim Kaendler, *circa* 1732–35, height overall 38½in (97.8cm)
London £105,000($194,250). 27.VI.78
From the collection of the late Robert von Hirsch

A Capodimonte snuff box with gold mounts, *circa* 1748, width $2\frac{1}{2}$in (6.5cm) London £12,500($23,125). 27.VI.78

A Vezzi Venice teapot and cover, incised *Mf* and inscribed *Ven^a*, *circa* 1723–27, height $5\frac{7}{8}$in (15cm) London £11,000($20,350). 25.X.77

A Worcester lobed dish painted by
Jefferyes Hammett O'Neale,
illustrating the Aesop fable of the
Bear and the Beehives, seal mark in
underglaze-blue, *circa* 1770,
diameter 9in (22.9cm)
London £1,500($2,775). 22.XI.77

An early Chelsea sauceboat, marked with incised triangle, *circa* 1745–49, width 7½in (19cm)
London £2,000($3,700). 11.X.77

One of a pair of Staffordshire saltglaze figures of hawks, *circa* 1750, height 12½in (31.7cm)
New York $8,500(£4,595). 28.X.77
From the collection of the late Edith Kane Baker

A Whieldon-type group of an oxherd on a water buffalo, *circa* 1750, width 9in (22.8cm)
New York $2,900(£1,568). 10.III.78
From the collection of Mr and Mrs Samuel Victor

This group is inspired by a Chinese original and the figure is intended to be the T'ang poet Li Tai Po

A Swansea chamberstick, *circa* 1814–22, diameter $4\frac{3}{4}$in (12cm)
London £860($1,591). 11.X.77

A Swansea biscuit figure of a ram, impressed SWANSEA and BEVINGTON & CO,
circa 1817–21, length $4\frac{1}{4}$in (10.8cm)
London £1,100($2,035). 11.X.77

A Ralph Wood group of a shepherd and shepherdess, *circa* 1770, height 11¼in (28.5cm)
£1,000($1,850)

Below left
A Pratt-type model of a cockerel after a Ralph Wood original, late eighteenth century,
height 9¼in (23.5cm)
£420($777)

Below right
A Prattware lion, late eighteenth century,
height 7¼in (18.4cm)
£680($1,258)

The pottery on this page was sold in London on 6 December 1977

A Martin Brothers bird, signed and dated *25.4.1903*, height 15in (38.1cm)
London £3,200($5,920). 19.IV.78
From the collection of Roy Aitken

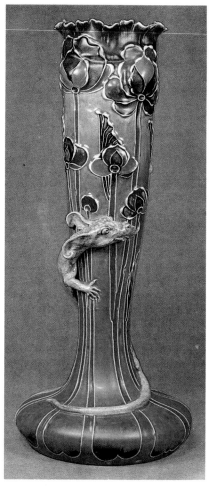

One of a pair of Wedgwood fairyland moonlight *Candlemas* vases, 1929, height 8½in (21.6cm)
London £1,450($2,683). 22.XII.77

A Mark V. Marshall vase, *circa* 1900, height 16¾in (42.5cm)
London £1,600($2,960). 20.IV.78
From the collection of the late
A. E. Snell

From left to right
A stoneware vase by Bernard Leach, impressed St Ives and *BL* seals, *circa* 1960, height 15in (38.1cm)
£1,600($2,960)

An earthenware jar by Bernard Leach, inscribed *East and West will Meet, Amen, 1923,* impressed St Ives and *BL* seals, height $5\frac{5}{8}$in (14.3cm)
£520($962)

A St Ives stoneware dish decorated by Bernard Leach, impressed St Ives seal and painted *BL*, *circa* 1960, diameter 13in (33cm)
£800($1,480)

A stoneware bottle vase by Shoji Hamada, affixed *Made in Japan* label and exhibition number, *circa* 1960, height $7\frac{1}{2}$in (19.1cm)
£700($1,295)

A stoneware vase by Bernard Leach, impressed St Ives and *BL* seals, *circa* 1960, height 13in (33cm)
£1,300($2,405)

This pottery was sold in London on 20 April 1978

A pair of bronze-gilt mounted covered urns with stands in Sèvres style, marked with interlaced Ls, late nineteenth century, height 44in (112cm)
New York $16,000 (£8,649). 14.VI.78

Furniture, Decorations and Textiles

A marquetry coiffeuse by Abraham Roentgen, made for Friedrich Augustus III, Elector of Saxony, dated *1769*, height 2ft 8½in (82.5cm)
London £200,000 ($370,000). 23.VI.78
From the collection of the late Robert von Hirsch

A Queen Anne inlaid and burr walnut
double dome bureau bookcase,
early eighteenth century, height
7ft 7in (231cm)
New York $13,500(£7,297). 14.I.78
From the collection of the late
Isabel Leib

A George III mahogany breakfront bookcase, mid eighteenth century, height 9ft 4½in (286cm)
New York $48,000 (£25,946). 15.IV.78
From the collection of the St Louis Art Museum

An early George III marquetry commode in the manner of Thomas Chippendale, *circa* 1765, height 2ft 9½in (85cm)
London £6,200($11,470). 2.XII.77
From the collection of the late Margherita, Lady Howard de Walden, CBE

A George III satinwood and marquetry secretaire bookcase, *circa* 1790,
height 6ft 10in (208cm)
London £18,500($34,225). 9.VI.78

A Florentine walnut intarsia table, *circa* 1500, height 2ft 7½in (80cm)
London £23,000 ($42,550). 23.VI.78
From the collection of the late Robert von Hirsch

A Florentine intarsia credenza, late fifteenth century, height 5ft 9in (175cm)
London £20,000 ($37,000). 23.VI.78
From the collection of the late Robert von Hirsch

A Venetian parcel-gilt walnut bureau cabinet, mid eighteenth century,
height 9ft 4in (284cm)
London £50,000($92,500). 23.VI.78
From the collection of the late Robert von Hirsch

A Dresden red-japanned bureau bookcase attributed to Martin Schnell, *circa* 1700,
height 7ft 3in (221cm)
London £50,000($92,500). 7.VII.78
From the collection of Gerald Hochschild

Two chairs from a suite of South German marquetry seat furniture, mid eighteenth century
London £14,000 ($25,900). 4.XI.77

A German marquetry commode attributed to Johann Friedrich and Heinrich Wilhelm Spindler, Berlin, mid eighteenth century, width 5ft 4in (163cm)
London £8,800 ($16,280). 9.XII.77

A Chippendale carved mahogany block-front chest of drawers, Massachusetts,
circa 1760–80, height 2ft 8½in (82.6cm)
New York $57,000(£30,811). 4.II.78
From the collection of the late Edward S. George

A carved and painted pine and oak chest, Eastern Massachusetts,
circa 1690–1710, height 2ft 7½in (80cm)
New York $50,000(£27,027). 29.IV.78
From the collection of Mabel B. Thatcher

An Oriental export black lacquer bureau cabinet, early eighteenth century,
height 7ft 10in (239cm)
Los Angeles $20,000(£10,811). 5.VI.78
From the collection of Mr and Mrs Eugene V. Klein

A pair of Louis XV ormolu-mounted K'ang Hsi celadon vases, *circa* 1745, height 2ft (60.6cm)
New York $90,000(£48,649). 25.II.78
From the collection of Henry Ford II

A pair of Louis XV ormolu candlesticks, after a design by Juste-Aurèle Meissonnier, mid eighteenth century, height 1ft (30.5cm)
$12,500(£6,757)

Centre
A Louis XV ormolu-mounted blanc de chine hexagonal pot and cover, mid eighteenth century, height $9\frac{7}{8}$in (25cm)
$11,000(£5,946)

These objects are from the collection of Henry Ford II and were sold in New York on 25 February 1978

A pair of Louis XV ormolu-mounted lacquer *encoignures*, signed *BVRB*, mid eighteenth century, height 3ft 1in (94cm)
New York $105,000(£56,757). 25.II.78
From the collection of Henry Ford II

Bernard van Risenburgh was received Master before 1730. Several pairs of lacquer *encoignures* by him are known to have survived, including a pair in the collection of Her Majesty The Queen

A Louis XV ormolu-mounted tulipwood and purplewood marquetry *bureau plat* attributed to
Joseph Baumhauer, mid eighteenth century, height 2ft 6in (76cm)
New York $82,000(£44,324). 25.II.78
From the collection of Henry Ford II

Joseph Baumhauer was received Master in 1764. The design of this piece closely resembles that of a
number of other tables signed *JOSEPH*, including one inlaid with Sèvres porcelain plaques at
Waddesdon Manor, Buckinghamshire

An early Louis XVI marquetry commode stamped *I.G. Schlichtig*, the marquetry panels attributed to
Georges Jansen, *circa* 1775, height 3ft 1in (94cm)
London £47,000($86,950). 30.VI.78

Jean-Georges Schlichtig and Georges Jansen were received Masters in 1765 and 1767 respectively

Two chairs from a suite of Louis XVI seat furniture covered with contemporary Beauvais tapestry,
one chair of which is stamped *J. Pothier*
Monte Carlo FF320,000(£36,571:$67,657). 22.V.78

Jean-Jacques Pothier was received Master in 1750

A Louis XV ormolu-mounted tulipwood and kingwood marquetry *secrétaire à abattant* attributed to
Bernard van Risenburgh, mid eighteenth century, height 4ft 5in (135cm)
New York $195,000(£105,405).25.II.78
From the collection of Henry Ford II

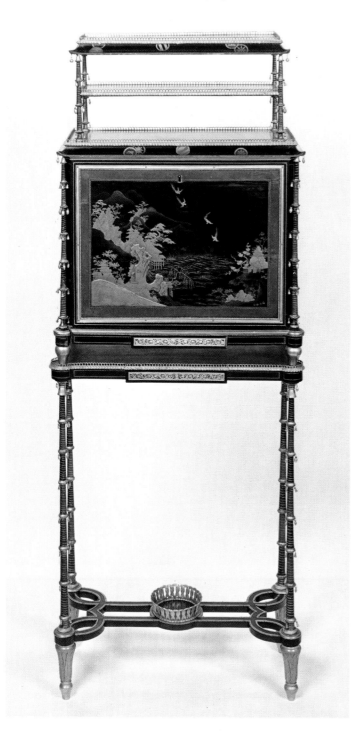

A Louis XVI ormolu-mounted black lacquer
and painted metal secretaire on stand, signed
M. Carlin JME, late eighteenth century
height 4ft 8½in (144cm)
New York $60,000(£32,432). 25.II.78
From the collection of Henry Ford II

Martin Carlin was received Master in 1766.
This piece reflects the influence of Oriental art
on eighteenth-century European taste and also
that of English designs on French furniture
such as are found in *The Gentleman and
Cabinet-maker's Director* by Thomas
Chippendale, first published in 1754

A Louis XVI ebony *bureau plat* stamped *G. Beneman*, late eighteenth century, height 2ft 6in (76cm)
Monte Carlo FF230,000 (£26,286:$48,629). 22.V.78

Guillaume Beneman was received Master in 1785

A Régence ormolu-mounted ebony *bureau plat*, early eighteenth century, height 2ft 6¾in (78cm)
Monte Carlo FF230,000 (£26,286:$48,629). 21.V.78

A Louis XVI thuyawood commode attributed to Adam Weisweiler, *circa* 1789, height 3ft (91.5cm)
London £27,000($49,950). 30.VI.78

An Empire ormolu-mounted mahogany side cabinet attributed to François-Honoré-Georges and Georges Jacob, early nineteenth century, height 3ft 6in (107cm)
New York $14,000(£7,568). 8.X.77

One of a pair of French red boulle side cabinets in the style of Louis XIV inlaid with brass and pewter, *circa* 1870, height 3ft (91.4cm)
London £7,500($13,875). 1.III.78

A French ormolu-mounted *meuble d'appui,* the plaque signed *Emile Guillemin* and dated *1867,*
height 5ft (152cm)
London £11,500($21,275). 2.XI.77

A German Dresden-mounted side cabinet, 1870s, height 4ft 5$\frac{1}{4}$in (135.5cm)
London £10,500($19,425). 21.VI.78

A French ormolu-mounted mahogany commode in the style of Charles Cressent, early twentieth century, height 3ft 1in (93.5cm)
London £5,200($9,620). 21.VI.78

This commode is a copy of one by Cressent at Waddesdon Manor, Buckinghamshire

Two from a set of three French bronze and gilt-bronze urns and covers in
the style of Louis XV, *circa* 1860, height 3ft 8in (112cm)
London £11,000 ($20,350). 21.VI.78

A detail from a *millefleurs* tapestry, French or Flemish, early sixteenth century,
2ft 9½in by 8ft (85cm by 244cm)
New York $33,000 (£17,838). 1.VI.78

A Gothic tapestry altar frontal with five episodes from the Life of Christ, Swiss or South German, mid fifteenth century, 2ft by 7ft 10in (61cm by 239cm)
£10,500 ($19,425)

A Gothic tapestry altar frontal with scenes from the Life of the Virgin, Swiss or South German, mid fifteenth century, 2ft 9½in by 5ft 10¼in (85cm by 178.5cm)
£14,000 ($25,900)

The tapestries on this page are from the collection of the late Robert von Hirsch and were sold in London on 23 June 1978.

A Brussels tapestry depicting *Samson and Delilah*, after Bernard van Orley, *circa* 1570, 3ft 3in by
3ft 1½in (99cm by 95cm)
London £15,000($27,750). 7.VII.78

Fig 1   *The Failure of Sir Gawain*
7ft 10in by 9ft 6in (239cm by 290cm)
£28,000 ($51,800)

This and the following two tapestries are from the collection of The Earl Grosvenor and were sold in London on 19 April 1978

Burne-Jones took the heraldic details for these tapestries from a sixteenth-century French publication *Devises des Chevaliers de la Table Ronde* by Gyron le Courtoise and, despite an earlier affirmation that the subjects should not be set in a specific period, based the costumes on plates in Henry Shaw's *Dresses and Decoration of the Middle Ages* of 1843

The Stanmore Hall tapestries

Linda L. A. Parry

In 1890 a set of tapestries was commissioned from the firm of Morris & Co by W. K. D'Arcy, an Australian mining engineer. It was to decorate the dining-room in Stanmore Hall, Middlesex, a house built in 1847 in the Tudor-Gothic style with later additions of 1888–90 by Brightwell Binyon. Morris & Co had redecorated most of the inside of the house since the D'Arcy family's occupation, and furnishings by such notable designers as W. R. Lethaby for Kenton & Co and William Morris and George Jack for Morris & Co, seen in Harry Bedford Lemere's contemporary photographs of the interior,[1] show that the patron was a man of definite taste and discrimination.

D'Arcy imposed no restrictions on the commission and the only limitation was the architecture of the room itself which contained a wide chimney breast and two double windows. It is clear from the outset that William Morris, director of the firm, and Edward Burne-Jones, designer of the tapestries, discussed all aspects of the work on equal terms, Morris contributing the technical expertise and Burne-Jones the artistic inspiration. A memorandum from Morris states: 'I have had a careful discussion with Mr Burne-Jones . . . and after considering the spaces to be filled, the light in the room and other circumstances . . . the subject chosen for illustration is the Quest of the Sancgreal'.[2] The Arthurian legends, as told by Malory, were not new to either Morris or Burne-Jones who had first discovered the romances while studying at Oxford some forty years earlier. Morris wrote that *The Quest of the Holy Grail* was chosen for two reasons; it was, he believed, the most beautiful and complete episode of the legends and being 'in itself a series of pictures' was the most suitable subject to illustrate.

Conforming with the nineteenth-century convention for dividing walls horizontally the tapestries were designed in two tiers. One narrative set, of figure compositions, was to hang from the cornice to the top of the dado and the other set, of verdures showing deer in woodland with the knights' shields suspended from branches, was designed to hang below these to the floor. These subsidiary tapestries not only helped to emphasise the importance of the narrative but their explanatory inscriptions also assisted in telling the tale.

Morris and Burne-Jones considered various different scenes, although it is not certain how many. However it is known that their original plan included an illustration of *The death of Galahad amid the Host in the City of Sarras* which was subsequently dropped. The finished set of six narrative scenes depicts *The Beckoning, The Knights departing* (Fig 3), *The Failure of Sir Gawain* (Fig 1), *The Failure of Sir Lancelot, The Ship* and *The Attainment of Sir Galahad* (Fig 2).[3]

Fig 2   *The Attainment of Sir Galahad*
7ft 10in by 24ft 8in (239cm by 632cm)
£40,000 ($74,000)

Burne-Jones's numerous studies for these designs are now well known and, as they were made specifically for tapestry, unlike most early tapestry designs which were adapted from stained-glass panels, their importance is recognised. Constantly aware of the scale of the room and its lighting, Burne-Jones's figures stretch the full height of the tapestries and in some cases the tops of the figures' heads are cut off so as to add height and dramatic effect when seen thirteen feet (400cm) above the ground. Various existing pencil and chalk drawings show changes in compositions and an early scheme for the second tapestry shows a background of tents and banners.[4]

The mille-fleurs foregrounds and all decoration on the clothing and figures were designed by J. H. Dearle (1860–1934), Morris's chief tapestry weaver and assistant, who was also responsible for the design of the verdure panels. The process of combining Burne-Jones's figure studies with Dearle's decoration was unique. The original designs, showing the composition of figures, were usually fifteen to twenty inches high (38cm to 50cm). They were photographed and the enlarged prints were then worked on and embellished by Burne-Jones and Dearle before being presented

to the weavers for transfer to the looms.[5]

There were three upright looms in the Merton Abbey Works of Morris & Co at the time and between 1894 and 1895 all three were employed on the Stanmore series. Three weavers worked on each loom using vegetable-dyed wools, silks and mohairs, the latter two to give richness in tone and variation in texture, on a warp of cotton. The tapestries were woven at a thickness of fourteen threads to the inch. Although the weavers strictly followed the designs from the cartoons before them at the looms, they were given a considerable latitude in the choice and arrangements of tints and the shading of colours, for as Morris said 'The executants themselves . . . [are] both in nature and training, artists, not merely animated machines'.[6]

Before the D'Arcy commission the continuation of tapestry manufacture at Merton Abbey was prejudiced through lack of work. The Stanmore series proved the turning-point and subsequently a number of panels from the same designs were ordered. In 1895–96 a partial set of four (excluding the first and fourth designs) and one verdure panel were woven for Laurence Hodson of Compton Hall, Wolverhamp-

Fig 3   *The Knights departing*
7ft 10in by 11ft 6in (239cm by 346cm)
£36,000($66,600)

ton, (now in the City Museum and Art Gallery, Birmingham), and in 1898 a full set of figure tapestries, without verdures and with *The Ship* and *The Attainment* woven into one panel, was made for Mr G. McCulloch, a friend of D'Arcy's. To stop further production W. K. D'Arcy bought the cartoons from Morris & Co at the end of the nineteenth century but on the death of her husband in 1920 Mrs D'Arcy returned them to the Merton Abbey workshops and three further panels were repeated.

Recognised by many as one of the most interesting decorative schemes of the nineteenth century the importance of the Stanmore Hall tapestries lies in the technical and stylistic innovations used by Morris and Burne-Jones. The prices three of the panels fetched in April indicate that their true significance is now well established.

[1] Now in the National Monuments Record, London
[2] See E. B. Bence-Jones's typescript in the Victoria and Albert Museum Library, London
[3] For photographs of the tapestries in situ see *Studio*, vol XV, 1899
[4] Lot 25, the Artist's Sale, Christies, 16 July 1898
[5] Photographic cartoons for part of the series are now in the William Morris Gallery, Walthamstow
[6] For the names of the weavers see H. C. Marillier, *History of the Merton Abbey Tapestry Works*, 1927

Clocks, Watches and Scientific Instruments

A blued steel and gilt-metal quarter-repeating alarum clock, signed *Tho: Tompion Lon:*,
late seventeenth century, height 8in (20.3cm)
London £29,000 ($53,650). 31.III.78

A walnut-veneered quarter-repeating bracket clock, signed *Joseph Knibb London*, circa 1690, height 12½in (31.8cm)
London £15,000($27,750). 31.III.78

An ormolu and porcelain perpetual calendar mantel clock, signed *Le Roy & fils. Pals.Ral.Gie.Montpensier Paris, circa* 1860, height 1ft 4¾in (42.6cm)
London £1,500($2,775). 21.VI.78

Below left
A calendar mantel clock, signed *Sarton, circa* 1820, height 2ft (61cm)
London £8,500($15,725). 3.II.78
From the collection of René Sarton

Below right
A George III chinoiserie japanned chiming bracket clock, signed *Ellicott, London*, late eighteenth century, height 2ft 2in (66cm)
Los Angeles $5,000(£2,703). 24.X.77

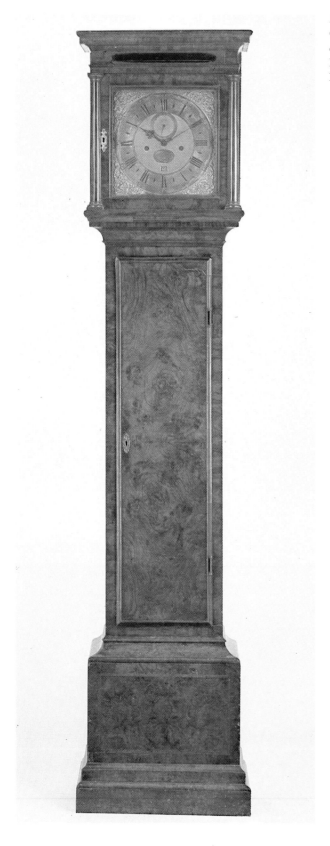

A walnut month longcase clock,
George Graham No. 635,
circa 1725, height 7ft 2in (218cm)
London £13,000 ($24,050). 31.III.78
From the collection of the Misses Mill

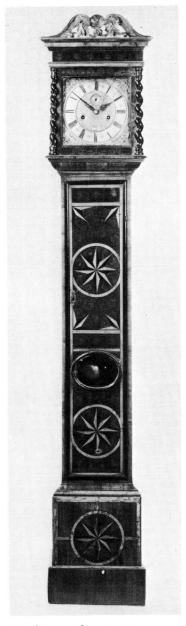

An olivewood parquetry
longcase clock, *circa* 1690,
height 6ft 10in (208cm)
London £3,800($7,030). 3.II.78

An oak longcase clock,
dated *1718*, height 9ft 7¾in (294cm)
Amsterdam Fl15,000(£3,529:$6,529).
15.IX.77

A George I walnut longcase clock,
signed *Jacob Massy, Leicester
Fields, London*, early eighteenth
century, height 7ft 8in (234cm)
London £2,500($4,625). 3.II.78
From the collection of His Grace
the Duke of Sutherland, TD

A George III gilt-metal and enamel quarter-striking musical automaton table clock,
signed *W.H. Craft*, 1796, height 3ft 4⅛in (102cm)
Zurich SFr220,000(£59,299:$109,703). 16.XI.77

A gold, enamel and diamond set watch by William Anthony, London, *circa* 1790, diameter 2⅝in (6.7cm) New York $13,000(£7,027). 1.III.78

BREGUET NO. 2808
A gold and enamel pair cased quarter-repeating ruby cylinder watch, diameter 2in (5cm) London £13,500($24,975). 7.VII.78

A silver and gilt-metal alarum verge watch by Thomas Ribart, Paris, early seventeenth century, length 2⅞in (7.3cm) London £12,500($23,125). 26.V.78

A gold quarter-repeating automaton watch by Dubois & Fils, *circa* 1800, diameter 2⅜in (6cm) London £26,000($48,100). 26.V.78

A Swiss gold and enamel quarter-repeating automaton singing bird watch, *circa* 1820, diameter 2½in (6.3cm) New York $31,000(£16,757). 14.XII.77

A repoussé silver verge clockwatch by
Johan Georg Hagen, Neus, *circa* 1720,
diameter 2½in (6.3cm)
London £4,400($8,140). 9.XII.77

LOUIS BERTHOUD NO. 53
A silver pocket chronometer, *circa* 1800,
diameter 2⅝in (6.7cm)
Zurich SFr95,000(£25,606 : $47,372). 16.XI.77

A gold half hunting cased keyless lever minute-repeating
perpetual calendar by E. A. Capt, diameter 2¼in (5.7cm)
London £10,000($18,500). 26.V.78

A gold hunting cased one minute tourbillon by Auguste
Courvoisier & Co, La Chaux de Fonds, diameter 2⅛in (5.3cm
London £7,200($13,320). 9.XII.78

A brass ring dial, signed and dated *I.A.M. 1697*, diameter 2⅛in (5.3cm) London £1,400($2,590). 26.V.78

A German silver-gilt trefoil-shaped combined perpetual calendar and spice box, early eighteenth century, width 2⅜in (6cm) London £920($1,702). 9.XII.77

A brass-gilt astronomical ring dial and compass by John Rowley, inscribed *Made by John Rowley Mathematical Instrument maker to his Royal Highness the Prince*, London, *circa* 1720, diameter of base 10in (25.4cm) New York $15,000(£8,108). 14.VI.78

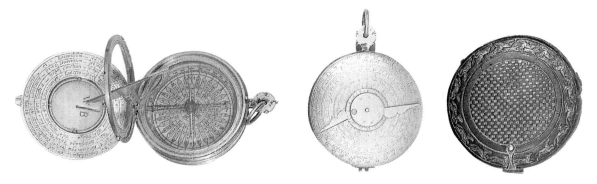

Two views of a gilt-metal compendium by Elias Allen, and its original gold-stamped leather case (far right), early seventeenth century, diameter 2½in (6.3cm)
London £7,500($13,875). 7.VII.78

A gilt-metal polyhedral sundial and clock, sixteenth century, diameter of base 3in (7.6cm)
London £6,200($11,470). 9.XII.77

One of John Russell's Selenographia, inscribed on the sphere *A Globe representing the visible surface of the Moon . . .* and *Invented by John Rufsell*, dated *June 14th 1797*, London, height 20⅜in (51.7cm)
London £11,500($21,275). 9.XII.77

Jewellery

An emerald brooch and a pair of emerald pendent earrings en suite, both set with
diamonds in gold filigree work, mid nineteenth century
London £72,000($133,200). 23.II.78

Fig 1
An emerald and diamond brooch by Rundell, Bridge and Rundell, London, *circa* 1820
London £250,000($462,500). 20.IV.78
From the collection of His Grace the Duke of Northumberland, KG, TD, FRS

The large emerald is decorated with Mughal carvings of stylised tulips and is believed to have
been brought to England by Clive of India whose grand-daughter married the third Duke of
Northumberland

Jewellery in an age of discovery, 1800–1900

Shirley Bury

The most international of all the decorative arts, jewellery, was profoundly affected as the Age of Enlightenment dissolved under the pressure of the wars following the French Revolution. The complex business of shipping, processing, and re-exporting raw materials and finished goods all over the world was impeded as the warring powers closed their ports or operated blockades. Parisian jewellers, who traditionally led the trade, could scarcely expect to attract clients during the Terror of 1793–94, when, it was said, a pair of silver shoe buckles was enough to mark out the wearer as a potential candidate for the guillotine.[1] Meanwhile, aristocratic French refugees, their estates sequestrated, were selling their jewellery all over Europe in an effort to finance themselves in exile. Unfortunately their goods saturated an already uncertain market and drove down the price of precious stones still further. Rundell & Bridge, the greatest of the goldsmithing firms to hold a royal warrant from the English monarch, George III, relieved the French of some of their jewellery at prices very favourable to themselves and made a handsome profit when the market recovered.[2] A similar sharp blow to the price of diamonds was experienced in the 1870s and '80s following the discovery of diamonds in South Africa. The situation was stabilised by the formation in 1888 of the de Beers Consolidated Mining Company which was large enough to control the flow of stones on to the market.

Rundell's dealt with rough stones in addition to making jewellery. Their trade connections were world-wide and the war between England and France strengthened the international importance of the firm as it encouraged the partners to develop markets outside Western Europe. Their work was unrivalled in England for its excellence. Rundell's chief designer was a diamond-setter named Philip Liebart, born in Liège, who had fled to England when his country was occupied by the French. Ironically, Liebart must have remounted the French jewels acquired by his employers. Re-setting was essential, for the mid 1790s saw the introduction of a new technique, diamonds set *à jour* (in open-backed mounts), the contemporary term being 'set transparent'. As Liebart remained with Rundell's throughout the 1820s, he was probably also concerned in resetting in a transparent diamond frame a fabulous carved Mughal emerald inherited by the grand-daughter of Clive of India (Fig 1).

Rundell's were always quick to adopt new techniques. In 1822 they installed a steam-engine in their diamond-cutting workshop in Spitalfields,[3] nearly three decades before this form of power was adopted in Amsterdam, the main centre of the

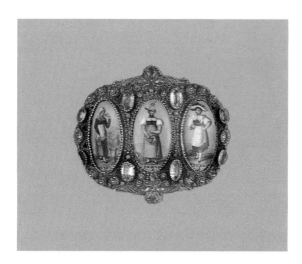

Fig 2
A gold brooch set with three Geneva
enamel miniatures, *circa* 1830
London £400($740). 24.XI.77

industry. Whether they experimented with platinum settings, as in France, is not known. Unhappily the firm ceased to exist when another new metal, aluminium, then more expensive than gold, was taken up by French jewellers in the 1850s.

The Parisian jewellery trade made a remarkable recovery following the appointment of Napoleon as First Consul in 1799. Both he and his wife Josephine had a predilection for jewels. Once, to gratify her passion for engraved gems, Napoleon had antique specimens removed from the national collections to be mounted in jewellery of the fashionable neo-classical type. The age of the large parure (or set) of jewellery had arrived. Ladies everywhere were soon wearing parures which might comprise a 'Spartan' or arched coronet, a necklace, earrings, brooch, buckle and a pair of bracelets or armlets, often set with cameos. The popularity of engraved gems is one of the many instances of early nineteenth-century fashions that persist throughout the century (see *Art at Auction* 1976–77, p 481). They were high fashion until the late 1830s throughout Europe and were still made, admired and worn thereafter, gaining widespread acceptance again from the 1870s when it was modish in some circles to hold diamonds in contempt because they were too freely available.

Another long-lived manifestation of the neo-classical style which originated in France and lasted until the 1850s was gold filigree jewellery with *cannetille* and *grainti* decoration. *Cannetille* consisted of thin gold wire spirals of beehive shape. It probably derived from the filigree work made during the Consulate when shortage of funds led jewellers to decorate the open borders of pendants and lockets with thin strips of gold wound into spirals. *Grainti* comprised coarse gold granules, often in graduated rows. The technique was probably inspired by the fine granulation of Greek and Etruscan jewellery. There the resemblance ended, for the elaborate nineteenth-century settings, later embellished further with applied leaves and florets in coloured golds, were used as a background for a profusion of coloured stones, enamels and cameos. The demand for this work was far too great for it not to be imitated by jewellers outside France. A Swiss brooch with enamels depicting regional costume illustrates the use of granules placed round bosses (Fig 2). Perhaps because this device was reminiscent of the cut steel ornaments made in England in the late eighteenth century and afterwards, English jewellers also appear to have employed it.

Until the 1870s and in a large proportion of cases after, formal occasions demanded the wearing of diamonds and pearls, the latter only marginally less costly than the former. These were often combined with coloured stones, increasingly also set transparent; emeralds, sapphires, rubies, peridots and opals were popular for this purpose. Topaz, amethyst, and, later, garnets, were prime favourites for secondary wear. Gold jewellery, with or without multi-coloured stones, was worn at informal parties. Sentimental jewellery, in which stones were so arranged that their initials spelled a name or a word such as 'Regard' (ruby, emerald, garnet, amethyst, ruby and diamond), was popular from about 1810–40. Lockets containing portrait miniatures and a curl of hair under glass were much worn; in the first three decades of the century they were suspended from a long gold chain, in the 1860s and '70s a short length of chain or a ribbon was in order.

Hair, the universal gauge of affection, was frequently used in jewellery, including memorial pieces which were especially admired in English and German-speaking countries. In the early years of the century mourning jewellery was still made to order, as in the past, but it was increasingly mass-produced from prefabricated components in later decades. This development reflected an enhanced demand: in England, for instance, George IV disliked black so intensely that both as Regent and King he cut short the accepted period of mourning when any relative died on the grounds that it was harmful to trade. He chose to ignore the interests of the mourning trade. His niece, Victoria, on the other hand, sedulously observed the conventions, and after the death of her Prince Consort in 1861 was never out of mourning for the rest of her long life. The makers of black enamelled jewellery, jet, cut steel, bog oak, Berlin ironwork and the like flourished accordingly. It is worth noting that the Queen's patronage encouraged the substitution of photographs for painted miniatures in jewellery. Her first commissions date from the early 1850s and, later, much of the mourning jewellery for Prince Albert was also set with photographs.

Parures of seed pearls, strung with horse-hair on mother-of-pearl frames, were produced in England and on the Continent in the late eighteenth and early nineteenth centuries, mainly by women. They continued to be made thereafter but only became high fashion again at the approach of the twentieth century. An invariable part of a Regency seed-pearl parure was a 'sprig', a stylised floral spray worn in the hair or on the bodice. Floral jewellery was also made in precious stones, in metals and other materials, throughout the century. The rage for naturalistic devices, which at first sight appears inimical to the neo-classical tradition, in fact partly stemmed from it. The vine, a popular motif in jewellery, was of impeccable classical origin. Butterflies, also popular, had the additional advantage of symbolising the soul in classical mythology. Naturalism also derived from the Romantic movement, which after considering Man in his natural setting had taken on the setting itself. At its least ambitious, the naturalistic style found expression in the flowers intermingling with scrolls which formed the staple decoration of the stamped gold jewellery in the rococo style turned out in quantity from the 1820s to the 1840s. As the style progressed from about 1830 to 1855, a spectacular imitation of nature was achieved with the aid of precious and semi-precious stones, augmented by enamel. Even when there was no attempt to simulate natural colours, the structure of plants and other motifs was

Fig 3
A gold, pearl, enamel and rose-
diamond pendant by Carlo
Giuliano, signed, *circa* 1875
London £1,700($3,145). 20.IV.78

Fig 4
A diamond stomacher brooch
designed as a spray of
convolvulus, *circa* 1840
Zurich SFr16,000(£4,313:$7,978).
17.II.78

realistically portrayed (Fig 3). This phase was succeeded by a return to a greater
degree of stylisation, until in the 1880s and 1890s it once again became permissible to
render organic forms naturalistically.

For all its charm, the most extreme form of naturalism was suspect in advanced
artistic circles where attitudes were serious and antiquarian. The people who attracted the attention of critics at national and international exhibitions were those who
had revived, in a scholarly and exact fashion, historic styles and techniques. They
included two Parisian jewellers, the German-born Charles Wagner, who in the 1830s
reintroduced niello decoration into Western Europe after a lapse of centuries, and
J.-D. Froment-Meurice, celebrated for his enamelled jewellery, embellished with miniature figure sculpture in the Gothic and Renaissance styles. Froment-Meurice met with

Fig 5
An enamel and rose-diamond demi-parure comprising a brooch
and matching earrings, French, late nineteenth century
London £680($1,258). 15.XII.77

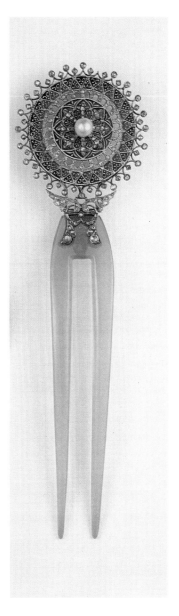

Fig 6
One of a pair of gold, *plique-à-jour* enamel and pearl hair ornaments
by Riffault, *circa* 1870
London £2,100($3,885). 15.XII.77

great success at the Great Exhibition of 1851. The revival of *champlevé* and *cloisonné* enamel was followed in the 1860s by one of the most difficult techniques, *plique-à-jour*, which was re-mastered by a happy accident in Paris when the backing plate of a *cloisonné* enamel fell away in the course of firing to reveal the stained-glass effect of *plique-à-jour*. Riffault, a skilled exponent of the technique produced the two fine hair ornaments (Fig 6) sold at Sotheby's last December.

The same antiquarian spirit led Italian jewellers to adopt as their models the Greek, Etruscan and Roman jewellery which literally lay beneath their feet. In the late eighteenth and early nineteenth centuries, when the excavation of Pompeii and Herculaneum was well under way, and Etruscan tombs were yielding their treasures, antique pieces were freely available. The diarist Charles Greville, visiting Pompeii in

Fig 7
Five gold and *cloisonné* enamel medallions with
beaded edges by Alexis and Lucien Falize,
signed, *circa* 1870
London £5,000 ($9,250). 20.IV.78

1830, was told that Napoleon's sister, Caroline Murat, had once put on a pair of gold bracelets as they were removed from a skeleton.

Although Sarno of Naples was one of the first to make archaeological jewellery in the early years of the century, the most distinguished practitioners of the genre were Fortunato Pio Castellani of Rome and his sons. The elder Castellani founded his firm in 1814 but began producing classical pieces only in the 1830s. It was not until about 1860 that his son Alessandro, a political exile from Rome, produced with the help of his craftsmen in his Neapolitan workshop a far closer approximation to the granulation of the ancients than the *grainti* of previous decades. The Castellanis' display at the International Exhibition of 1862 established their reputation to the extent that leading jewellers everywhere felt bound to emulate them. Their work in other styles was never as popular.

Two of Alessandro's craftsmen at Naples afterwards achieved independent success. Giacinto Melillo, the younger of the two, was not as innovatory as the elder, Carlo Giuliano, who was transferred to London by Alessandro in about 1860 and installed in a workshop in Soho. As befitted a dependent, he continued to work in the approved classical manner, but later, having severed his connection with Alessandro, he evolved an individual style, combining delicate enamel work with precious stones. The originality of his pendant (Fig 4) becomes clear when it is compared with a

Fig 8
Above A gold *plique-à-jour*
enamel *plaque de collier*,
French, *circa* 1900
London £5,000($9,250).
21.IV.78
Below A gold necklace by
The Guild of Handicrafts
Ltd, English, *circa* 1900
London £1,100($2,035).
21.IV.78

charming but more openly historicist French demi-parure in the Louis XVI style of about the same date (Fig 5). Carlo died in 1895 and his sons Carlo and Arthur continued the business until the late Edwardian era.

In the 1870s and '80s the vogue for Japonaiserie spread over North America and Europe with remarkable speed. The most original contributions to Japanese-inspired design were made by Tiffany & Co of New York and Alexis Falize and his son Lucien of Paris (Fig 7). Japanese design survived to influence the development of Arts and Crafts jewellery and of continental Art Nouveau. Indeed, though national differences in style appear to be more marked in 1900 than heretofore, it is remarkable, when they are analysed, how much they are found to rely upon the common stock of antiquarian studies built up over the century (Fig 8).

[1] H. Vever, *La Bijouterie française au XIXᵉ Siècle*, vol 1, 1906
[2] G. Fox, [An Account of] the firm of Rundell, Bridge & Co, the Crown Jewellers & Goldsmiths on Ludgate Hill, [*circa* 1845]. Original ms. in the Baker Library, Harvard University; photocopy in the Victoria and Albert Museum Library, London
[3] Mr John Culme kindly informs me that Rundell's insured the property in Brick Lane, together with the steam engine and other machinery, on 25 February 1822 with the Sun Insurance Company. Guildhall Library, Ms. no. 11936/492

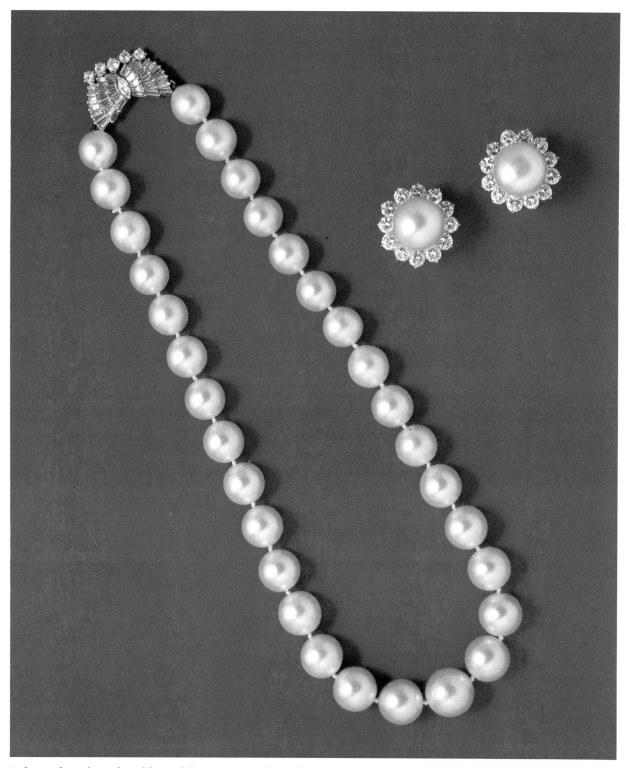

Left A cultured pearl necklace of thirty-one pearls graduating from 1.08cm to 1.35cm, with a platinum and diamond clasp, $30,000(£16,216)
Right A pair of cultured pearl and diamond earclips mounted in platinum, the pearls measuring approximately 1.46cm, $13,000(£7,027)

The jewellery on this page is from the collection of the late Dorothy Clerk and was sold in New York on 25 May 1978

A diamond and cultured pearl necklace by Van Cleef & Arpels, the diamonds weighing
approximately 86.25 carats, the pearl drops measuring approximately from 1.42cm to 1.9cm
New York $110,000(£59,460). 8.XII.77

A diamond bracelet with eight marquise-shaped, sixteen pear-shaped and
sixteen round diamonds, weighing approximately 40.5, 28.5 and 12 carats
respectively
New York $450,000 (£243,243). 12.X.77
From the collection of the late Edith Kane Baker

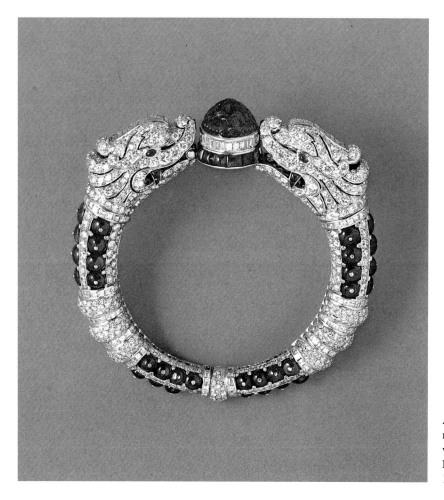

A French Art Deco diamond and
ruby bangle, the diamonds
weighing approximately 46 carats
New York $29,000 (£15,676).
13.X.77

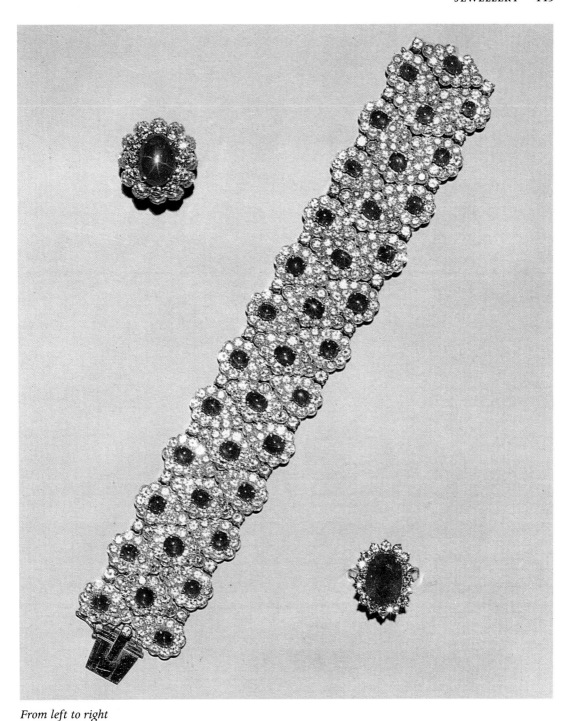

From left to right
A star ruby and diamond ring, the ruby weighing 10.64 carats, HK$100,000(£11,561:$21,388)
A star ruby and diamond bracelet, the rubies weighing approximately 36.75 carats and the diamonds weighing approximately 34 carats, HK$110,000(£12,717:$23,526)
A ruby and diamond cluster ring, the ruby weighing 8.26 carats, HK$85,000(£9,827:$18,180)

The jewellery on this page was sold in Hong Kong on 30 November 1977

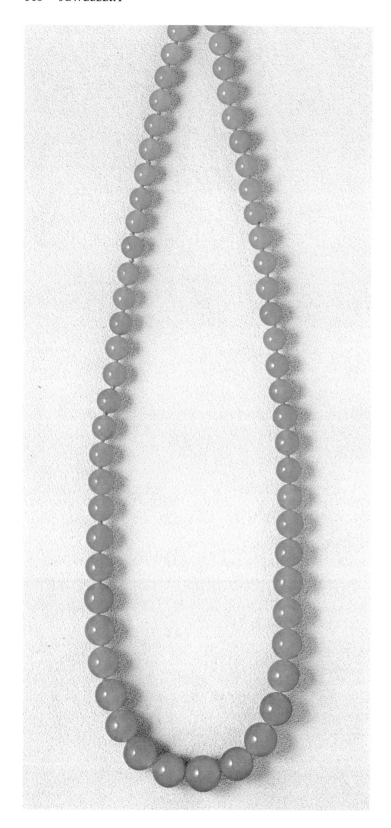

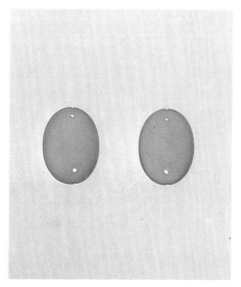

A pair of cabochon jades of Imperial emerald green colour, measuring 2.05cm by 1.5cm
Hong Kong HK$1,200,000(£138,728: $256,647). 30.XI.77

A pair of jade and diamond earclips, the jade cabochons measuring 1.7cm by 1cm
Hong Kong HK$75,000(£8,671:$16,041). 26.V.78

A jade bead necklace of ninety-six beads graduating from approximately 0.36cm to 0.99cm
New York $140,000(£75,676). 12.IV.78

An Art Deco crystal, lapis and diamond
pendant by T. B. Starr Inc
New York $7,500 (£4,054). 24.V.78
From the collection of the late
Jean F. Hance

A diamond and carved emerald lapel
watch
New York $12,000 (£6,486). 24.V.78

An emerald and diamond brooch, the
emerald weighing approximately
4.46 carats
New York $55,000 (£29,730). 8.XII.77

A pair of emerald and diamond pendent
earrings by Meister, the emeralds
weighing 6.4 and 6.68 carats respectively
Zurich SFr800,000 (£215,633:$398,921).
17.XI.77

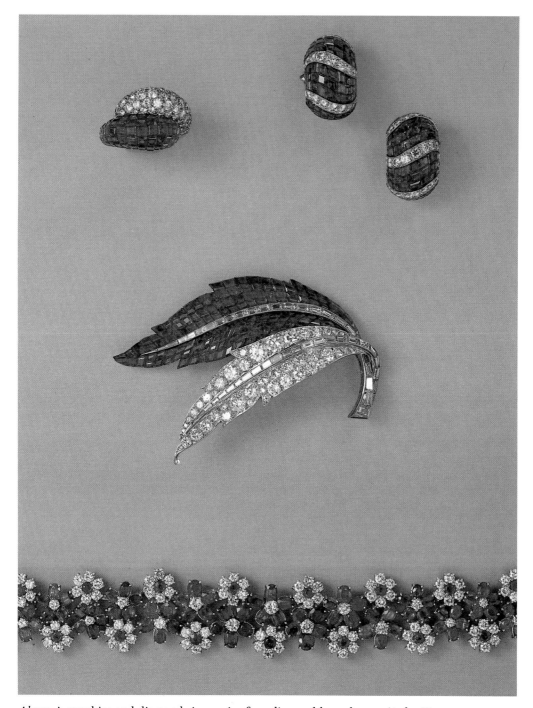

Above A sapphire and diamond ring, pair of earclips and brooch en suite by Van
Cleef & Arpels
SFr20,000(£5,391:$9,973), SFr18,000(£4,852:$8,976), SFr40,000(£10,782:$19,946)
Below A sapphire and diamond bracelet mounted in 18 carat gold
SFr18,000(£4,852:$8,976)

The jewellery on this page was sold in St Moritz on 18 February 1978

Above left A necklet set with a ruby, a sapphire and a diamond on a platinum chain
SFr210,000(£56,604:$104,717)
Centre left An unmounted fancy yellow step-cut diamond weighing 4.99 carats
SFr38,000(£10,243:$18,950)
Right An emerald and diamond flower brooch by Cartier, SFr50,000(£13,477:$24,933)
Below An Art Deco diamond and coloured stone bracelet, SFr90,000(£24,259:$44,879)

The jewellery on this page was sold in Zurich on 17 November 1977

1. A diamond (21.61 carats) ring, St Moritz SFr1,250,000(£336,927:$623,315). 17.II.78
2. An emerald and diamond cross-over ring, Zurich SFr58,000(£15,633:$28,921). 3.V.78
3. A diamond (approx 5.9 carats) ring, New York $50,000(£27,027). 13.IV.78
4. A diamond (15 carats) ring by Cartier, Zurich SFr800,000(£215,633:$398,922). 3.V.78
5. A star sapphire (46.34 carats) and diamond ring, Hong Kong HK$130,000(£15,029:27,803). 30.XI.77
6. A diamond (approx 16.5 carats) ring, New York $210,000(£113,514). 13.IV.78
7. A cat's eye (49.29 carats), Hong Kong HK$140,000(£16,185:$29,942). 30.XI.77
8. A sapphire (approx 30 carats) ring, Zurich SFr300,000(£80,863:$149,597). 17.XI.77
9. An emerald ring by Cartier, Zurich SFr160,000(£43,127:$79,784). 3.V.78
10. An emerald ring by Van Cleef & Arpels, St Moritz SFr125,000(£33,693:$62,332). 18.II.78
11. An emerald (approx 10.95 carats) and diamond ring, New York $170,000(£91,892). 13.IV.78
12. A diamond (approx 15.35 carats) ring, New York $335,000(£181,081). 25.V.78
13. A sapphire (approx 20 carats) and diamond ring by Cartier, New York $95,000(£51,351). 12.IV.78
14. A sapphire (33.81 carats) and diamond ring, Zurich SFr180,000(£48,518:$89,757). 3.V.78
15. A sapphire (approx 8.46 carats) and diamond cluster ring, Zurich SFr78,000(£21,024:$38,895). 3.V.78
16. A sapphire (approx 19.75 carats) and diamond ring, New York $105,000(£56,757). 12.IV.78

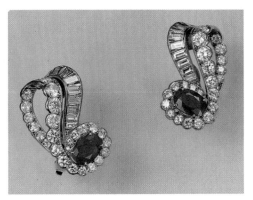

A ruby and diamond cluster ring by
Harry Winston
SFr180,000(£48,518:$89,758)

A pair of ruby and diamond earclips
by Cartier
SFr16,000(£4,313:$7,979)

A pair of emerald and diamond pendent
earrings by Cartier
SFr160,000(£43,127:$79,785)

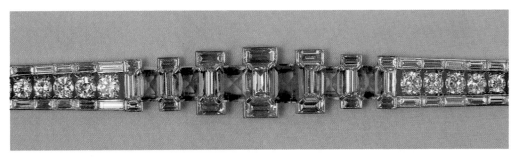

An emerald and diamond bracelet by Cartier, SFr150,000(£40,431:$74,797)

The jewellery on this page was sold in Zurich on 3 May 1978

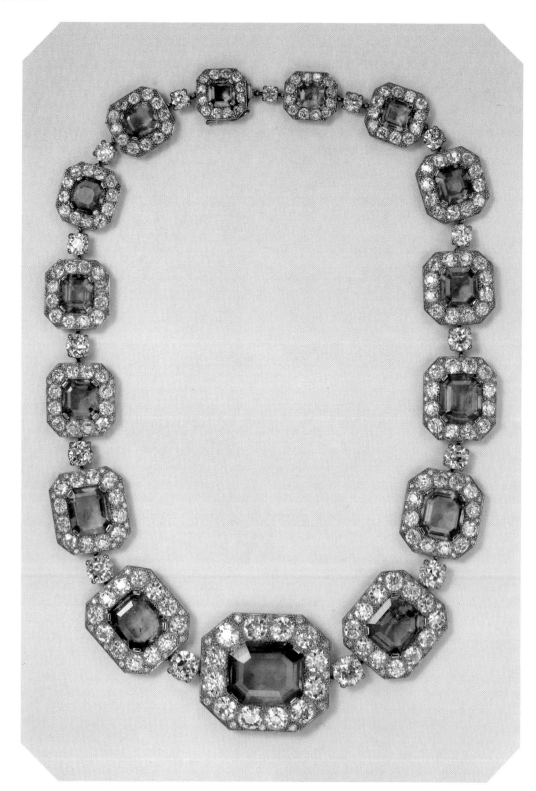

An emerald and diamond necklace by Cartier, the three centre emeralds
weighing 23.35, 10.93 and 10.67 carats respectively
St Moritz SFr1,800,000(£485,175:$897,574). 18.II.78

Glass and Paperweights

A Venetian enamelled beaker,
circa 1495, height 4⅝in (11.7cm)
London £55,000($101,750).
2.VI.78
From the collection of the late
Robert von Hirsch

This beaker was probably made
for the marriage of Michael
Behaim and Katerina Lochnerin
of Nuremberg in 1495. It is
decorated with three cusped
panels, one of which contains
the arms and crest of Behaim,
another with figures of
St Michael slaying Lucifer and
the third, which is shown in
this view, with St Catherine and
the head of the Emperor
Maximinius

Two views of a gilt and enamelled armorial *Stangenglas* and cover, inscribed *HANS PRAVN VON NVRNBERG*, German or possibly Venetian, *circa* 1598, height 15½in (39.5cm)
London £22,000($40,700). 26.VI.78
From the collection of the late Magdalene Sharpe Erskine

One of a pair of Hausmaler flasks by Ignaz Preissler, *circa* 1720–30, height 8½in (21.5cm)
London £11,000($20,350). 5.XII.77
This depiction of the youthful Bacchus is taken from a woodcut by Jost Amman
(1539–1591) published in his *Kunstbuchlin* in 1578

A roemer engraved in diamond-point, Rhenish or Netherlandish, early seventeenth century, height $4\frac{5}{8}$in (11.8cm)
London £20,000($37,000). 26.VI.78
From the collection of the late Magdalene Sharpe Erskine

A Bohemian enamelled blue-glass tankard, dated *1608*, height 6¼in (16cm)
London £4,600($8,510). 5.XII.77

A St Louis flower weight,
diameter 2⅞in (7.3cm)
New York $4,100(£2,216).
25.IV.78

A Baccarat magnum flat-bouquet
weight, diameter 3½in (8.9cm)
New York $4,000(£2,162). 25.IV.78

A St Louis flat-bouquet weight,
diameter 2½in (6.4cm)
London £2,800($5,180). 3.VII.78

A yellow Baccarat wheat-flower
weight, diameter 3in (7.6cm)
London £1,600($2,960). 3.VII.78

A three-dimensional flower weight, probably St Louis,
diameter 2¾in (7cm)
London £7,500($13,875). 3.VII.78

From left to right
Three Beilby enamelled glasses, *circa* 1770:
A wine glass, height 5⅞in (15cm), £1,150($2,128)
A masonic firing glass, height 3⅛in (8cm), £1,000($1,850)
A wine glass, height 6in (15.2cm), £380($703)

From left to right
One of a pair of gilt cruet bottles and stoppers decorated by James Giles, *circa* 1770, height 7¼in (18.4cm) £500($925)
An engraved green-tinted goblet, *circa* 1750, height 7in (17.8cm), £220($407)
One of a pair of blue-tinted gilt urns and covers, *circa* 1790, height 9¼in (23.5cm), £380($703)
A composite-stem part-coloured wine glass, *circa* 1750, height 6⅛in (15.6cm), £500($925)
A blue-glass gilt rose-water sprinkler decorated in the manner of James Giles, *circa* 1770, height 8½in (21.6cm), £240($444)

The glass on this page is from the collection of the late Jeffrey Rose and was sold in London on 6.III.78

A *gem* cameo-glass bowl by Thomas Webb & Sons, *circa* 1885, diameter $4\frac{1}{4}$in (10.8cm)
London £850($1,572). 19.I.78

Art Nouveau and Art Deco

L'oiseau de feu, a glass lamp designed by René Lalique, signed, 1920s, height 16¾in (42.5cm)
London £3,800($7,030). 21.IV.78
From the collection of Martin Battersby

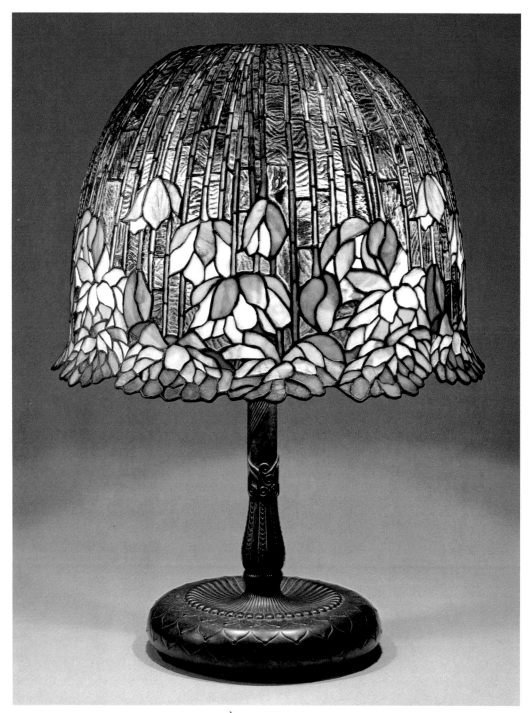

A Tiffany Favrile glass and bronze flowering lotus lamp, the base impressed *Tiffany Studios New York 262*, *circa* 1899–1920, height 25in (63.5cm)
New York $60,000(£32,432). 21.VI.78
From the collection of the late Charles E. Conville

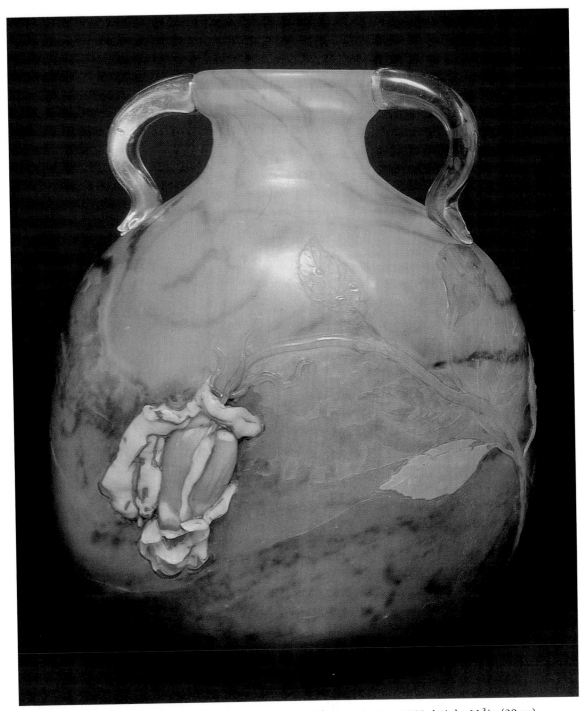

An applied and carved *Rose de France* vase by Emile Gallé, signed, *circa* 1900, height 11¾in (30cm)
Monte Carlo FF 163,000 (£18,629:$34,464). 8.X.77

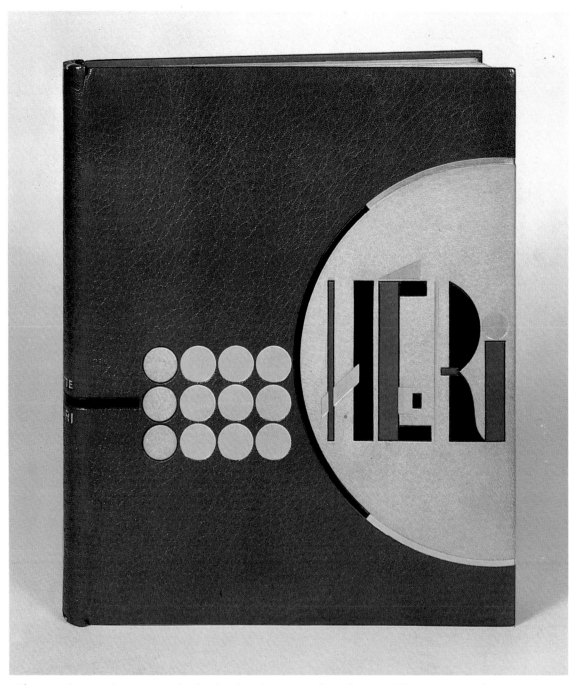

Chéri by Colette with Moroccan leather binding by Rose Adler, illustrated by Marcel Vertès,
stamped inside *Rose Adler 1931* and *A Jeanne Dor*, Paris, 1929, height 11in (28cm)
Monte Carlo FF50,000(£5,714:$10,571). 8.X.77

A red lacquer cigar box on a table stand by Jean Dunand, the table veneered with *ébène de Macassar*, signed, *circa* 1925, overall height 18¼in (46.5cm)
Monte Carlo FF95,000(£10,857:$20,086). 8.X.77

A Pullman parlour-car, no 4163, constructed by Entreprises Industrielles Charantaises, France, the interior decorated by René Lalique and René Prou, 1929
Monte Carlo FF360,000(£41,143: $76,115)

Musical Instruments

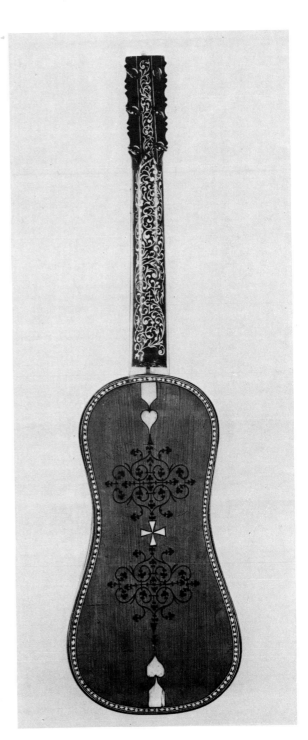

A guitar by Matheus Epp, Strasbourg, 1643,
length of back 17¾in (45.1cm)
London £2,500 ($4,625). 17.IX.77

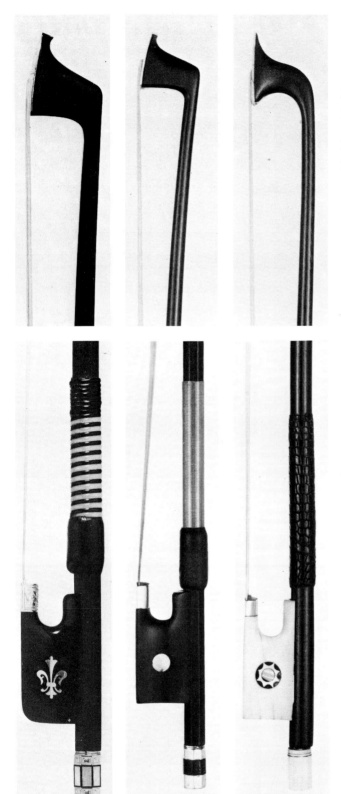

From left to right
A chased and gold-mounted violoncello bow
by W. E. Hill and Sons, 85 grams
London £1,050 ($1,943). 17.XI.77

A silver-mounted violin bow by a maker of the
Tourte School, Paris, *circa* 1820–40, 60 grams
London £3,400 ($6,290). 16.V.78

A gold and ivory-mounted violin bow by Xavier
Tourte l'aîné, Paris, *circa* 1770, 55 grams
London £1,300 ($2,405). 16.V.78

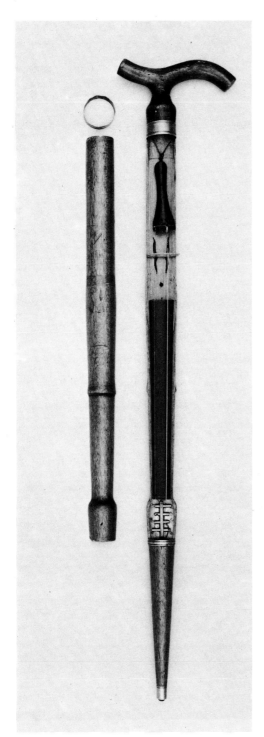

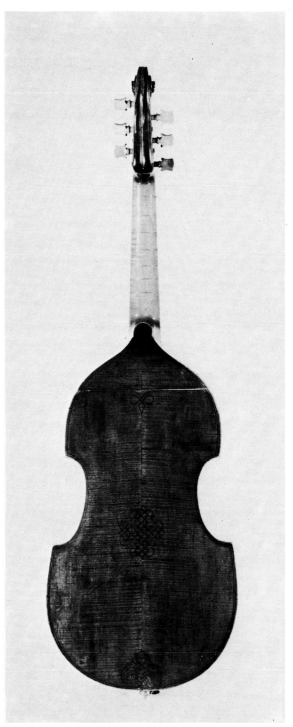

A German walking-stick violin, mid nineteenth century, length 34¾in (88.3cm)
London £1,400($2,590). 16.V.78

A bass viola da gamba by Barak Norman, London,
labelled *Barak Norman at the Bass Violin, St Paul's
Churchyd., London 17*8*, early eighteenth century,
length of back 28⅞in (73.4cm)
London £13,000($24,050). 16.V.78

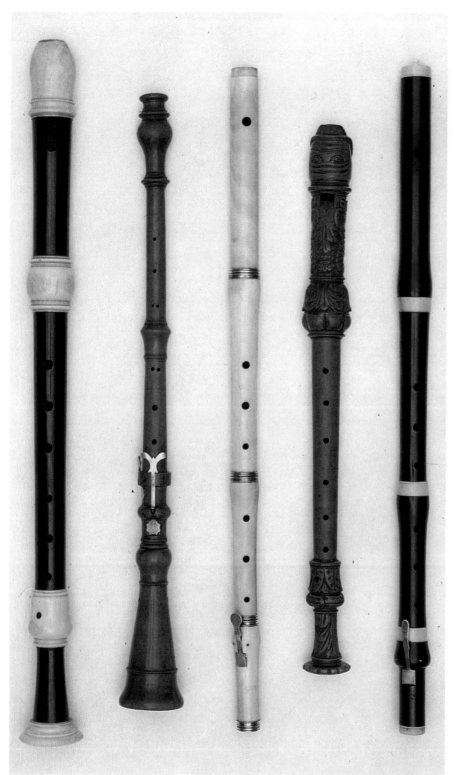

From left to right
An ebony tenor recorder by
Richard Haka, Amsterdam,
late seventeenth century,
length 25¼in (64.2cm)
£5,400 ($9,990)

A two-keyed boxwood oboe by
Goulding & Co, London, *circa*
1800, length 22⅛in (56.2cm)
£3,600 ($6,660)

An ivory one-keyed flute by
Thomas Stanesby Junior,
London, *circa* 1730, sounding
length 22in (55.9cm)
£8,500 ($15,725)

A boxwood treble (alto)
recorder, German, early
eighteenth century,
length 20in (50.8cm)
£3,800 ($7,030)

A one-keyed ebony flute by
Heinrich Grenser, Dresden, mid
eighteenth century, sounding
length 20$\frac{15}{16}$in (53.2cm)
£2,600 ($4,810)

These instruments were sold in
London on 16 May 1978

Two views of the 'Gillott' violin by Joseph Guarneri del Jesu, Cremona, 1734, labelled *Joseph Guarnerius fecit Cremona anno 1734*, length of back $13\frac{15}{16}$in (35.4cm)
London £115,000($212,750). 17.XI.77

The 'Ex-Cobbett' violin by Antonio Stradivari, Cremona, 1721, labelled *Antonius Stradivarius Cremonensis faciebat Anno 1721*, length of back 14in (35.6cm)
New York $130,000(£70,270). 11.IV.78

A violin by Antonio Stradivari, Cremona, 1708, labelled *Antonius Stradivarius Cremonensis faciebat Anno 1708*, length of back 14in (35.6cm)
London £58,000($107,300). 16.V.78

Collectors' Sales

A Great Auk set up by Rowland Ward, *circa* 1880, height 20in (51cm)
London £4,200($7,770). 21.IX.77
From the collection of the University of Durham

This species became extinct in 1844

An American Victor typewriter, *circa* 1895, width 12in (30.5cm) London £600($1,110). 7.VI.78

An American Watling *Rol-a-tor* one-armed bandit, *circa* 1930, height 26in (66cm) London £320($592). 26.V.78

A German 24½-inch Polyphon disc musical box, 1880–1900, height 59in (150cm) London £2,700($4,995). 14.IV.78

A French Vichy musical automaton
depicting *Pierrot serenading the moon*, late
nineteenth century, height 20in (51cm)
London £2,300($4,255). 26.V.78

The Pierrot character can be traced back
to *circa* 1665 when the role was brought
from France to Italy and became popular
at fairs. The original robust country lad
later developed into a love-sick youth
pining from unrequited love, often
represented singing ballads under a
waning moon

An English 3-inch scale live
steam coal-fired Burrell single-
cylinder traction engine,
1976–77, length 43in (109cm)
London £2,000($3,700).
3.III.78

The model is based on an
original dating from *circa* 1900
and has been modelled with
the contemporary style of
round front axle

A musical automaton of a French dandy, height of figure 27½in (70cm)
New York $6,000(£3,243). 6.VI.78

Four dolls from a group of nine representing the wedding of Princess Mary and H.R.H. Duke of York (later King George V), late nineteenth century, height of each approximately 12in (30.5cm)
London £1,100($2,035).
5.V.78

A French bisque doll, possibly by Petit & Dumontier, 1870–80, height 23½in (60cm)
London £1,350($2,498). 13.I.78

A French Jumeau doll, in its original box, height 27½in (70cm)
Amsterdam Fl 5,200(£1,224: $2,264). 14.IX.77

Postage Stamps

UNITED STATES OF AMERICA, 1847 5c brown,
unused marginal block of four
New York $5,500(£2,973). 11.I.78

CANADA, 1851 12d black, used pair
New York $40,000(£21,622). 28.IX.77

CANADA, 1857 7½d yellow-green, unused top marginal pair
with full original gum
New York $15,000(£8,108). 28.IX.77

CAPE OF GOOD HOPE, 1853 1d brick red on slightly blued paper, two blocks of four tied to entire
from Port Elizabeth to Cape Town
Johannesburg R2,200(£1,375:$2,544). 14.IV.78

GREAT BRITAIN, 1902 £1 dull blue-green unused marginal block of four with original gum
London £2,200($4,070). 9.XI.77

Photographs

GUSTAVE LE GRAY
Un effet de soleil
Albumen print from collodion on glass negative, mounted on card with blind stamped
photographer's credit *Photographie Gustave Le Gray & C, Paris* and with printed title label
Un effet de soleil – Ocean No 23, printed in red ink with facsimile signature, 1856,
12¾in by 16⅜in (32.5cm by 41.6cm)
London £4,200 ($7,770). 28.VI.78

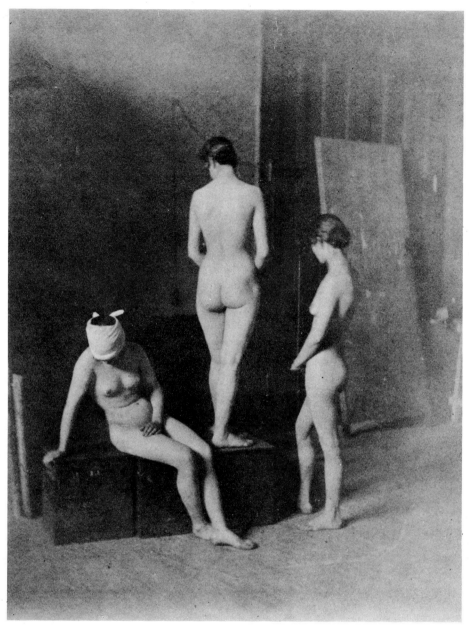

THOMAS EAKINS
Three female nudes
Albumen contact print, mounted on card, *circa* 1883, 4⅞in by 3⅝in (12.4cm by 9.2cm)
New York $11,000 (£5,946). 10.XI.77
From the collection of Joseph Seraphin

Eakins probably used the Scovill camera, which he purchased in 1883, for this
photograph. Few photographs of female models by Eakins have survived which,
until recently, led historians to the conclusion that he preferred the male to the
female figure. However, it is now known that a friend destroyed many of Eakins'
photographs of female nudes immediately after Mrs Eakins' death thus leaving an
unbalanced representation of his photographic work. This photograph, which is one
of the twenty-one given by Eakins to Edward H. Coates, is the only known print of
this subject

IRVING PENN
Portrait of Cecil Beaton
Bromide print, the reverse stamped in ink with photographer's credit *Photograph by Penn* and Condé Nast credit,
1940s, 10⅜in by 10in (26.5cm by 25.6cm)
London £700($1,295). 21.XI.77

Portraits by Sir Cecil Beaton

Colin Ford

Early in 1977, Sotheby Parke Bernet concluded negotiations to buy from Sir Cecil Beaton his photographic stock-in-trade: all the negatives and positives in his possession (except those of royalty), his collection of pictures by other photographers (including many portraits of Sir Cecil himself), his scrapbooks of snapshots and pictures clipped from magazines and newspapers. It was an historic purchase. For the first time, the auctioneers were to give a photographer a studio sale, or sales, just like those of painters over the centuries. They were also to become photographic dealers, retaining the negatives in order to publish prints, individually and in portfolios, as well as providing copies for publication and exhibition. No British photographer of our time has more surely earned such recognition. For half a century the credit *Cecil Beaton photograph* has been a stamp of style, artistry, wit, imagination and an unsurpassed sense of design.

Cecil Beaton began to photograph his family with a simple camera in the 1920s. Inspired by the then popular postcards of theatre actresses, his earliest published picture was of a fellow undergraduate, Edward Lebas (known as 'Boy'), dressed as an elegant lady; and a self-portrait in a fashionable gown was taken at about the same time. After coming down from Cambridge, Beaton took an office job at his father's insistence but, away from the office, experimented with settings, posing his sisters Nancy and Baba against mirrors and polished mahogany, cushioned in cellophane and shiny cloth and even under a Victorian glass dome. Celebrities cheerfully submitted themselves to his fantasies: William Walton (Fig 1), Margot Asquith and Lady Loughborough all in front of art deco painted backgrounds, Edith Sitwell in a four-poster or playing a harp or recumbent on a tiled floor in flowered brocade, flanked by stone cherubs and clasping a bunch of arum lilies, for all the world like some medieval tomb effigy (Fig 2). This exuberant visual imagination was soon being exercised on more and more fashionable sitters and in 1928 Beaton had his first Bond Street exhibition. Aged only twenty-two, he was on his way to becoming one of the world's best-known photographers.

'Before my time a photographer was despised as a nonentity who crawled under a black velvet cloth and pressed a button.' (*Cecil Beaton's Scrapbook*, Batsford, 1937)

Late in 1929, the young photographer sailed to the United States and about the time of the first of his many visits to Hollywood augmented his 3A pocket folding Kodak with something more professional. This and the ready availability of studio sets,

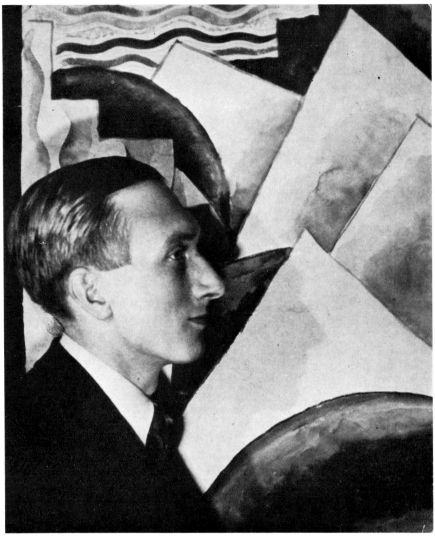

Fig 1
CECIL BEATON
William Walton the composer whose 'Facade' & 'Portsmouth Point' were played at the recent Siena Festival
Bromide print, the reverse stamped in ink with photographer's credit
Cecil Beaton Photograph and fully titled in pencil in Beaton's hand, 1926,
11⅜in by 9⅜in (29cm by 23.9cm)
London £260($481). 21.XI.77

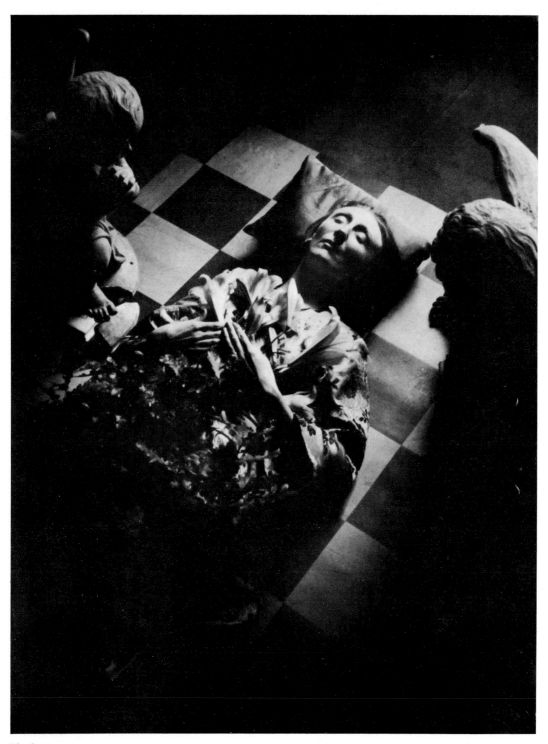

Fig 2
CECIL BEATON
Edith Sitwell recumbent
Bromide print, mounted on heavy grey paper, various annotations on the reverse, 1927,
$14\frac{5}{8}$in by $10\frac{7}{8}$in (37.2cm by 27.7cm)
London £750($1,388). 21.XI.77

Fig 3
CECIL BEATON
Marlene Dietrich
Bromide print, the reverse stamped in ink with photographer's credit *Cecil Beaton Photograph*
and titled in ink, 1935, 12⅛in by 15⅜in (30.8cm by 39cm)
London £420($777). 30.VI.78

props and lights brought a new richness and gloss to his work. His portraits of film stars were as sleek and glamorous as publicity stills by George Hurrell, George Hoyningen-Heune and Eugene Richee but his bold compositions and individual décors (often the exotic trappings of movie-making) saved him from being as stereotyped as they (Fig 3). In these and his growing number of fashion photographs Beaton's touch was becoming assured, his mastery complete. In 1939 he was given the accolade of being asked to photograph the Queen. His portraits of her had an elegance and style revolutionary in royal photography as did those of the present Queen taken in the 1960s. He was to become the supreme photographer royal, the twentieth century's nearest equivalent of the great state portraitists of the past.

'I was later to take pictures of Her Majesty [Queen Elizabeth, the Queen Mother] that were in contrast to any that had been taken before; against a painted background she was wearing a black velvet crinoline with tiara and diamonds like robins' eggs around her throat.' (*Happy and Glorious, 130 Years of Royal Photographs*, National Portrait Gallery, 1977)

After the outbreak of war, Beaton was at first frustrated and embarrassed by the feeling that he could make no significant contribution, but gradually he saw his photographs of air raid damage and RAF operations come to serve useful purposes (Fig 4). One, of a terror-stricken little girl in a hospital bed, was used as a *Life* cover and an influential American Red Cross poster. Later in the war he made memorable pictures in the Middle East, India and China.

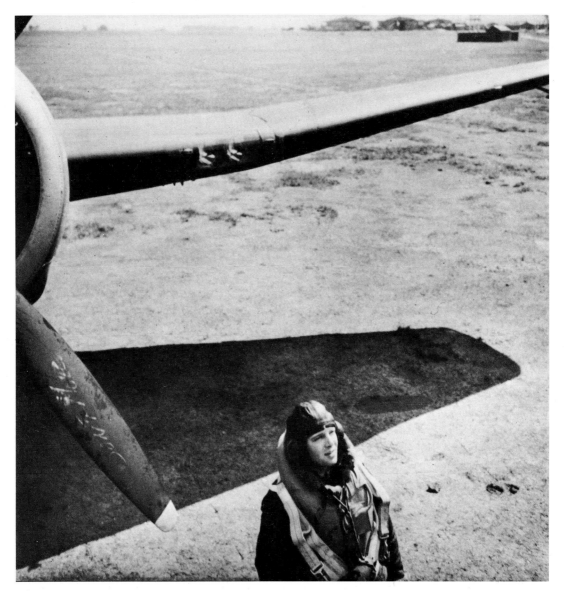

Fig 4
CECIL BEATON
One of five studies of RAF activities
Bromide prints, the reverse of each stamped in ink with photographer's credit *Cecil Beaton Photograph* and with various pencil titles and annotations, 1941, three $10\frac{1}{4}$in by $9\frac{3}{4}$in (25.9cm by 24.9cm), two 8in by $7\frac{3}{4}$in (20.4cm by 19.7cm)
London £38($70). 30.VI.78

Beaton's post-war photographs are usually said to be more direct and straightforward than his pre-war ones and editors certainly saw a new 'reality' in such fashion shots as that of a Paris model wearing trousers in a backyard. However, Beaton had always taken some pictures that seemed to be simple, some influenced by Bertram Park, master of sombre, moody lighting, others by E. O. Hoppé, whose results depended on restrained good taste and controlled tones and textures. Nevertheless, Beaton's flights of fancy were now more disciplined. He no longer seemed to be trying out effects for their own sake but was in complete technical and aesthetic control of them. Beaton never had his own studio nor, after the early years, made his own prints; 'I don't have the time', he told Erwin Blumenfeld in 1936, 'Besides, there are others who do it so much better'. Nevertheless, he became as much a master of the technique of visualising and taking photographs as anyone in the history of the medium.

> 'Designer of scenery and costumes for ballet and opera, and for many theatrical productions (London and New York stage); including sets and costumes for *Lady Windermere's Fan*, *Quadrille*, *The Grass Harp*; *The School for Scandal* (Comédie Française); costumes for *My Fair Lady* (New York, London); films: *Gigi*, *The Doctor's Dilemma*, *My Fair Lady*.' (*Who's Who*, A. and C. Black, 1978)

Beaton had included a number of 'my somewhat amateur stage designs' in his 1928 exhibition and after the war he devoted more time to the theatre. Indeed, one could say that a sense of theatre has impelled his whole life – and his photography. We are told that when Henry Irving read a script (even one by Shakespeare) his main concern was to find opportunities to make 'effects' with scenery, costumes and acting. Beaton appears to have approached assignments in the same spirit; even in the war he 'was trying to find groups or settings that would compose themselves into a design'. In some of his portraits the design seems almost more important than the sitter's own personality: one of Henry Moore, for instance, seated in an ornate caned armchair (to be sold next season) is a fine, simple, clear composition but it seems to have little to do with the tough, stocky Yorkshireman and his sculpture. From this and many of Beaton's later portraits, elaborate backgrounds and clever decorations have been banished and the strength of design emerges more clearly than ever. In 1968 the Queen was photographed in this strikingly plain style (Fig 5).

> 'The morning papers all published my new photographs of the Queen wearing a naval boat cloak. As these were quite different from any that I had taken of her before, they caused a stir and were incidentally good publicity for my exhibition at the National Portrait Gallery, a collection of about six hundred of my photographs taken over the last forty years. It has been an amazing success and seems to have been enjoyed by old and young alike.' (*The Parting Years 1963–74*, Weidenfeld and Nicolson, 1978)

Beaton Portraits was the National Portrait Gallery's first ever photographic exhibition and it heralded a newly serious consideration in Britain of the art of photography. Sir Cecil (he was knighted in 1972) was once again in the lead as photography took a new direction.

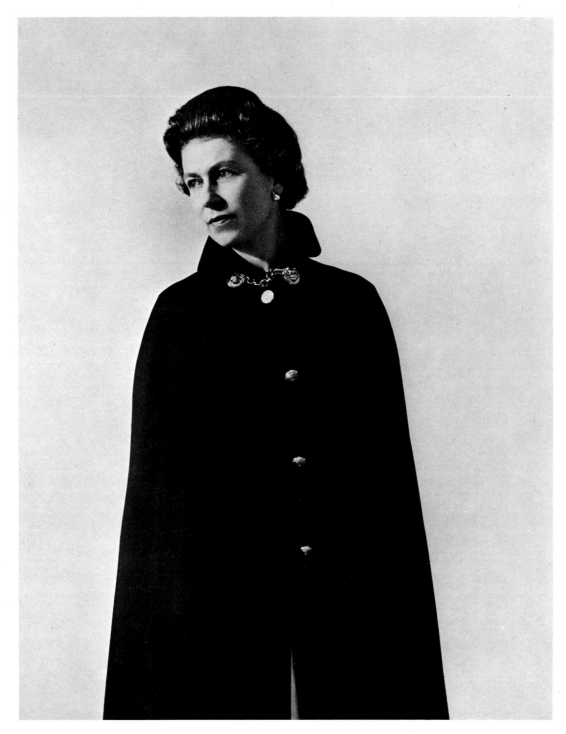

Fig 5
CECIL BEATON
Her Majesty Queen Elizabeth II wearing a blue naval boat cloak, 1968
A print of this photograph is in the collection of the National Portrait Gallery, London

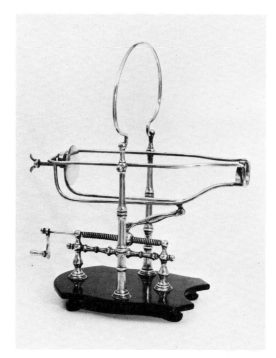

Left
A Belgian silver-plated decanting cradle, *circa* 1900
London £2,000($3,700). 2.V.78

Right
An Edward Thomason's 1802 patent type corkscrew
London £190($352). 2.V.78

From left to right
Rüdesheimer Berg 1893 (one bottle), London £42($78). 28.IX.77
Gilka Kümmel *circa* 1900 (one bottle), London £36($67). 8.III.78
Believed Cherry Liqueur mid to late eighteenth century (one bottle), London £28($52). 8.III.78
Sandeman 1955 (one three-bottle magnum), London £92($170). 28.IX.77
Alicante *circa* 1820 (one bottle), originally from the Tuileries Palace, London £100($185). 30.XI.77

Wine Sales

The Wine Department has completed another very successful season with net sales reaching £1,465,040 ($2,710,324). During the year, the total number of lots offered was nearly 13,000. Fifteen sales took place in the United Kingdom, three were held overseas and an additional small sale of Californian wines was conducted in Los Angeles for the Californian Museum of Science and Technology. Of the three overseas, one was in Amsterdam, one at Nederburg in South Africa and the third reintroduced sales to Zurich. At Nederburg, the fourth annual auction of Rare Cape wines comprising over 6,500 cases was conducted on behalf of Stellenbosch Farmers' Wineries, with every lot sold for a total of R368,905 (£230,566:$426,546).

Although sterling has strengthened against the American dollar, there has been little sign of decreased buying from the States. The situation has in fact been the contrary, with the older wines fetching higher and higher prices. Interest from Germany and Switzerland has increased as the quality of the sales has become more widely reported.

Private cellars at home still provide the bulk of the lots of interesting, older wines, with claret and vintage port traditionally predominating. However, this is likely to change as the rarer bottles are sold and consumed. New reserves are being formed but future generations will not find the wealth of old bottles in the abundance found today. Recently, several of the largest and most important collections have been consigned from the United States and France, where several other fine cellars are known to exist.

It is generally only the high prices that are reported here but it should be remembered that the considerable bulk of the wine sold is around £20 per case.

Among some of the most interesting wines sold during the season were: one jeroboam Château Pétrus 1971, £205 ($379); nine bottles Château Lafite 1945, £1,035 ($1,915) per dozen; one bottle Château d'Yquem 1861, £200 ($370); one bottle Romanée Conti 1952, £68 ($126); one bottle Madeira, Grand Cama de Lobos, vintage 1789, £155 ($287); one dozen bottles Cockburn 1912, from the cellars of Sherborne Castle, £375 ($694); one bottle Tokay Essence 1834, from a cellar walled-up during the Hungarian Revolution of 1849, £105 ($194); one magnum Cognac Grande Fine Champagne (de Réserve) 1811, £360 ($666).

Collectors' items increased in popularity and contributed nearly £30,000 to the sale total. Rare old corkscrew prices rose significantly and a Belgian silver-plated decanting cradle fetched the remarkable price of £2,000 ($3,700).

Veteran and Vintage Vehicles

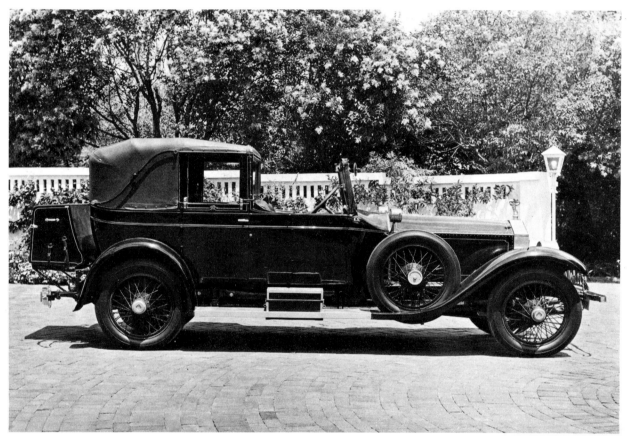

A 1923 Springfield Rolls-Royce Silver Ghost Salamanca
Donington Park £38,300 ($70,855). 29.IX.77

Sotheby's were the first major auction house to recognise the importance of early motor vehicles and held regular sales for car enthusiasts from 1965 to 1972. The Department of Veteran, Vintage and Special Interest Motor Cars was re-formed in 1977 and the vehicles on these two pages represent a résumé of its activities since it recommenced business so successfully in May of that year.

A Ford 1903 twin cylinder Model A
Johannesburg R13,000(£8,125:$15,031). 20.V.77

This is reputed to be the first Ford imported into South Africa

A 1923 Blue Label long chassis Bentley three-litre tourer
Donington Park £11,000 ($20,350). 22.IV.78

This car was found in a Shropshire barn in which it had lain for thirty to forty years and was sold totally unrestored

Index